BUCK ROGERS®

VOLUME 1: FUTURE SHOCK

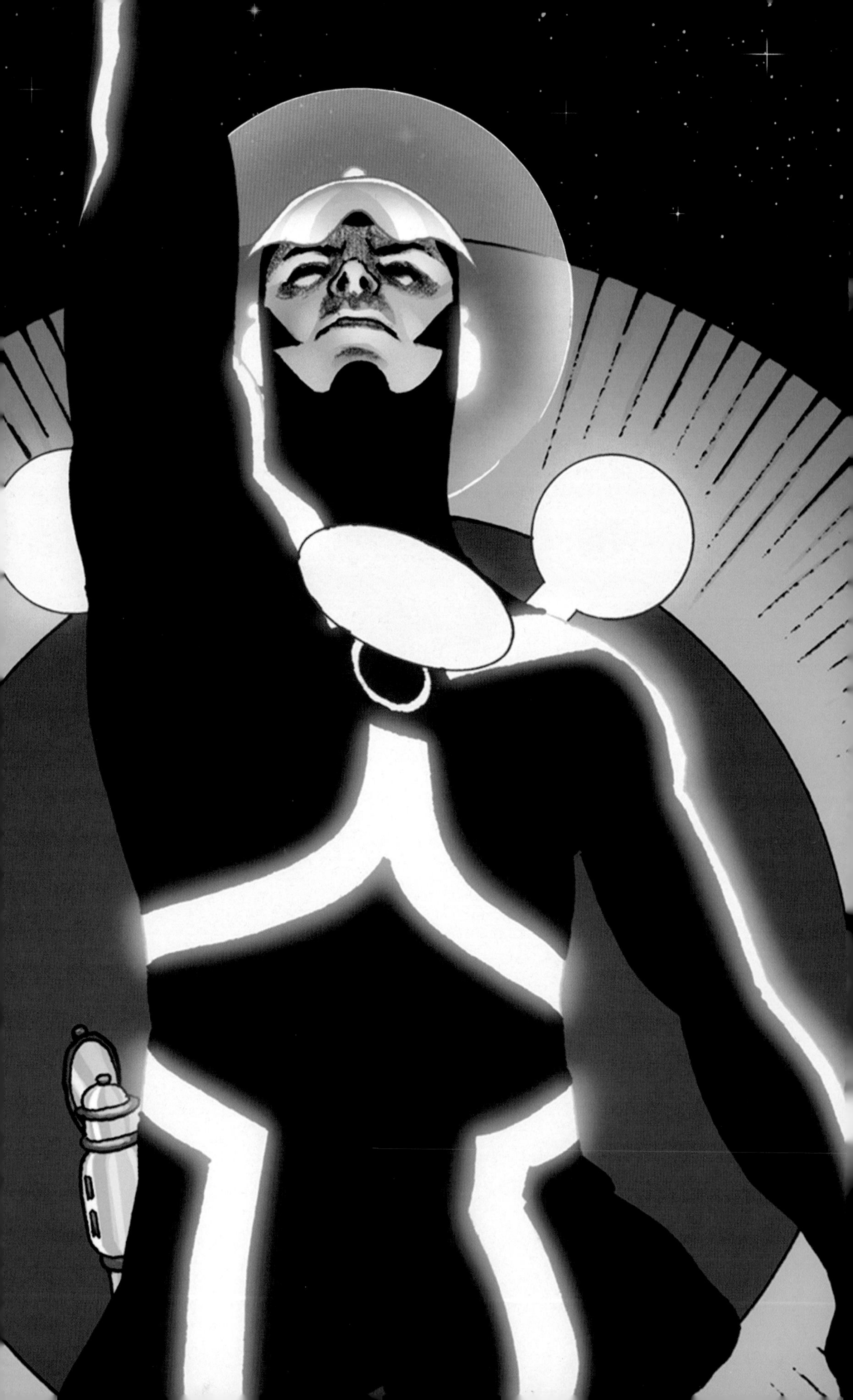

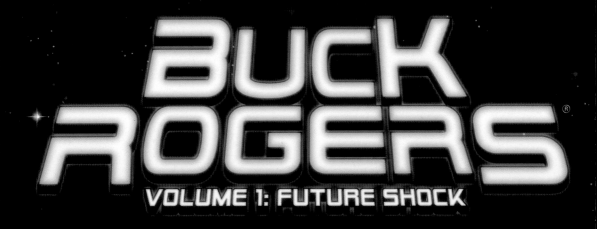

BUCK ROGERS®

VOLUME 1: FUTURE SHOCK

Written by
SCOTT BEATTY

Illustrated by
CARLOS RAFAEL

Colored by
CARLOS LOPEZ

Lettered by
SIMON BOWLAND

Cover by
JOHN CASSADAY

Collection design by
JASON ULLMEYER

Special thanks to
FLINT DILLE of the Dille Family Trust,
RICHARD LEIBOWITZ and **HOWARD BLISS**
of Union Entertainment
HARRIS MILLER II, SCOTT CHERRIN
and **LESLIE LEVINE**

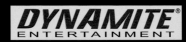

DYNAMITE ENTERTAINMENT

DYNAMITE ENTERTAINMENT
NICK BARRUCCI • PRESIDENT
JUAN COLLADO • CHIEF OPERATING OFFICER
JOSEPH RYBANDT • EDITOR
JOSH JOHNSON • CREATIVE DIRECTOR
JASON ULLMEYER • GRAPHIC DESIGNER

Hardcover ISBN-10: 1-60690-106-0
Hardcover ISBN-13: 978-1-60690-106-9
Softcover ISBN-10: 1-60690-107-9
Softcover ISBN-13: 978-1-60690-107-6

First Printing

10 9 8 7 6 5 4 3 2 1

For information regarding press, media rights, foreign rights, licensing, promotions, and advertising e-mail:
marketing@dynamiteentertainment.com

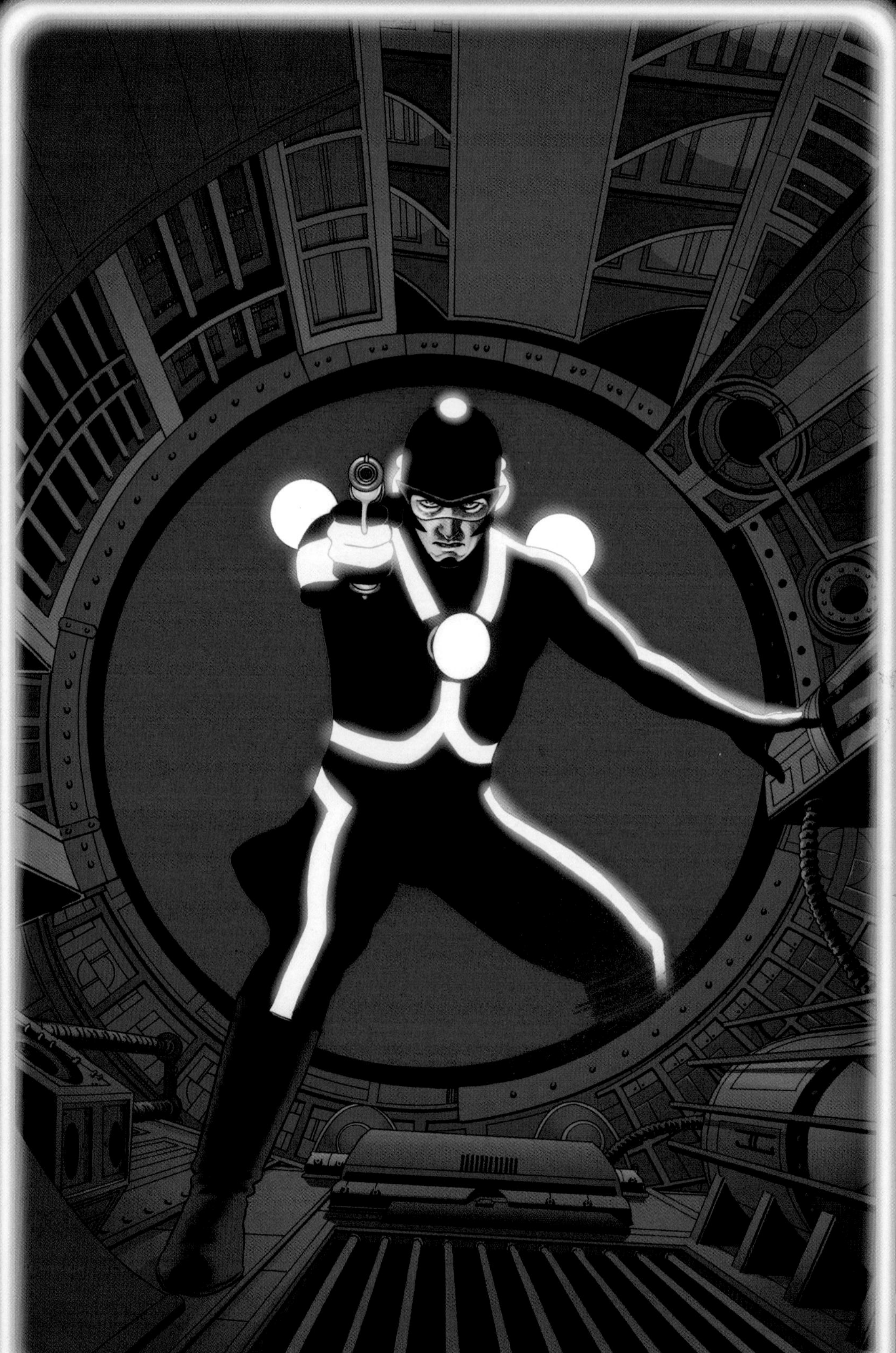

ISSUE ONE: One Giant Leap...

COVER BY JOHN CASSADAY

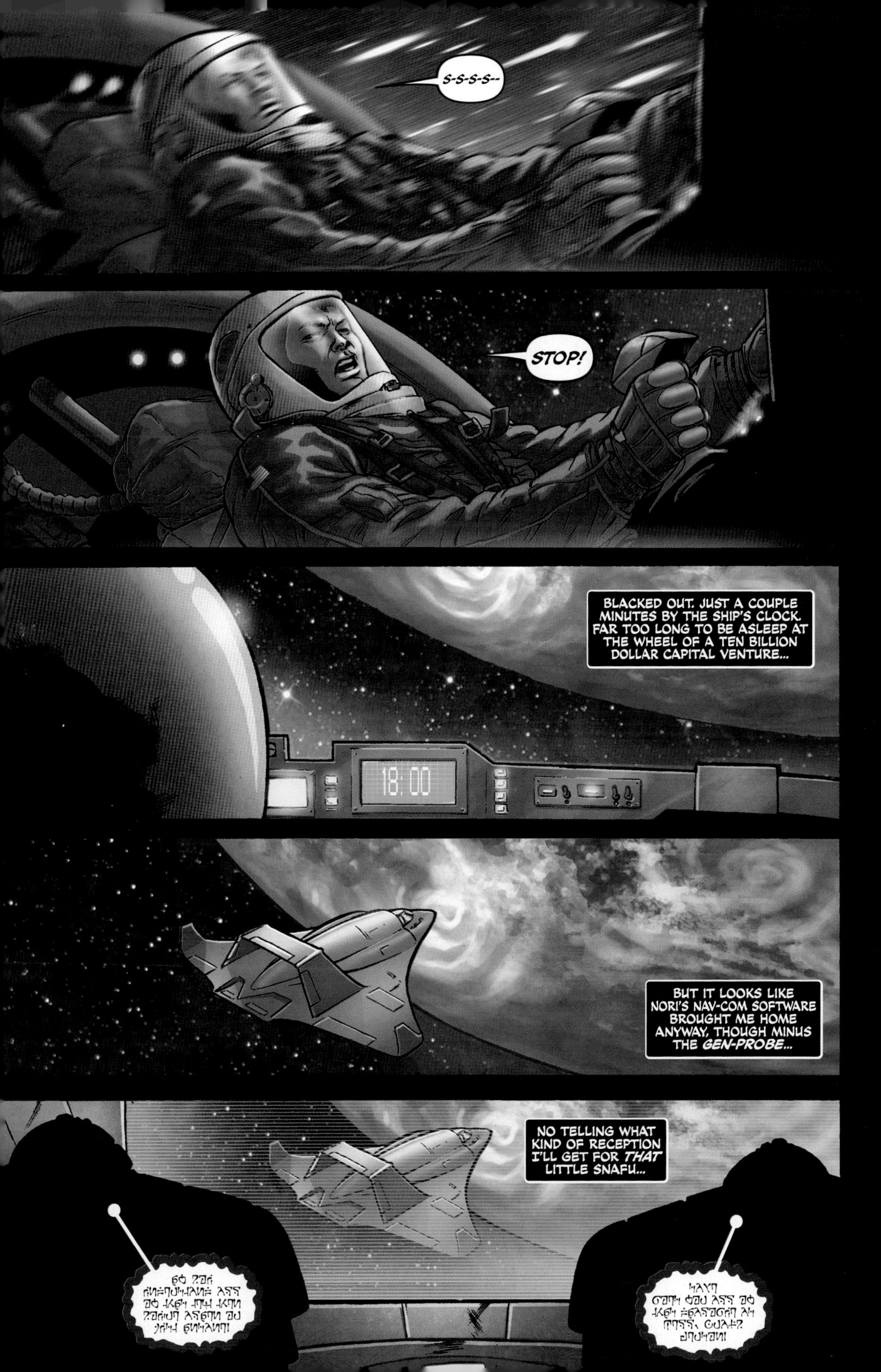
S-S-S-S--
STOP!
BLACKED OUT. JUST A COUPLE MINUTES BY THE SHIP'S CLOCK. FAR TOO LONG TO BE ASLEEP AT THE WHEEL OF A TEN BILLION DOLLAR CAPITAL VENTURE...
18:00
BUT IT LOOKS LIKE NORI'S NAV-COM SOFTWARE BROUGHT ME HOME ANYWAY, THOUGH MINUS THE *GEN-PROBE*...
NO TELLING WHAT KIND OF RECEPTION I'LL GET FOR *THAT* LITTLE SNAFU...

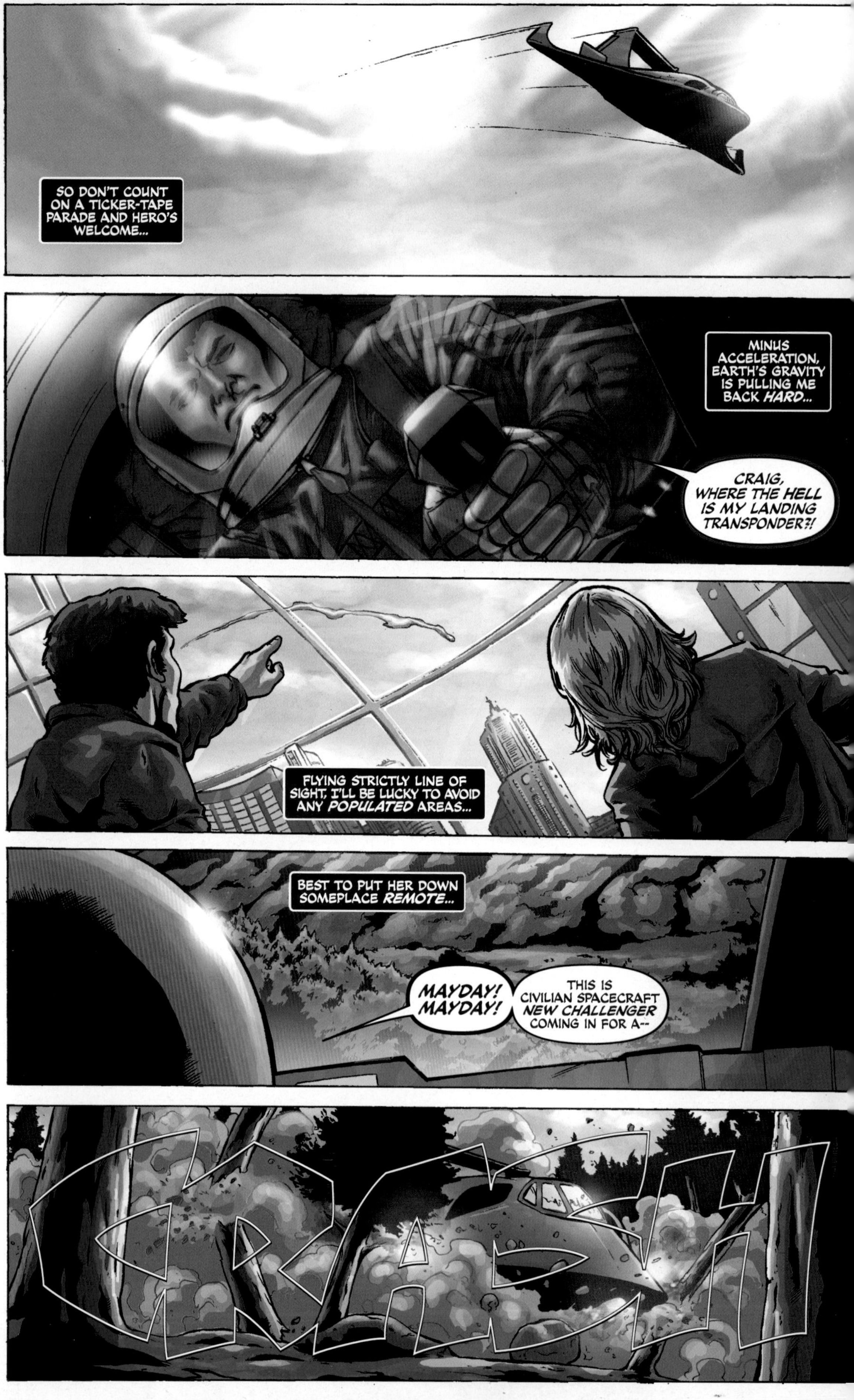
SO DON'T COUNT ON A TICKER-TAPE PARADE AND HERO'S WELCOME...
MINUS ACCELERATION, EARTH'S GRAVITY IS PULLING ME BACK HARD...
CRAIG, WHERE THE HELL IS MY LANDING TRANSPONDER?!
FLYING STRICTLY LINE OF SIGHT, I'LL BE LUCKY TO AVOID ANY POPULATED AREAS...
BEST TO PUT HER DOWN SOMEPLACE REMOTE...
MAYDAY! MAYDAY!
THIS IS CIVILIAN SPACECRAFT NEW CHALLENGER COMING IN FOR A--
CRASH

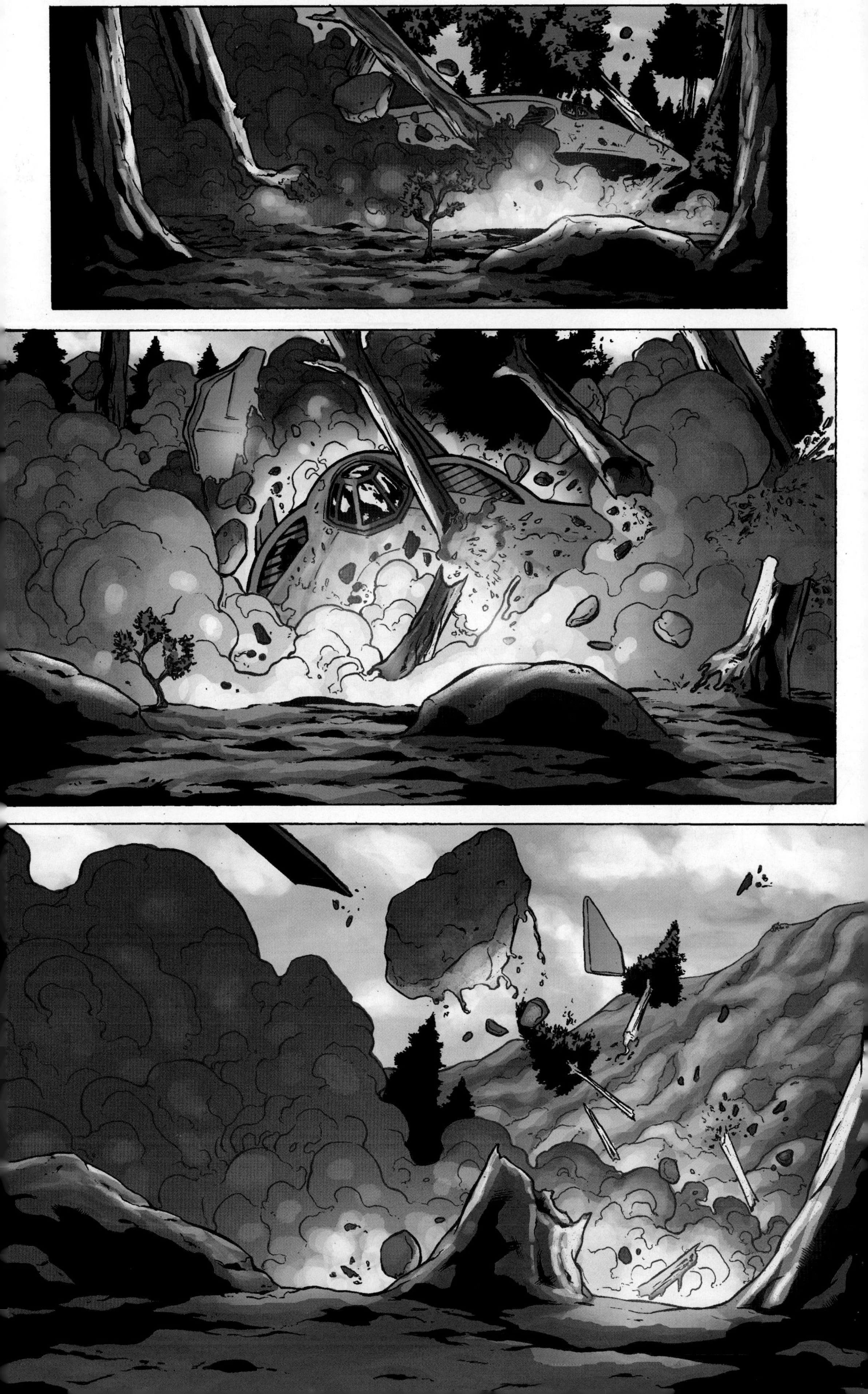

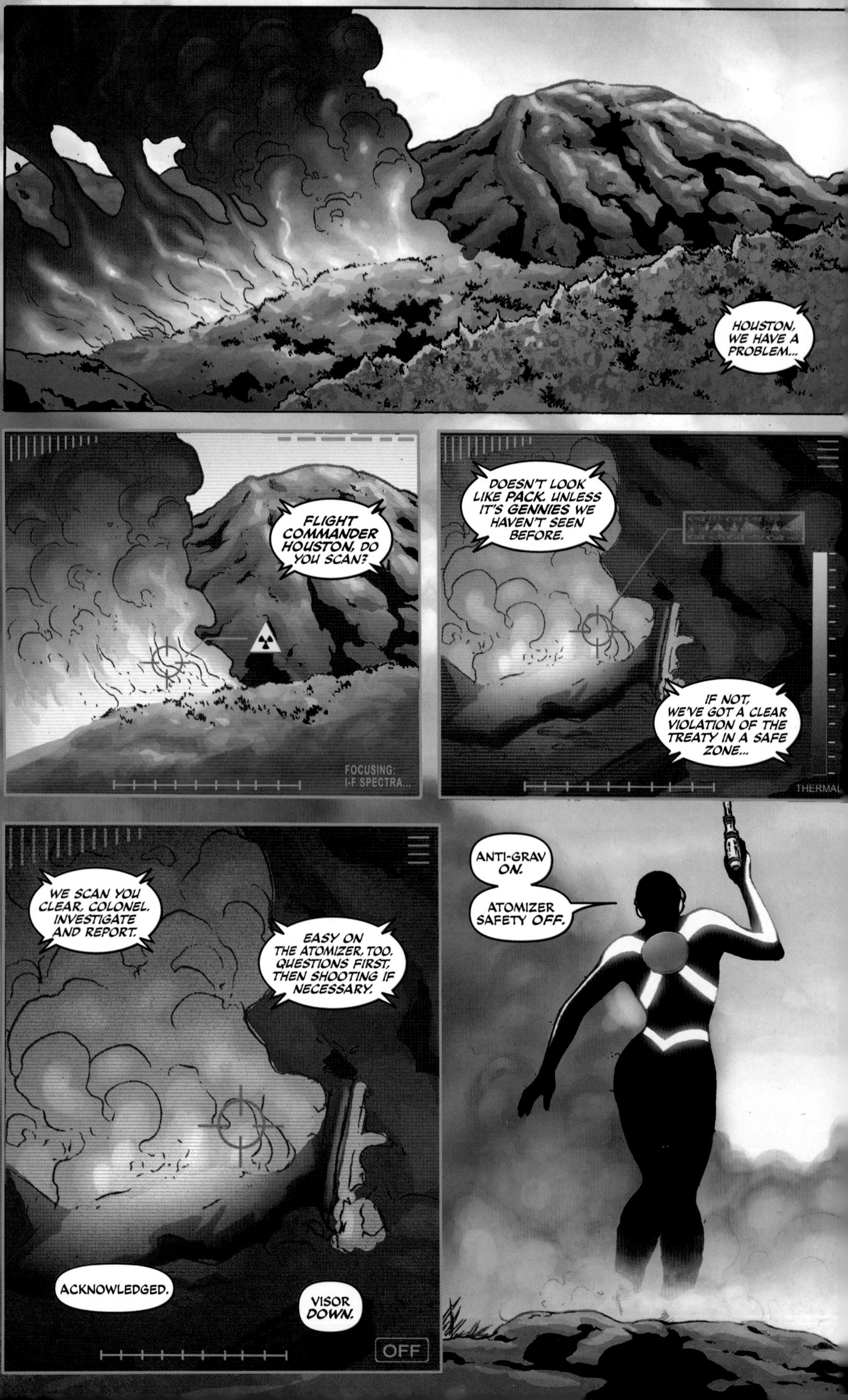
HOUSTON, WE HAVE A PROBLEM...
FLIGHT COMMANDER HOUSTON, DO YOU SCAN?
FOCUSING: I-F SPECTRA...
DOESN'T LOOK LIKE PACK. UNLESS IT'S GENNIES WE HAVEN'T SEEN BEFORE.
IF NOT, WE'VE GOT A CLEAR VIOLATION OF THE TREATY IN A SAFE ZONE...
THERMAL
WE SCAN YOU CLEAR, COLONEL. INVESTIGATE AND REPORT.
EASY ON THE ATOMIZER, TOO. QUESTIONS FIRST, THEN SHOOTING IF NECESSARY.
ACKNOWLEDGED.
VISOR DOWN.
OFF
ANTI-GRAV ON.
ATOMIZER SAFETY OFF.

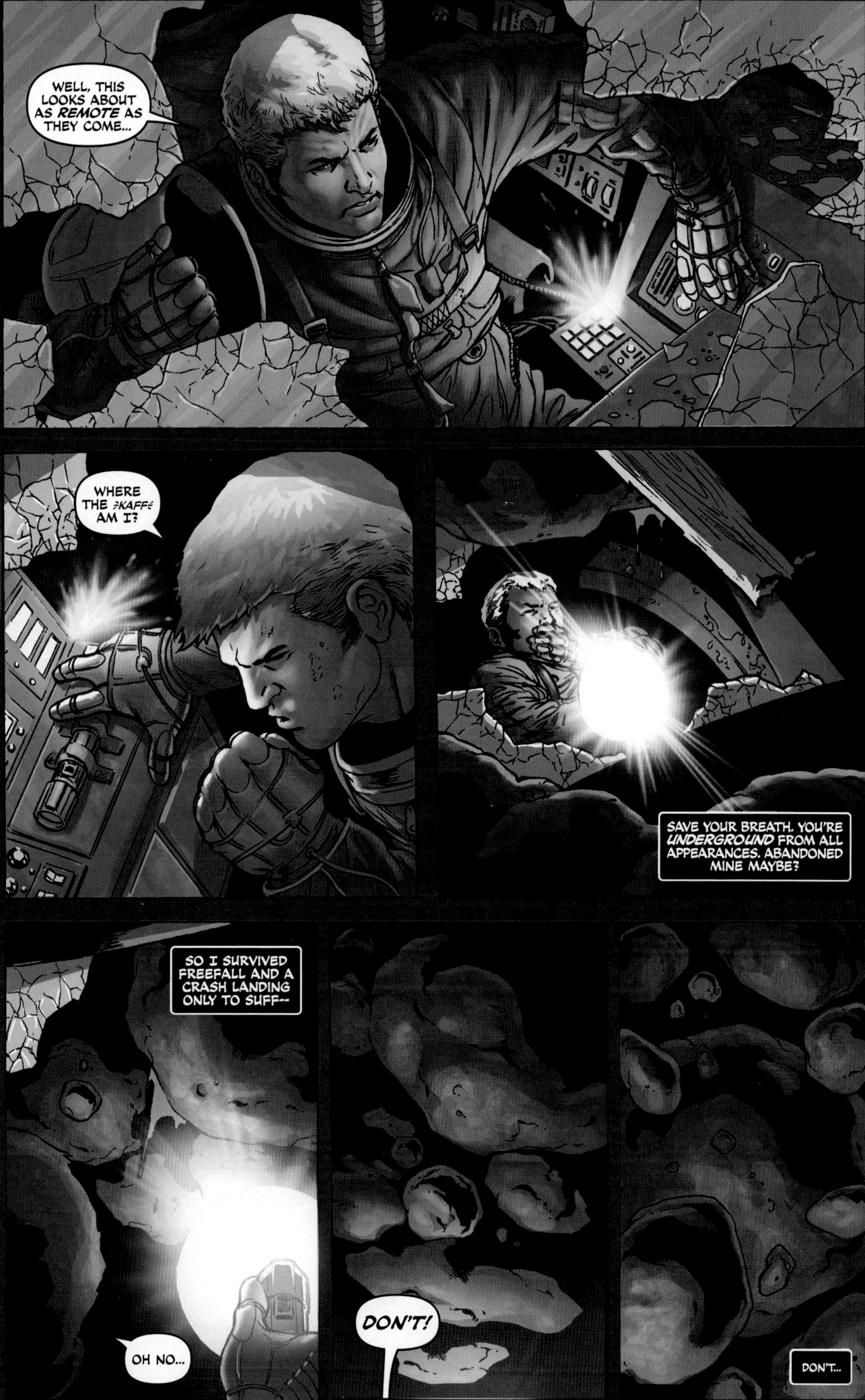
WELL, THIS LOOKS ABOUT AS *REMOTE* AS THEY COME...
WHERE THE ≠KAFF≠ AM I?
SAVE YOUR BREATH. YOU'RE *UNDERGROUND* FROM ALL APPEARANCES. ABANDONED MINE MAYBE?
SO I SURVIVED FREEFALL AND A CRASH LANDING ONLY TO SUFF--
OH NO...
DON'T!
DON'T...

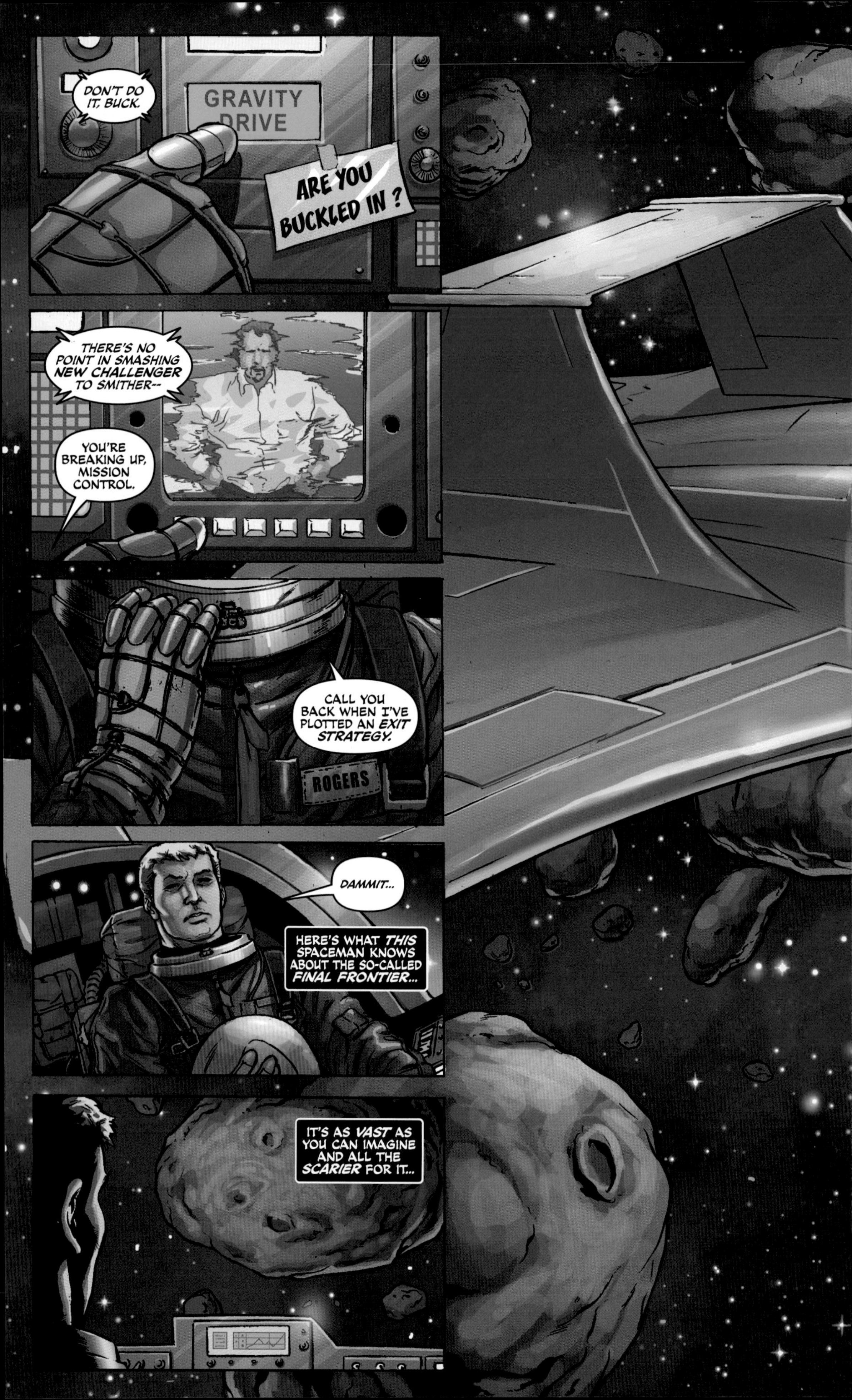
GRAVITY DRIVE
DON'T DO IT, BUCK.
ARE YOU BUCKLED IN ?
THERE'S NO POINT IN SMASHING NEW CHALLENGER TO SMITHER--
YOU'RE BREAKING UP, MISSION CONTROL.
CALL YOU BACK WHEN I'VE PLOTTED AN EXIT STRATEGY.
ROGERS
DAMMIT...
HERE'S WHAT THIS SPACEMAN KNOWS ABOUT THE SO-CALLED FINAL FRONTIER...
IT'S AS VAST AS YOU CAN IMAGINE AND ALL THE SCARIER FOR IT...

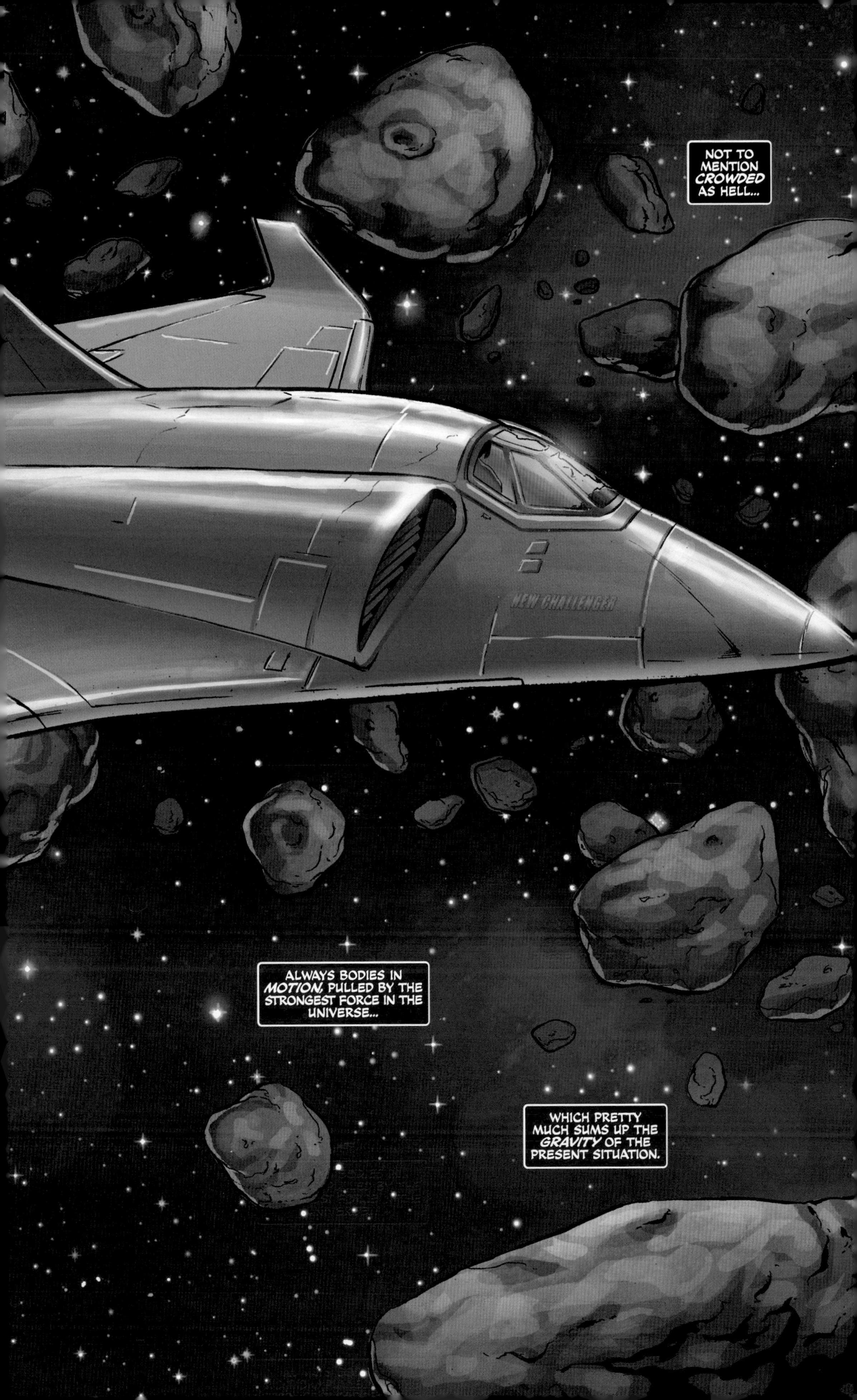
NOT TO MENTION CROWDED AS HELL...
NEW CHALLENGER
ALWAYS BODIES IN MOTION, PULLED BY THE STRONGEST FORCE IN THE UNIVERSE...
WHICH PRETTY MUCH SUMS UP THE GRAVITY OF THE PRESENT SITUATION.

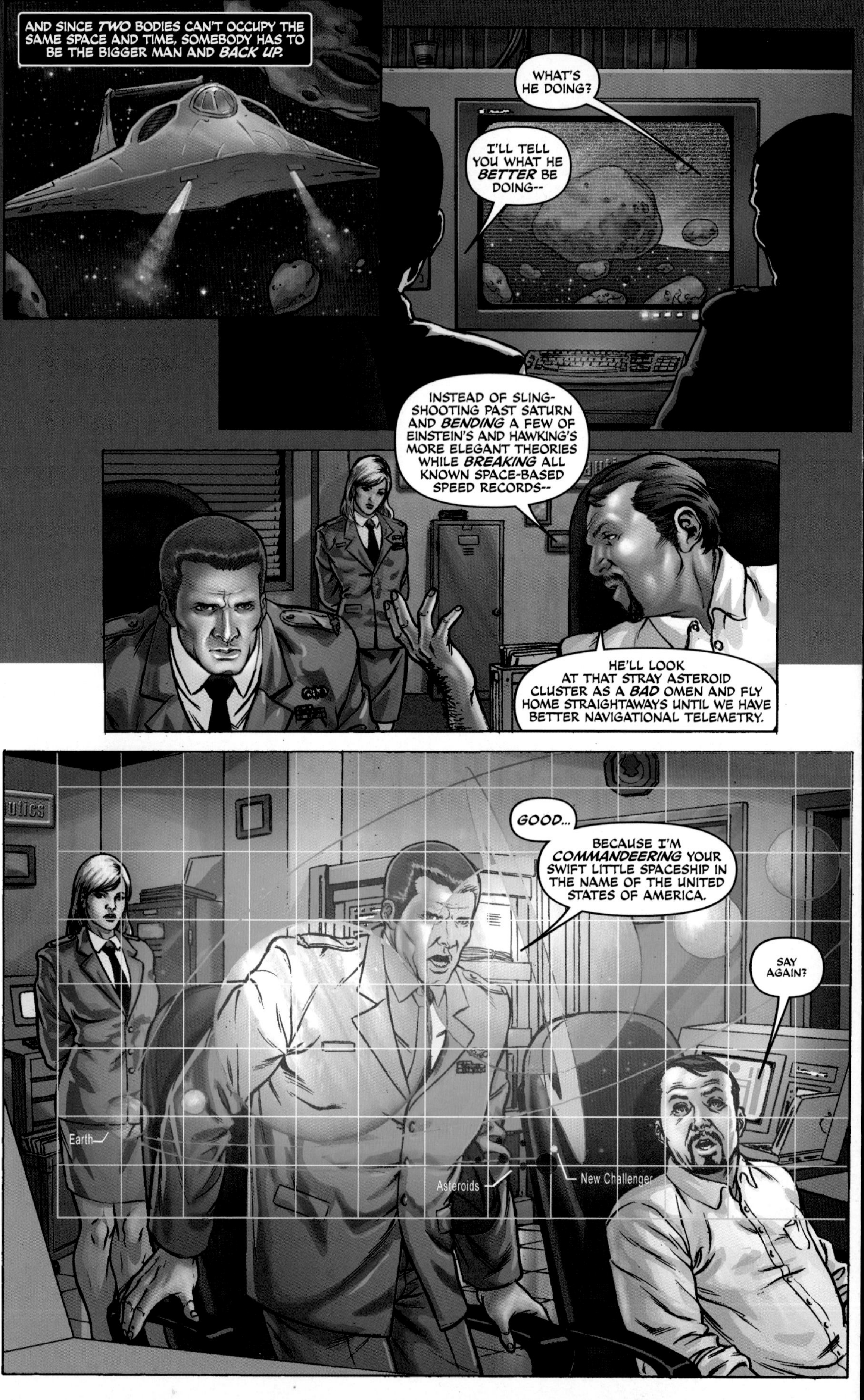
AND SINCE TWO BODIES CAN'T OCCUPY THE SAME SPACE AND TIME, SOMEBODY HAS TO BE THE BIGGER MAN AND BACK UP.
WHAT'S HE DOING?
I'LL TELL YOU WHAT HE BETTER BE DOING--
INSTEAD OF SLING-SHOOTING PAST SATURN AND BENDING A FEW OF EINSTEIN'S AND HAWKING'S MORE ELEGANT THEORIES WHILE BREAKING ALL KNOWN SPACE-BASED SPEED RECORDS--
HE'LL LOOK AT THAT STRAY ASTEROID CLUSTER AS A BAD OMEN AND FLY HOME STRAIGHTAWAYS UNTIL WE HAVE BETTER NAVIGATIONAL TELEMETRY.
GOOD...
BECAUSE I'M COMMANDEERING YOUR SWIFT LITTLE SPACESHIP IN THE NAME OF THE UNITED STATES OF AMERICA.
SAY AGAIN?
Earth
Asteroids
New Challenger

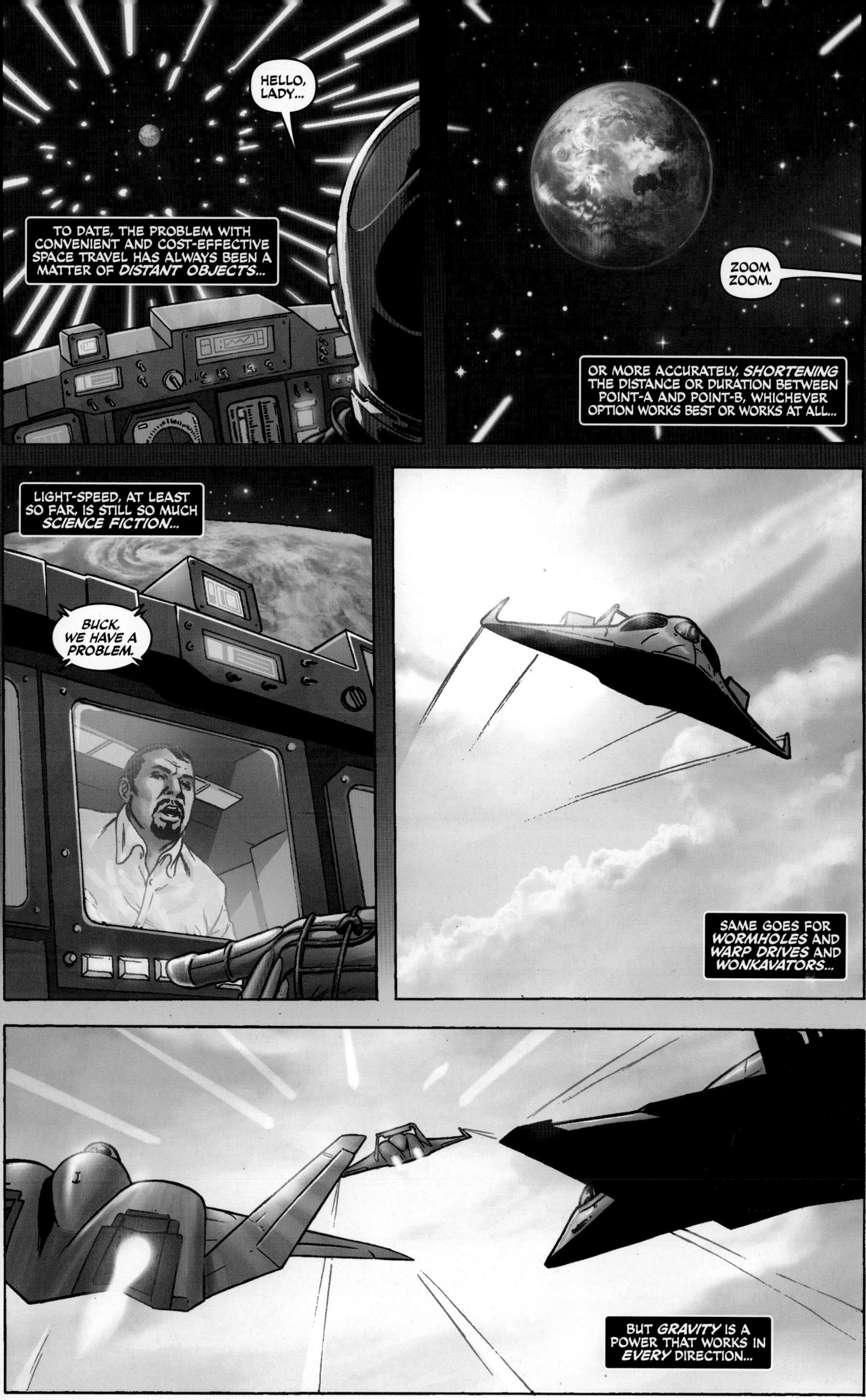
HELLO, LADY...
TO DATE, THE PROBLEM WITH CONVENIENT AND COST-EFFECTIVE SPACE TRAVEL HAS ALWAYS BEEN A MATTER OF *DISTANT OBJECTS*...
ZOOM ZOOM.
OR MORE ACCURATELY, *SHORTENING* THE DISTANCE OR DURATION BETWEEN POINT-A AND POINT-B, WHICHEVER OPTION WORKS BEST OR WORKS AT ALL...
LIGHT-SPEED, AT LEAST SO FAR, IS STILL SO MUCH *SCIENCE FICTION*...
BUCK, WE HAVE A PROBLEM.
SAME GOES FOR *WORMHOLES* AND *WARP DRIVES* AND *WONKAVATORS*...
BUT *GRAVITY* IS A POWER THAT WORKS IN *EVERY* DIRECTION...

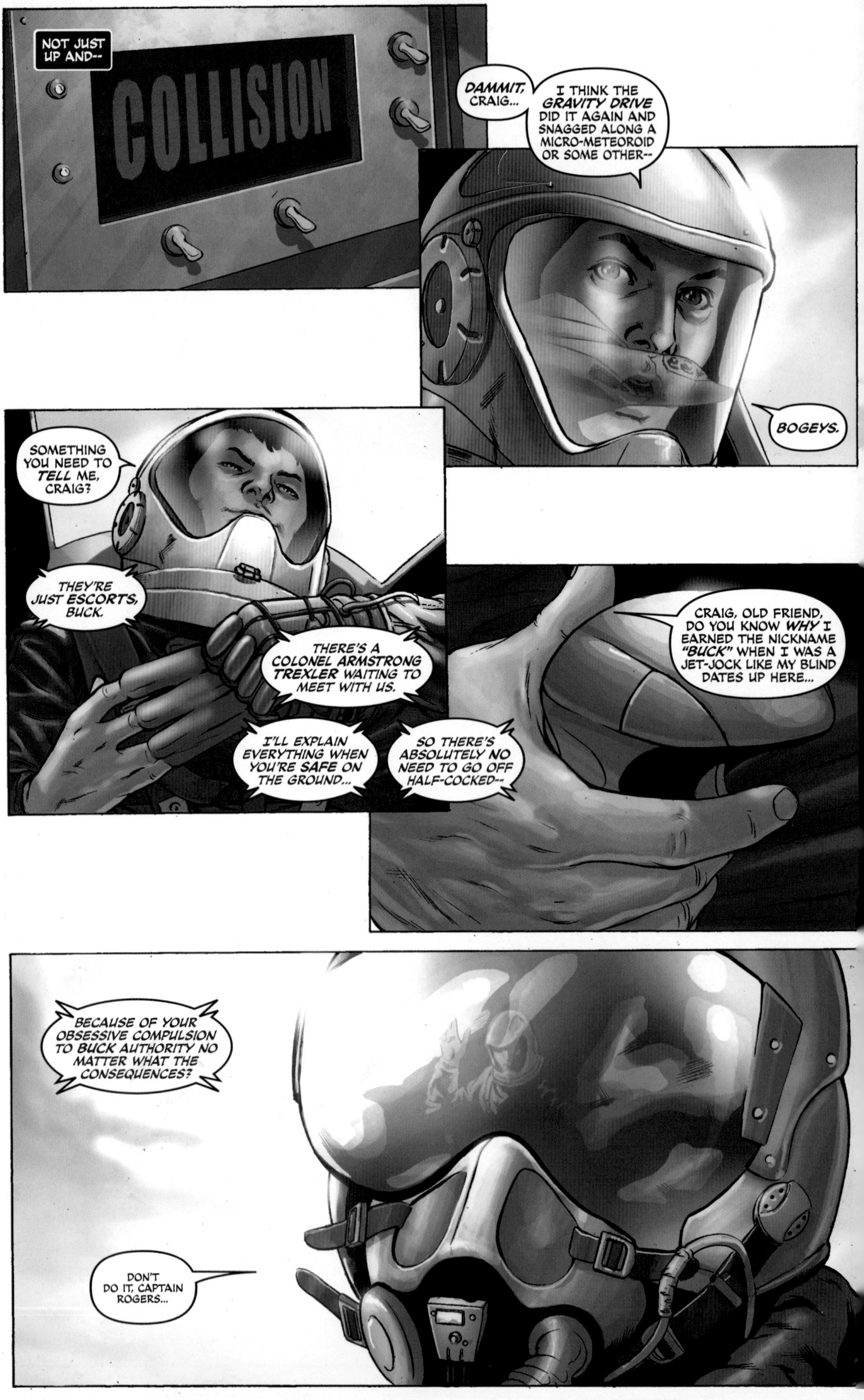
NOT JUST UP AND--
COLLISION
DAMMIT, CRAIG...
I THINK THE GRAVITY DRIVE DID IT AGAIN AND SNAGGED ALONG A MICRO-METEOROID OR SOME OTHER--
BOGEYS.
SOMETHING YOU NEED TO TELL ME, CRAIG?
THEY'RE JUST ESCORTS, BUCK.
THERE'S A COLONEL ARMSTRONG TREXLER WAITING TO MEET WITH US.
I'LL EXPLAIN EVERYTHING WHEN YOU'RE SAFE ON THE GROUND...
SO THERE'S ABSOLUTELY NO NEED TO GO OFF HALF-COCKED--
CRAIG, OLD FRIEND, DO YOU KNOW WHY I EARNED THE NICKNAME "BUCK" WHEN I WAS A JET-JOCK LIKE MY BLIND DATES UP HERE...
BECAUSE OF YOUR OBSESSIVE COMPULSION TO BUCK AUTHORITY NO MATTER WHAT THE CONSEQUENCES?
DON'T DO IT, CAPTAIN ROGERS...

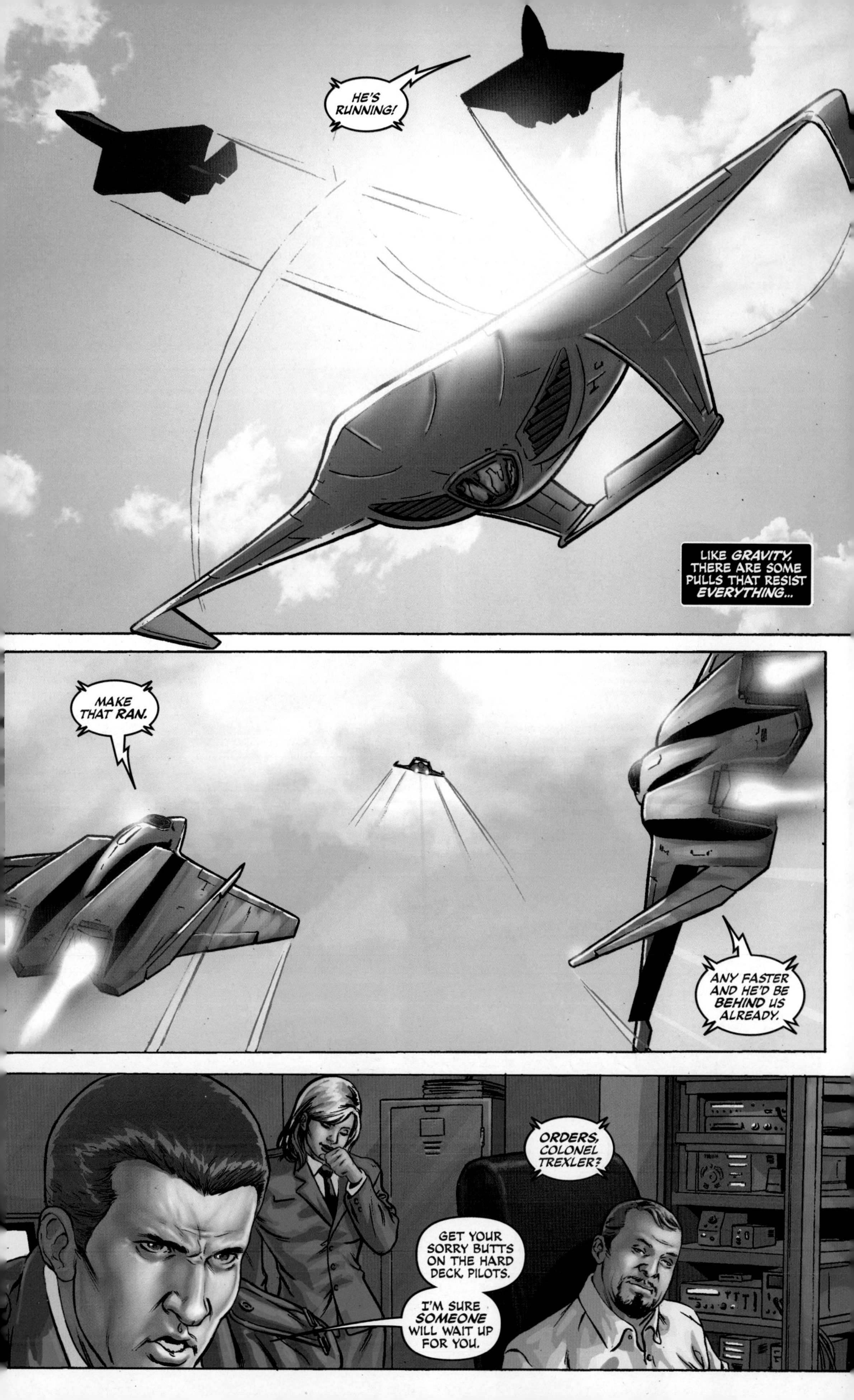
HE'S RUNNING!
LIKE GRAVITY, THERE ARE SOME PULLS THAT RESIST EVERYTHING...
MAKE THAT RAN.
ANY FASTER AND HE'D BE BEHIND US ALREADY.
ORDERS, COLONEL TREXLER?
GET YOUR SORRY BUTTS ON THE HARD DECK, PILOTS.
I'M SURE SOMEONE WILL WAIT UP FOR YOU.

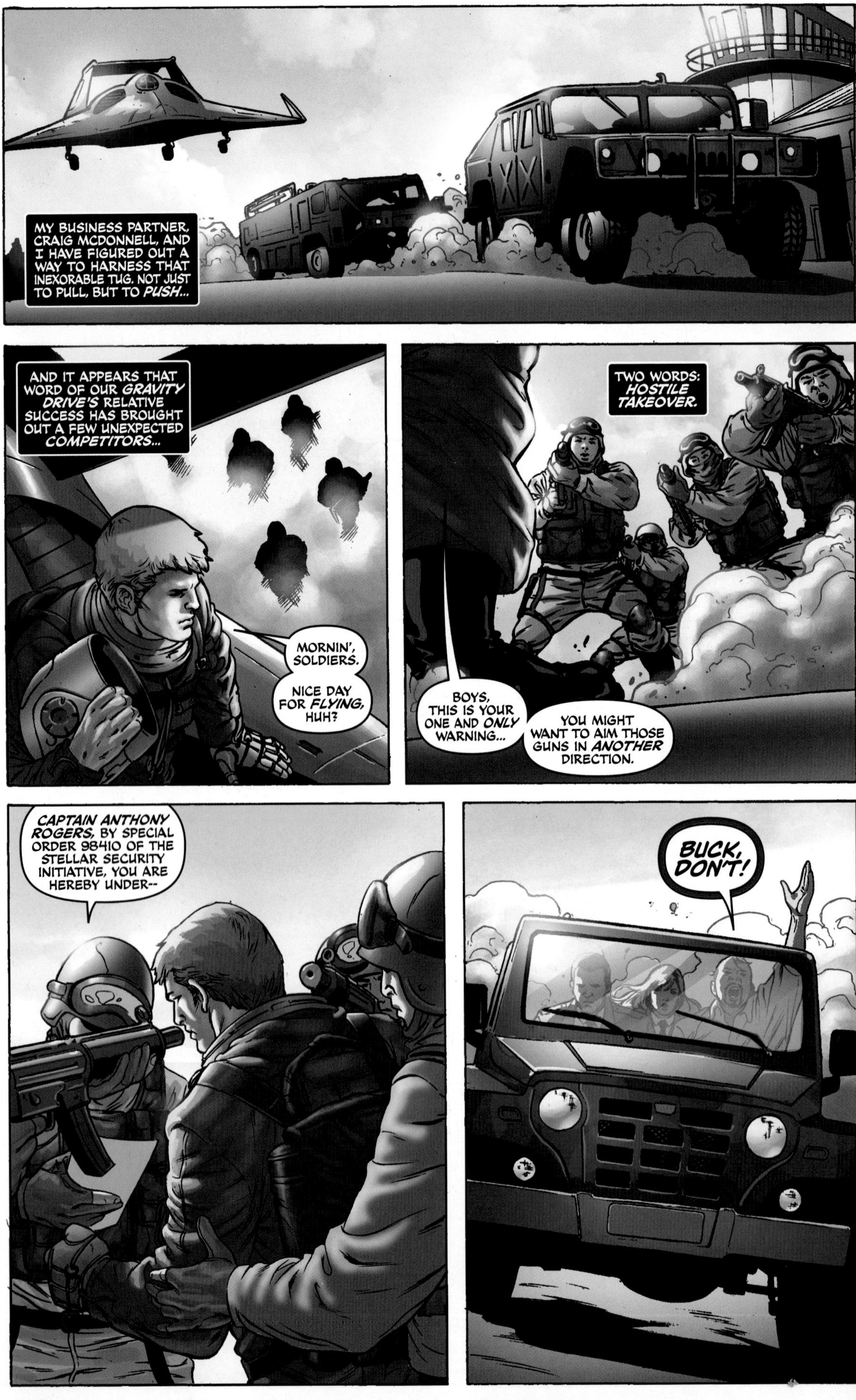
MY BUSINESS PARTNER, CRAIG MCDONNELL, AND I HAVE FIGURED OUT A WAY TO HARNESS THAT INEXORABLE TUG. NOT JUST TO PULL, BUT TO *PUSH*...
AND IT APPEARS THAT WORD OF OUR *GRAVITY DRIVE'S* RELATIVE SUCCESS HAS BROUGHT OUT A FEW UNEXPECTED *COMPETITORS*...
MORNIN', SOLDIERS.
NICE DAY FOR *FLYING*, HUH?
TWO WORDS: *HOSTILE TAKEOVER.*
BOYS, THIS IS YOUR ONE AND *ONLY* WARNING...
YOU MIGHT WANT TO AIM THOSE GUNS IN *ANOTHER* DIRECTION.
CAPTAIN ANTHONY ROGERS, BY SPECIAL ORDER 98410 OF THE STELLAR SECURITY INITIATIVE, YOU ARE HEREBY UNDER--
BUCK, DON'T!

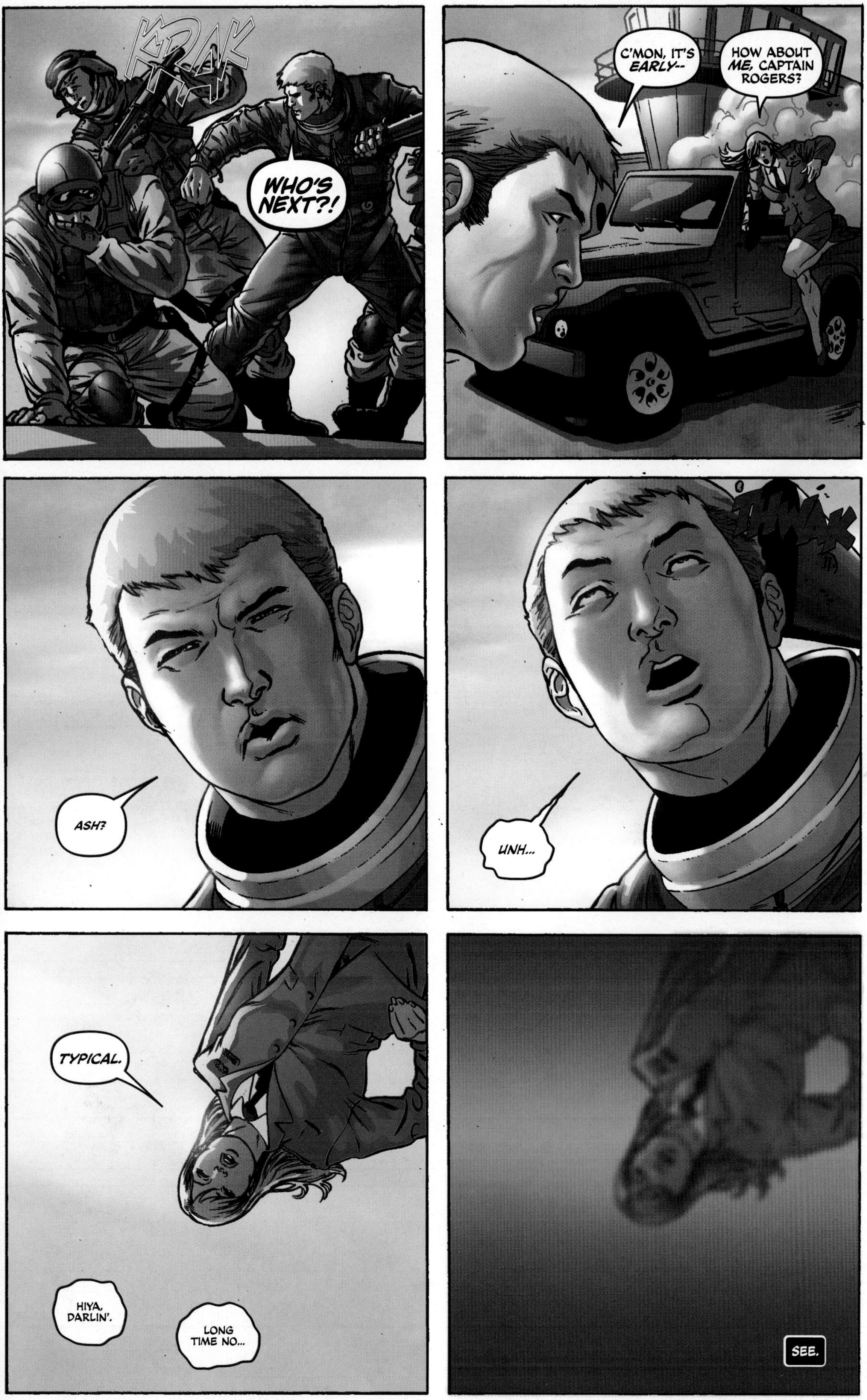
KRAK
WHO'S NEXT?!
C'MON, IT'S EARLY--
HOW ABOUT ME, CAPTAIN ROGERS?
ASH?
THWAK
UNH...
TYPICAL.
HIYA, DARLIN'.
LONG TIME NO...
SEE.

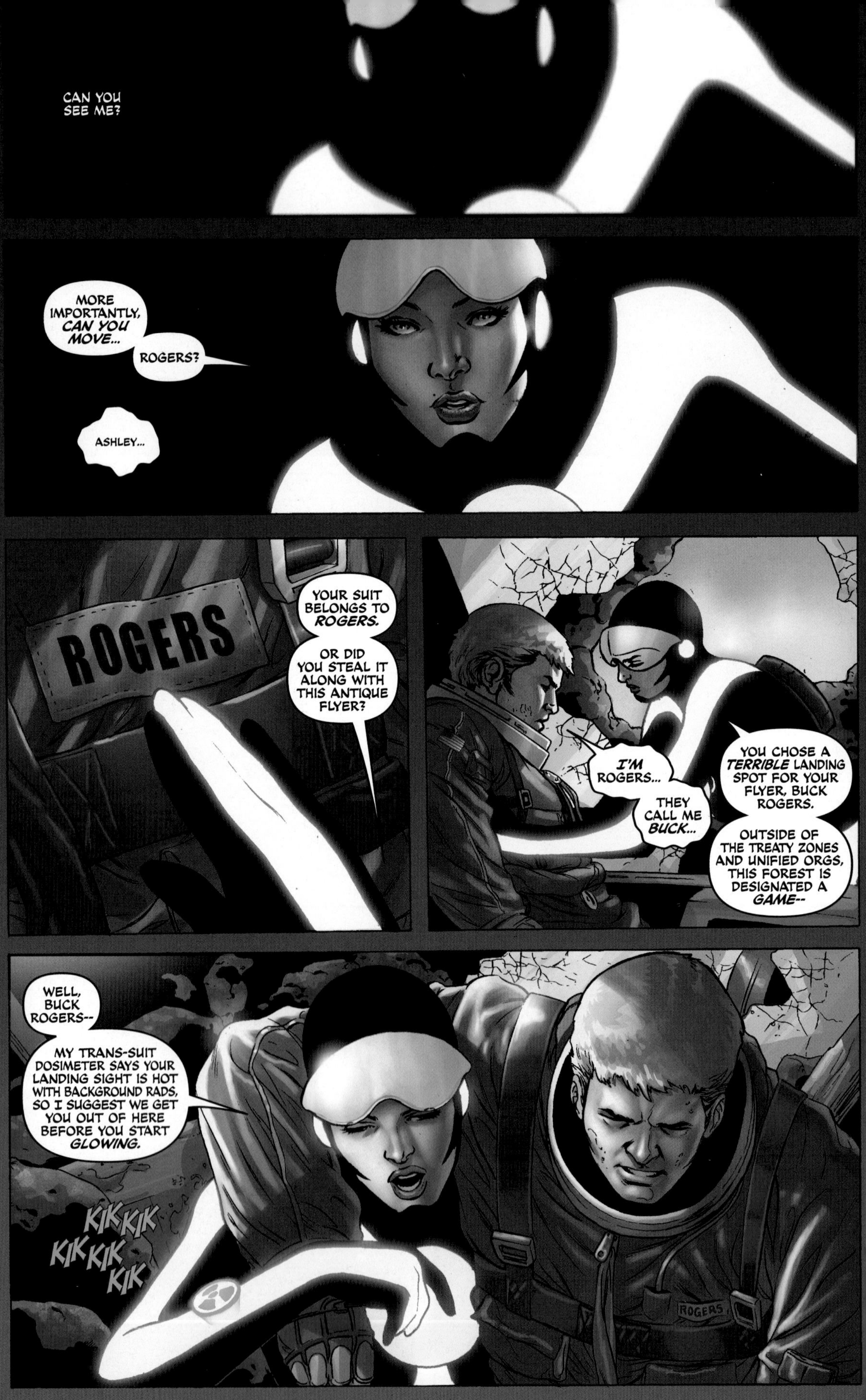
CAN YOU SEE ME?
MORE IMPORTANTLY, CAN YOU MOVE...
ROGERS?
ASHLEY...
ROGERS
YOUR SUIT BELONGS TO ROGERS.
OR DID YOU STEAL IT ALONG WITH THIS ANTIQUE FLYER?
I'M ROGERS...
THEY CALL ME BUCK...
YOU CHOSE A TERRIBLE LANDING SPOT FOR YOUR FLYER, BUCK ROGERS.
OUTSIDE OF THE TREATY ZONES AND UNIFIED ORGS, THIS FOREST IS DESIGNATED A GAME--
WELL, BUCK ROGERS--
MY TRANS-SUIT DOSIMETER SAYS YOUR LANDING SIGHT IS HOT WITH BACKGROUND RADS, SO I SUGGEST WE GET YOU OUT OF HERE BEFORE YOU START GLOWING.
KIK KIK KIK KIK KIK KIK
ROGERS

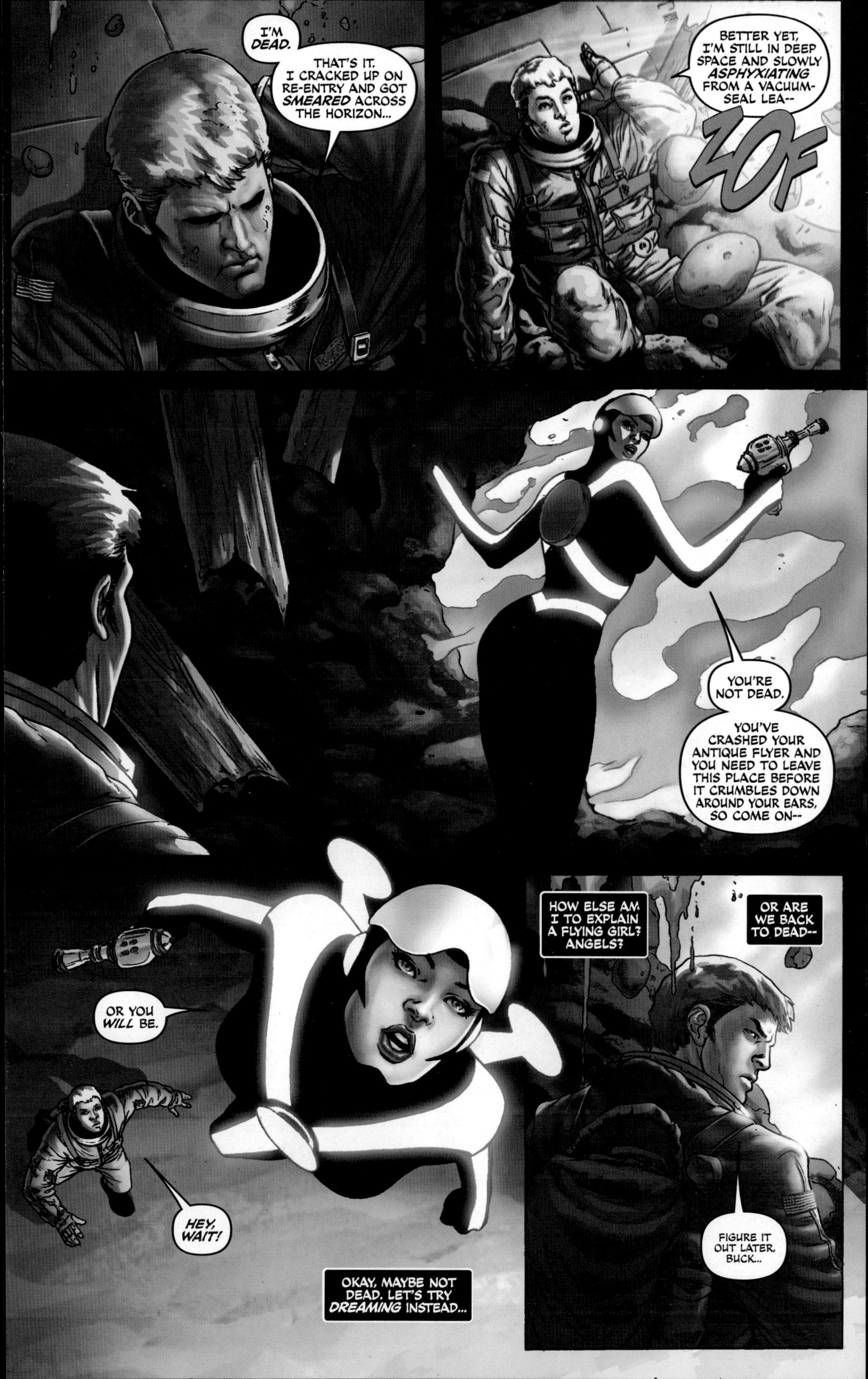
I'M DEAD.
THAT'S IT. I CRACKED UP ON RE-ENTRY AND GOT SMEARED ACROSS THE HORIZON...
BETTER YET, I'M STILL IN DEEP SPACE AND SLOWLY ASPHYXIATING FROM A VACUUM-SEAL LEA--
ZOF
YOU'RE NOT DEAD.
YOU'VE CRASHED YOUR ANTIQUE FLYER AND YOU NEED TO LEAVE THIS PLACE BEFORE IT CRUMBLES DOWN AROUND YOUR EARS, SO COME ON--
OR YOU WILL BE.
HEY, WAIT!
OKAY, MAYBE NOT DEAD. LET'S TRY DREAMING INSTEAD...
HOW ELSE AM I TO EXPLAIN A FLYING GIRL? ANGELS?
OR ARE WE BACK TO DEAD--
FIGURE IT OUT LATER, BUCK...

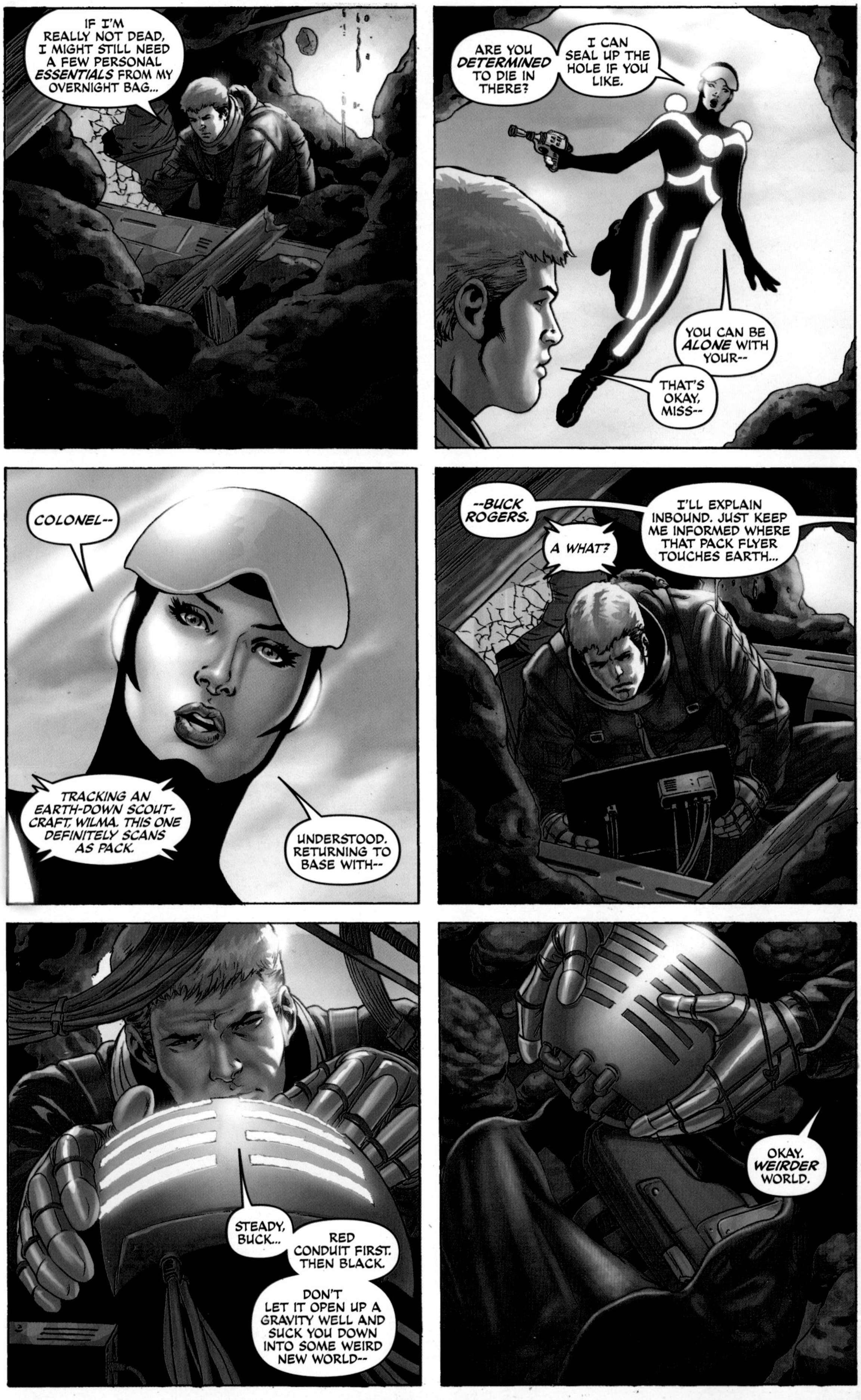
IF I'M REALLY NOT DEAD, I MIGHT STILL NEED A FEW PERSONAL *ESSENTIALS* FROM MY OVERNIGHT BAG...
ARE YOU *DETERMINED* TO DIE IN THERE?
I CAN SEAL UP THE HOLE IF YOU LIKE.
YOU CAN BE *ALONE* WITH YOUR--
THAT'S OKAY, MISS--
COLONEL--
TRACKING AN EARTH-DOWN SCOUT-CRAFT, WILMA. THIS ONE DEFINITELY SCANS AS PACK.
UNDERSTOOD. RETURNING TO BASE WITH--
--BUCK ROGERS.
A WHAT?
I'LL EXPLAIN INBOUND. JUST KEEP ME INFORMED WHERE THAT PACK FLYER TOUCHES EARTH...
STEADY, BUCK...
RED CONDUIT FIRST. THEN BLACK.
DON'T LET IT OPEN UP A GRAVITY WELL AND SUCK YOU DOWN INTO SOME WEIRD NEW WORLD--
OKAY. *WEIRDER* WORLD.

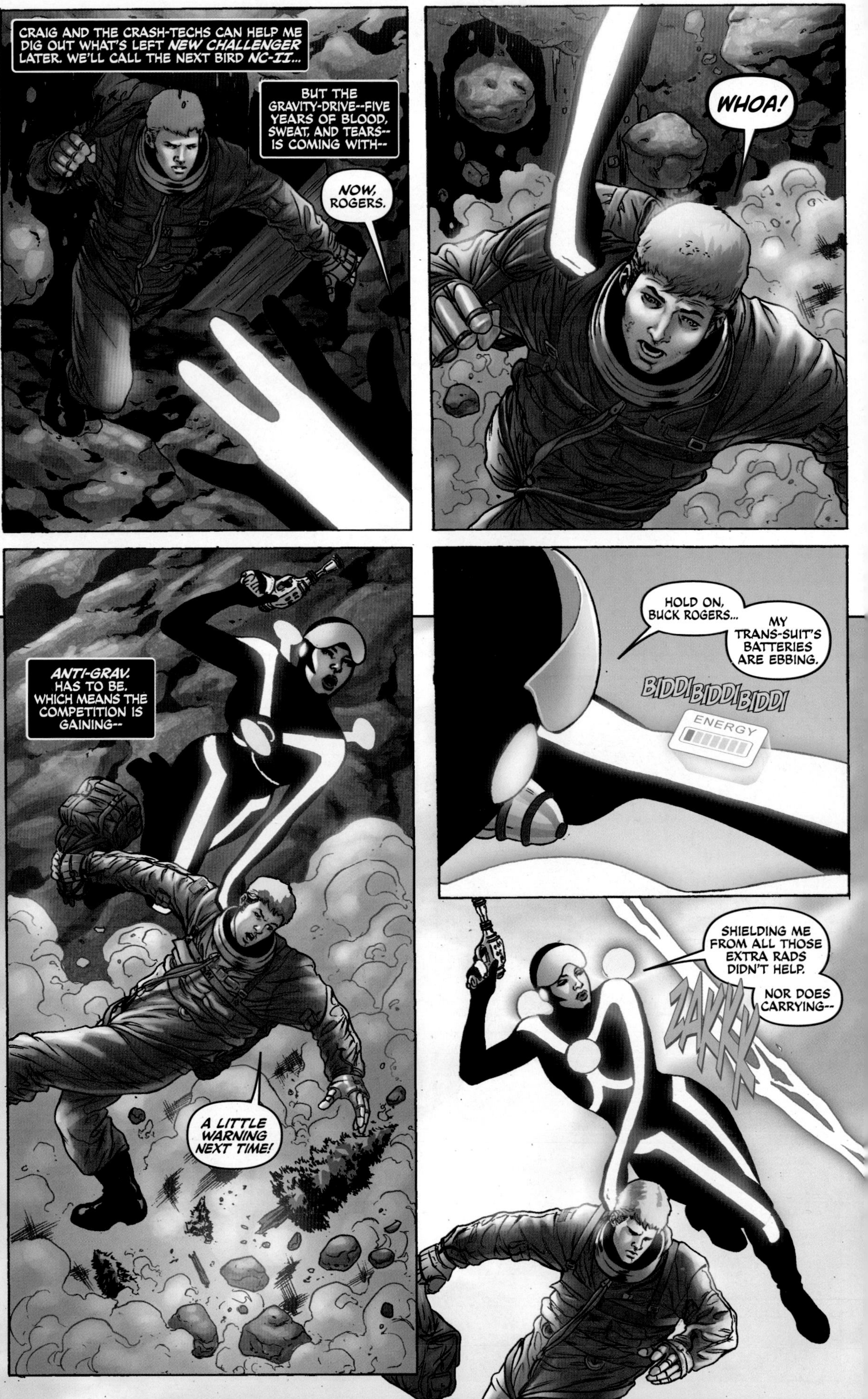
CRAIG AND THE CRASH-TECHS CAN HELP ME DIG OUT WHAT'S LEFT NEW CHALLENGER LATER. WE'LL CALL THE NEXT BIRD NC-II...
BUT THE GRAVITY-DRIVE--FIVE YEARS OF BLOOD, SWEAT, AND TEARS--IS COMING WITH--
NOW, ROGERS.
WHOA!
ANTI-GRAV. HAS TO BE. WHICH MEANS THE COMPETITION IS GAINING--
A LITTLE WARNING NEXT TIME!
HOLD ON, BUCK ROGERS...
MY TRANS-SUIT'S BATTERIES ARE EBBING.
BIDDI BIDDI BIDDI
ENERGY
SHIELDING ME FROM ALL THOSE EXTRA RADS DIDN'T HELP.
NOR DOES CARRYING--
ZAKKK

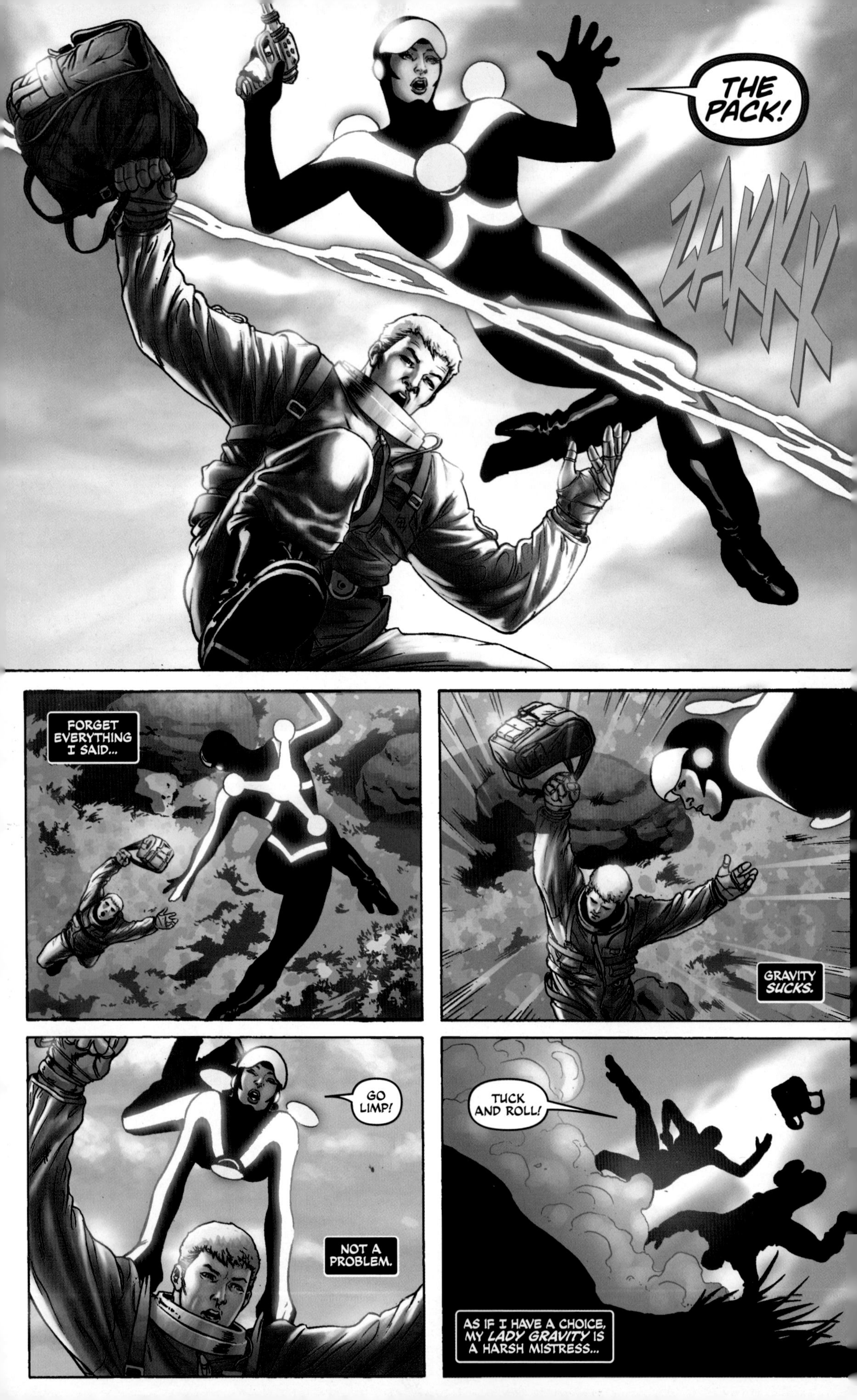
THE PACK!
ZAKKK
FORGET EVERYTHING I SAID...
GRAVITY SUCKS.
GO LIMP!
NOT A PROBLEM.
TUCK AND ROLL!
AS IF I HAVE A CHOICE, MY LADY GRAVITY IS A HARSH MISTRESS...

AND MY ANGEL IN BLACK?

WHO *ARE* YOU?

MY NAME IS *COLONEL WILMA*--

WAIT, WHERE'S MY KNAPSACK?!

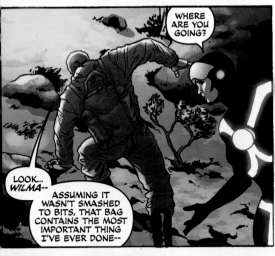

WHERE ARE YOU GOING?

LOOK... *WILMA*-- ASSUMING IT WASN'T SMASHED TO BITS, THAT BAG CONTAINS THE MOST IMPORTANT THING I'VE EVER DONE--

OR *WILL* DO.

BINGO. COME TO PAPA--

BEAR.

DO AS I TELL YOU AND PERHAPS *ONE* OF US WILL AVOID THE ABATTOIR SHIPS...

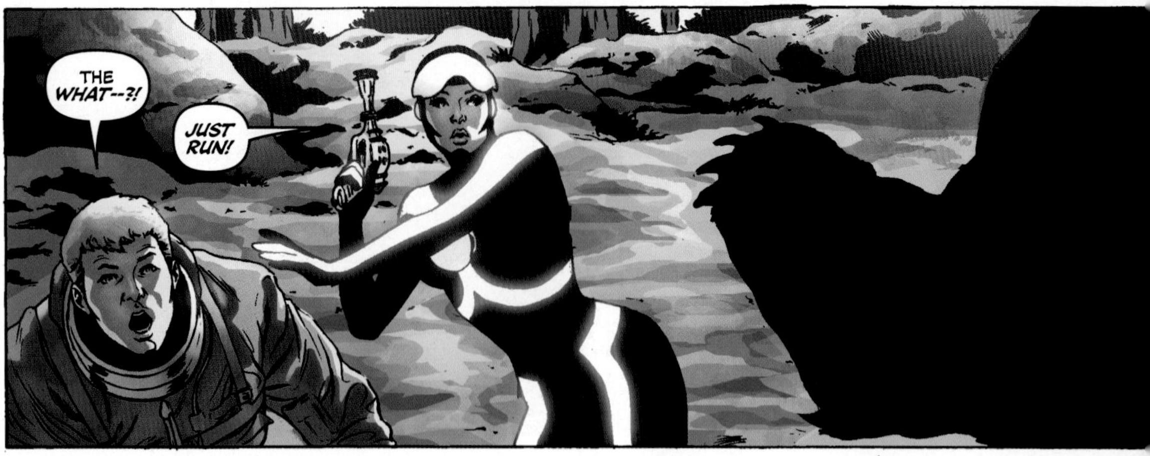
THE WHAT--?!
JUST RUN!

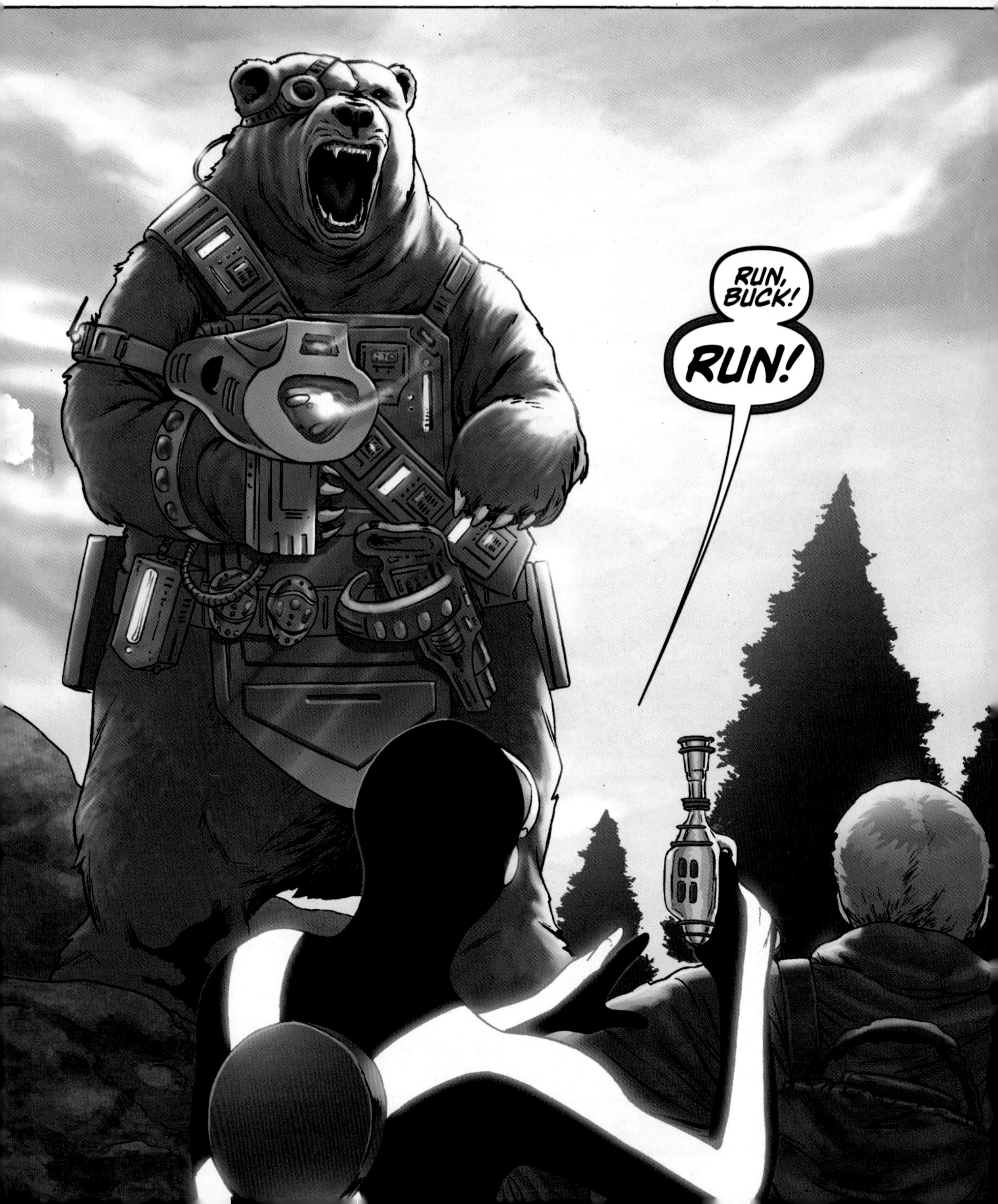
RUN, BUCK!
RUN!

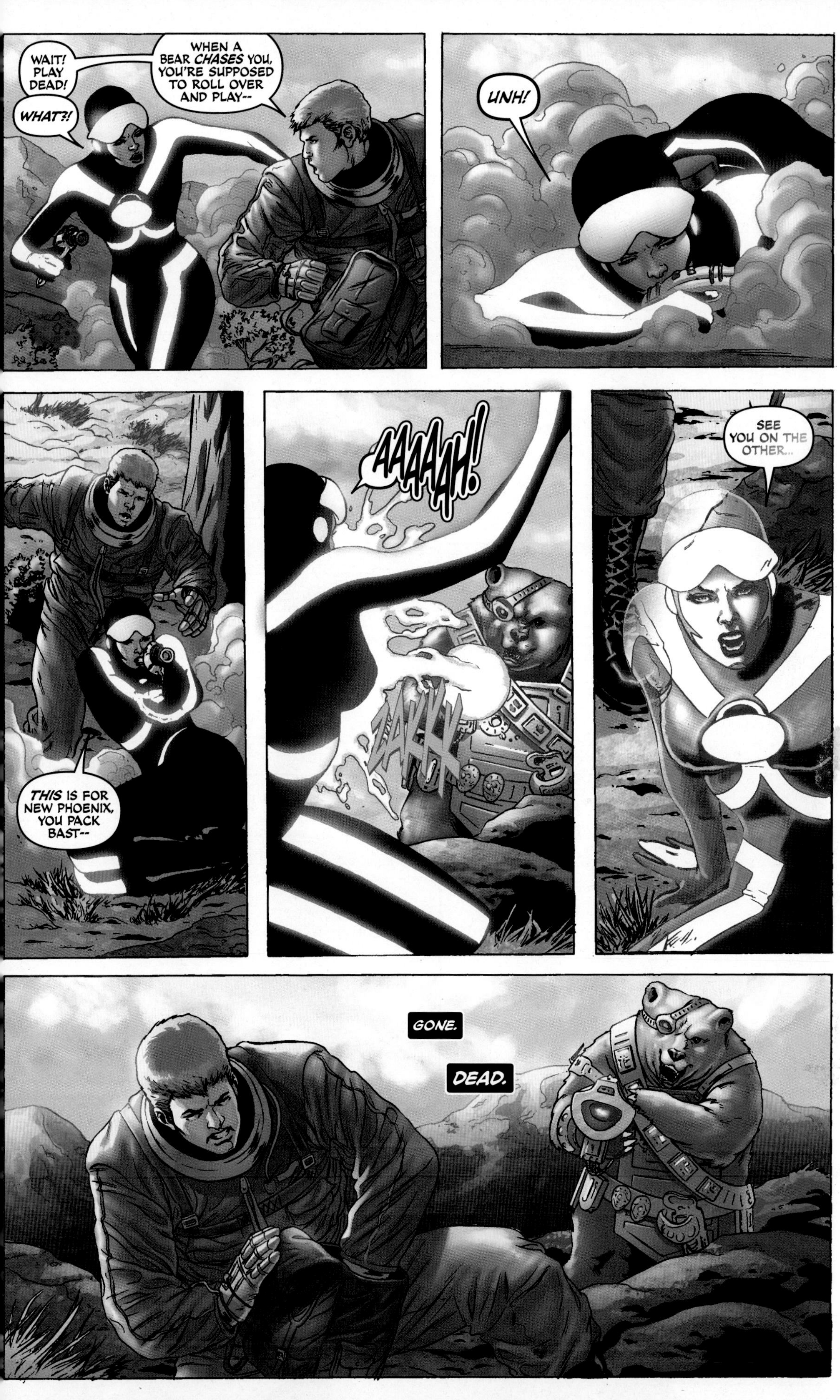

WHEN A BEAR CHASES YOU, YOU'RE SUPPOSED TO ROLL OVER AND PLAY--
WAIT! PLAY DEAD!
WHAT?!
UNH!
THIS IS FOR NEW PHOENIX, YOU PACK BAST--
AAAAAH!
ZAKKK
SEE YOU ON THE OTHER...
GONE.
DEAD.

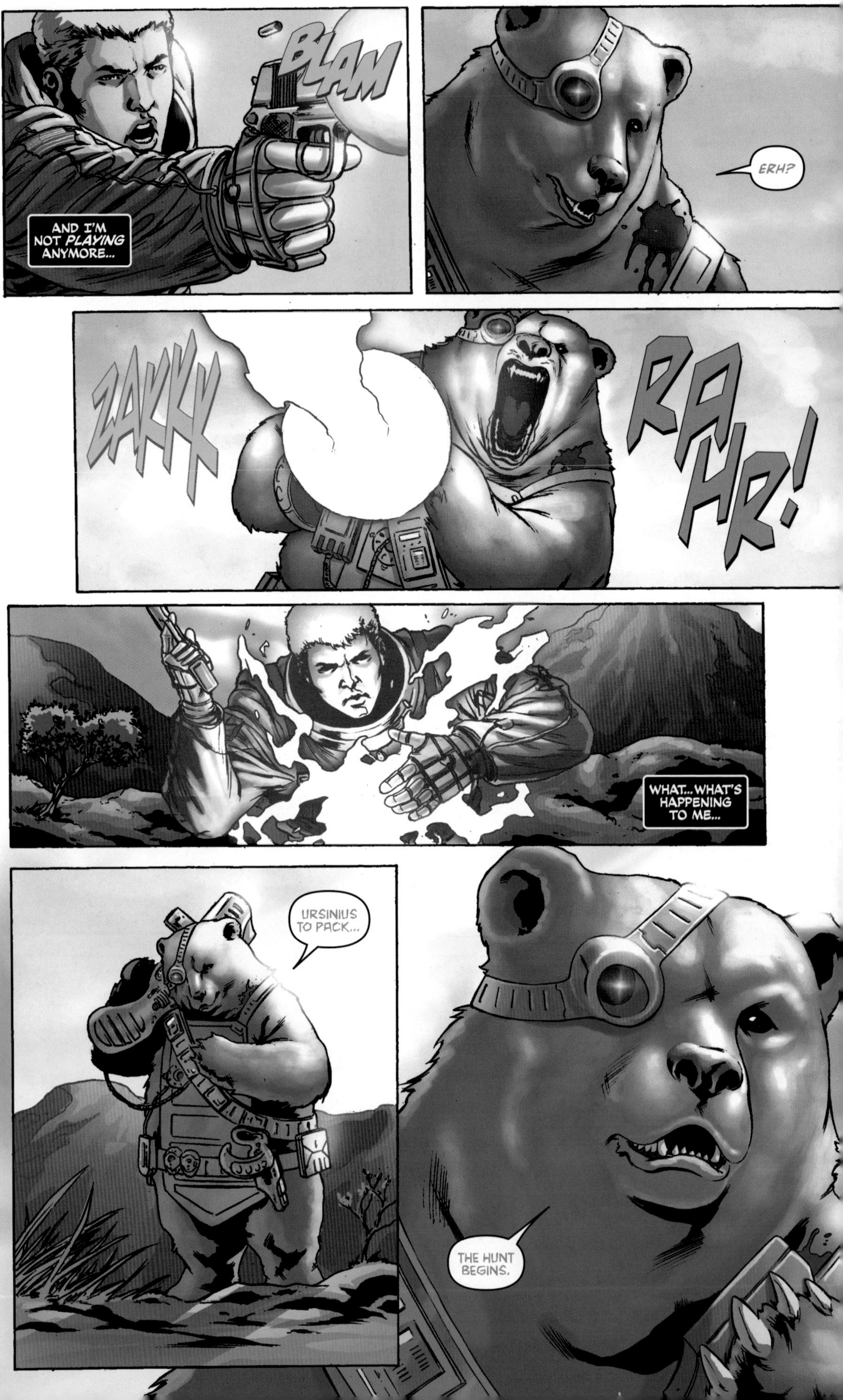
BLAM
AND I'M NOT PLAYING ANYMORE...
ERH?
ZAKKK
RAHR!
WHAT... WHAT'S HAPPENING TO ME...
URSINIUS TO PACK...
THE HUNT BEGINS.

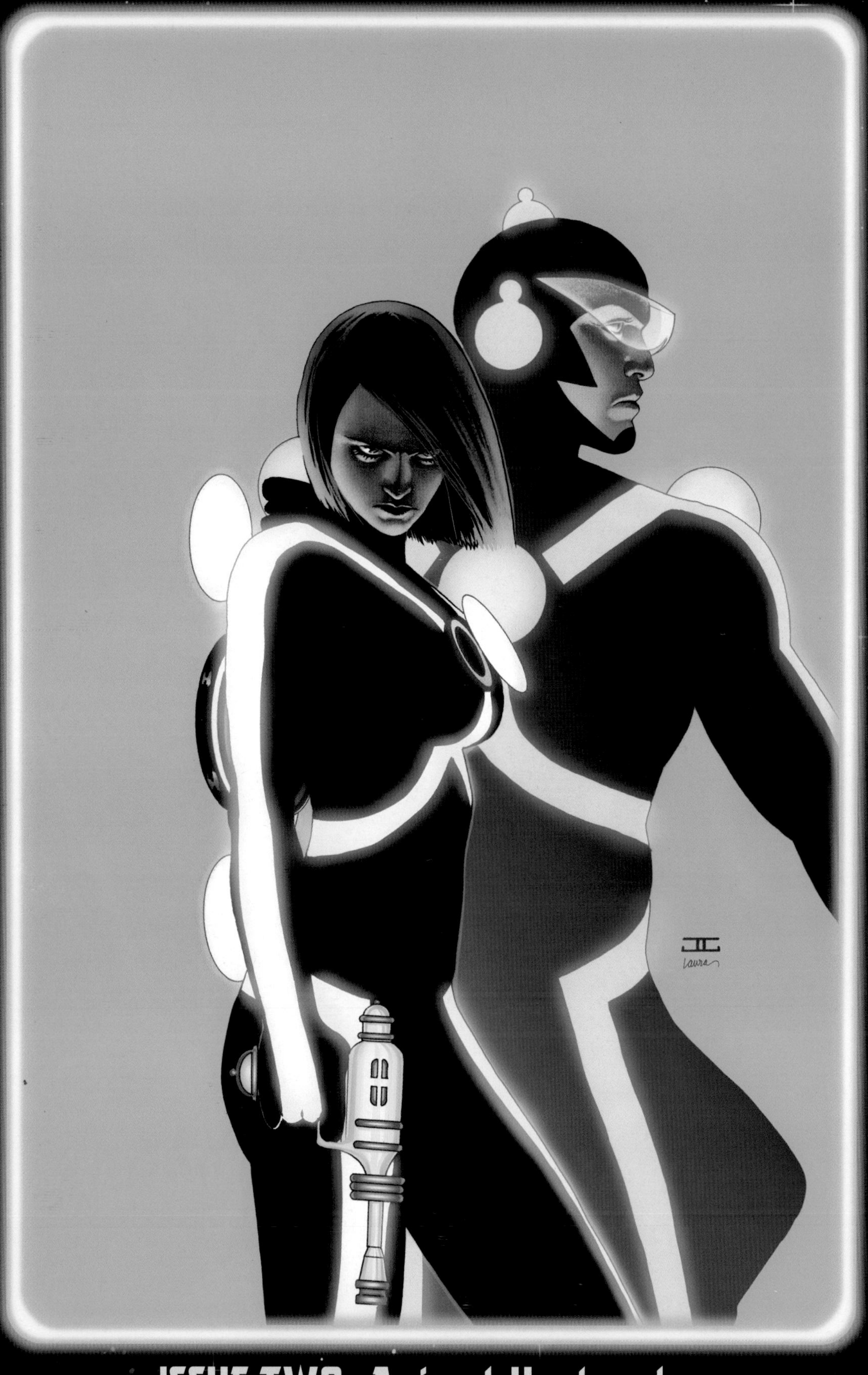

ISSUE TWO: Animal Husbandry

COVER BY JOHN CASSADAY

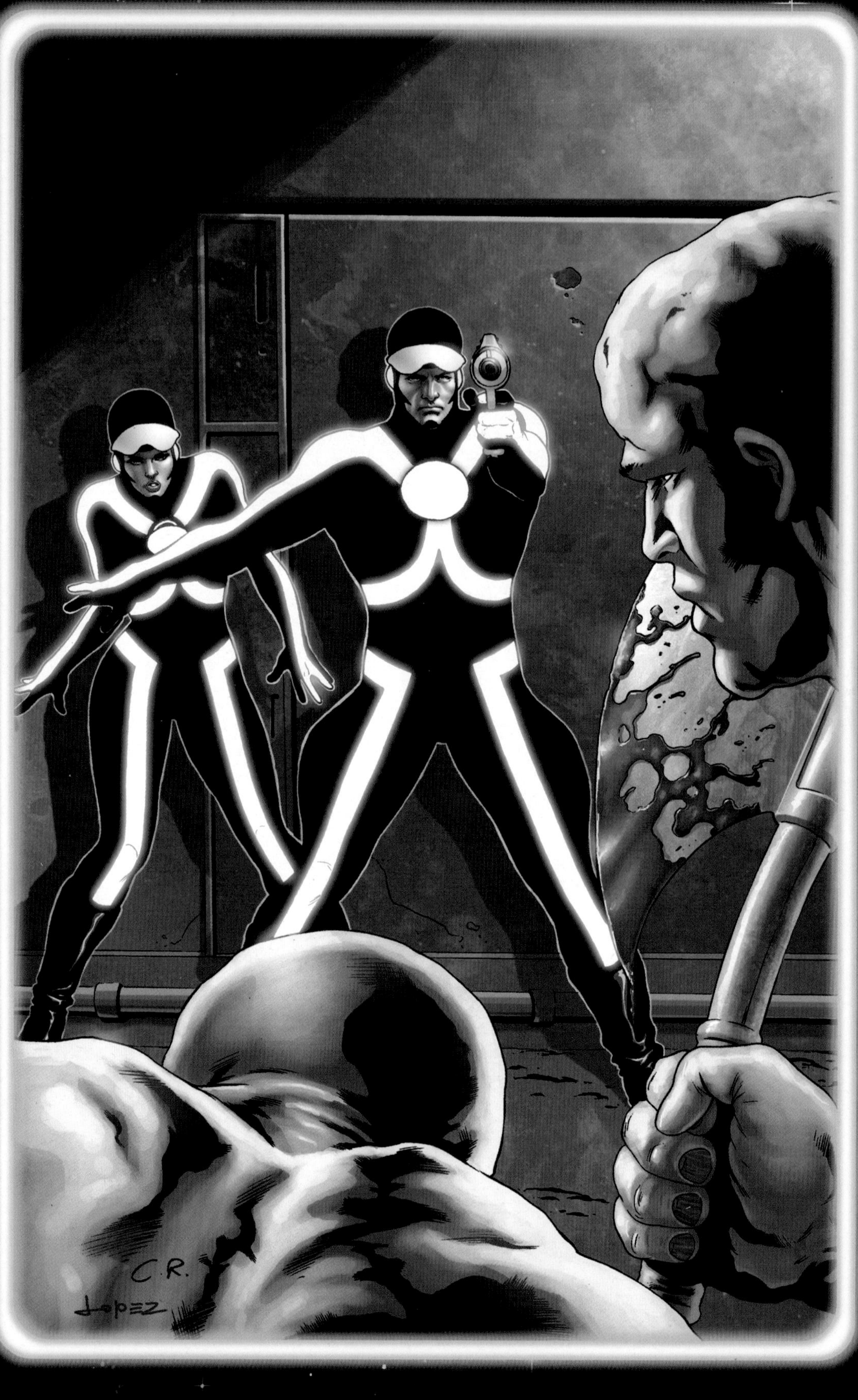
C.R.
Lopez

ALTERNATE COVER BY CARLOS RAFAEL

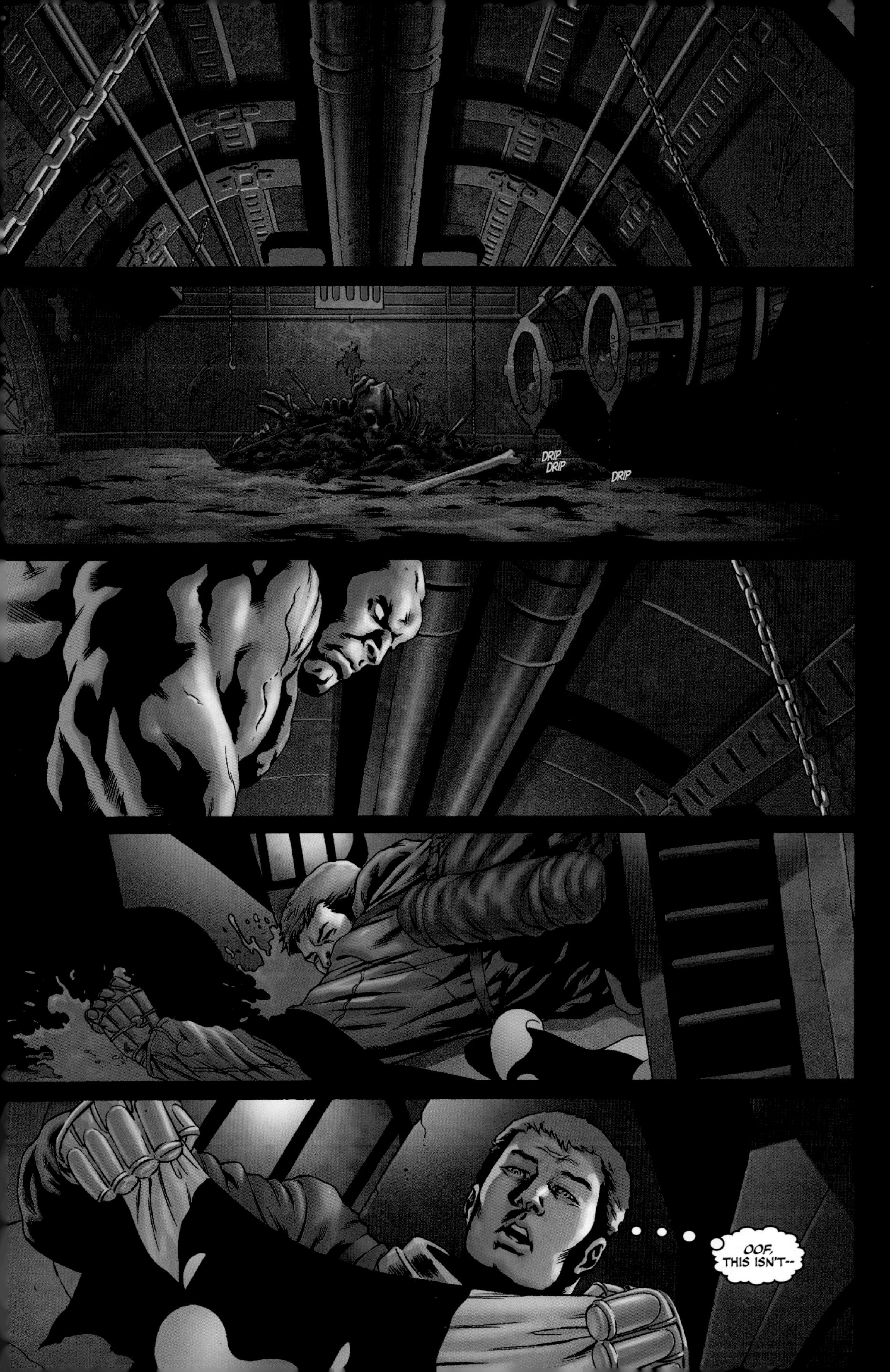
DRIP
DRIP
DRIP
OOF, THIS ISN'T--

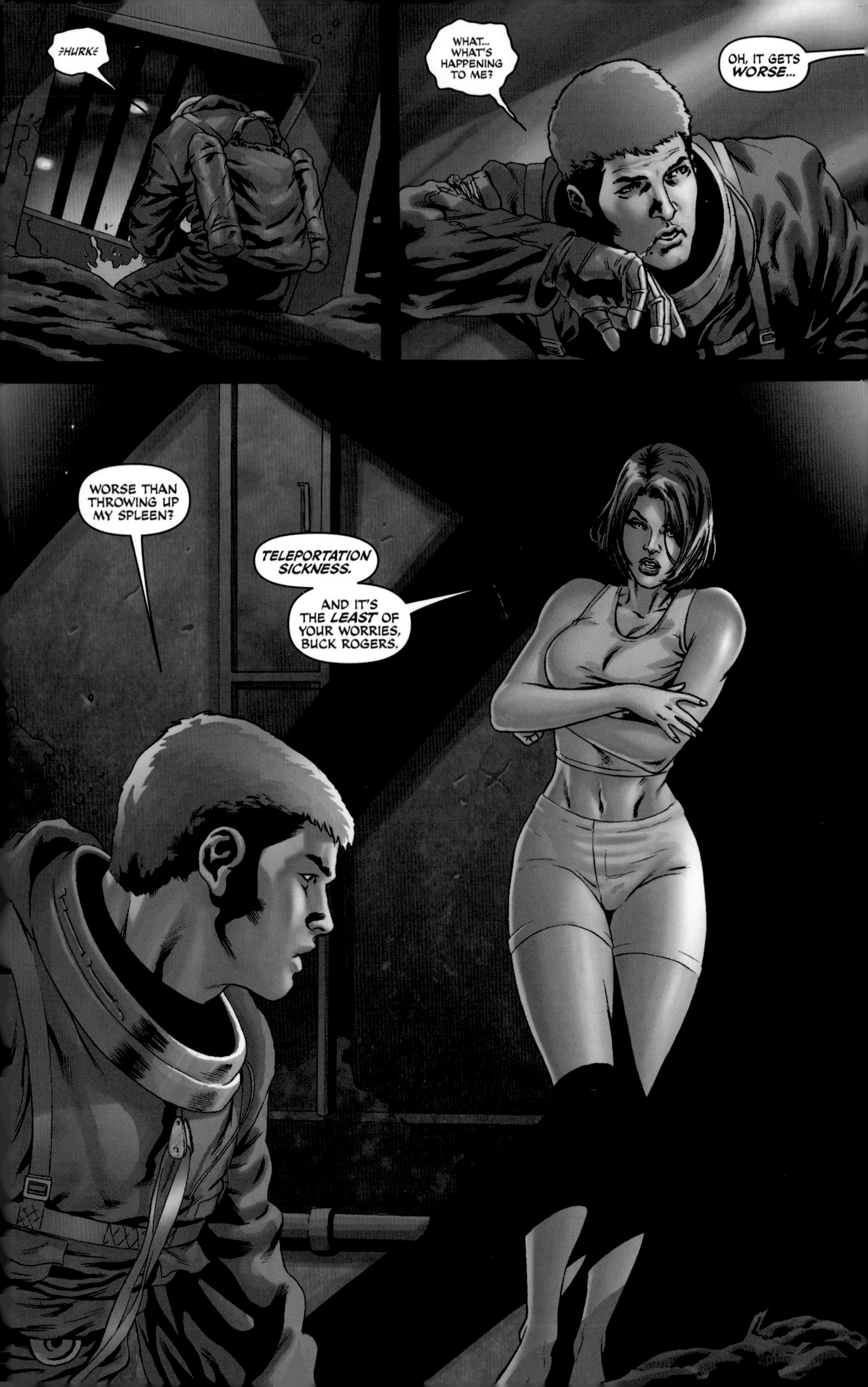

≥HURK≤
WHAT... WHAT'S HAPPENING TO ME?
OH, IT GETS *WORSE*...
WORSE THAN THROWING UP MY SPLEEN?
TELEPORTATION SICKNESS.
AND IT'S THE *LEAST* OF YOUR WORRIES, BUCK ROGERS.

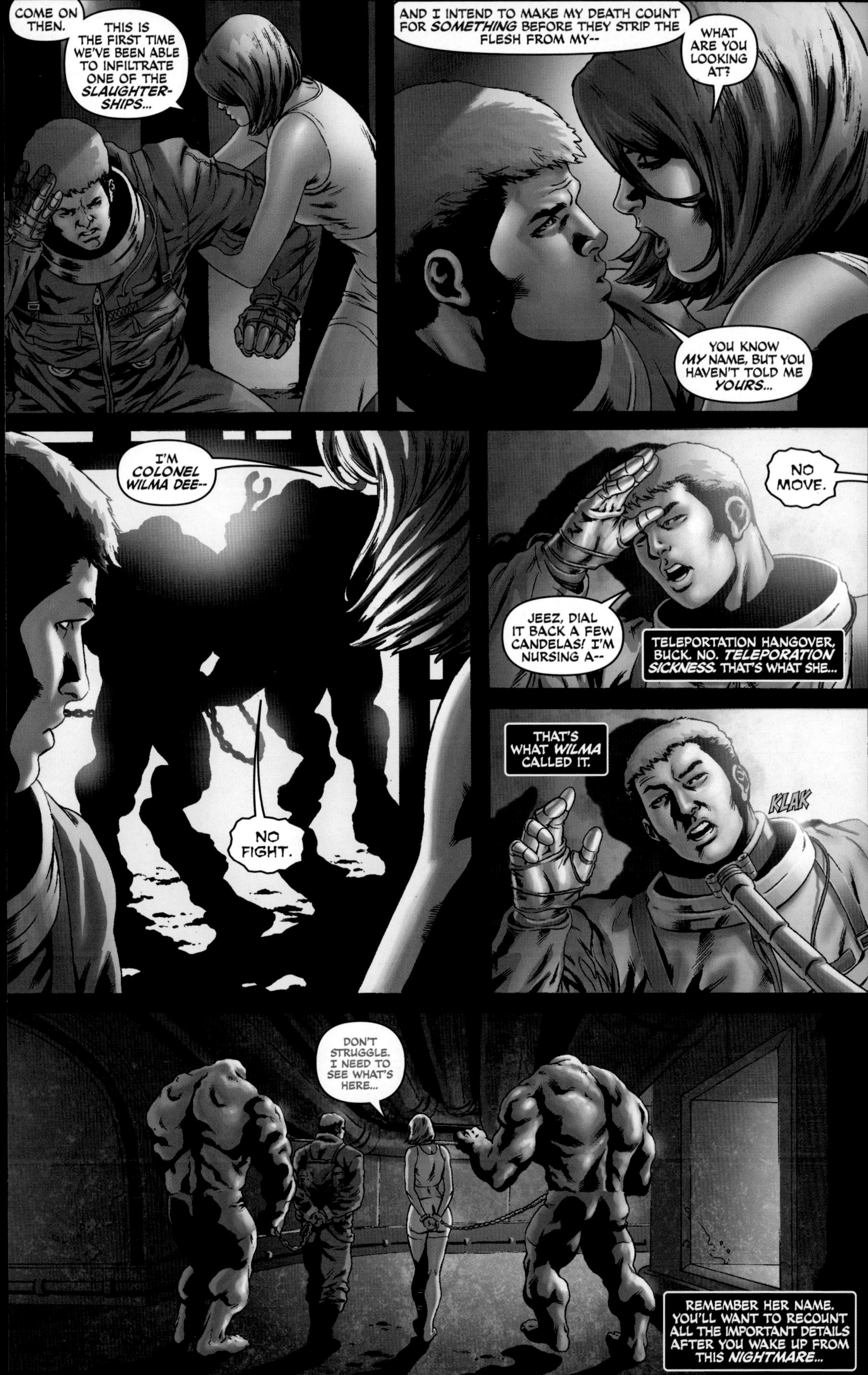
COME ON THEN.
THIS IS THE FIRST TIME WE'VE BEEN ABLE TO INFILTRATE ONE OF THE *SLAUGHTER-SHIPS*...
AND I INTEND TO MAKE MY DEATH COUNT FOR *SOMETHING* BEFORE THEY STRIP THE FLESH FROM MY--
WHAT ARE YOU LOOKING AT?
YOU KNOW *MY* NAME, BUT YOU HAVEN'T TOLD ME *YOURS*...
I'M *COLONEL WILMA DEE*--
NO FIGHT.
NO MOVE.
JEEZ, DIAL IT BACK A FEW CANDELAS! I'M NURSING A--
TELEPORTATION HANGOVER, BUCK. NO. *TELEPORATION SICKNESS*. THAT'S WHAT SHE...
THAT'S WHAT *WILMA* CALLED IT.
KLAK
DON'T STRUGGLE. I NEED TO SEE WHAT'S HERE...
REMEMBER HER NAME. YOU'LL WANT TO RECOUNT ALL THE IMPORTANT DETAILS AFTER YOU WAKE UP FROM THIS *NIGHTMARE*...

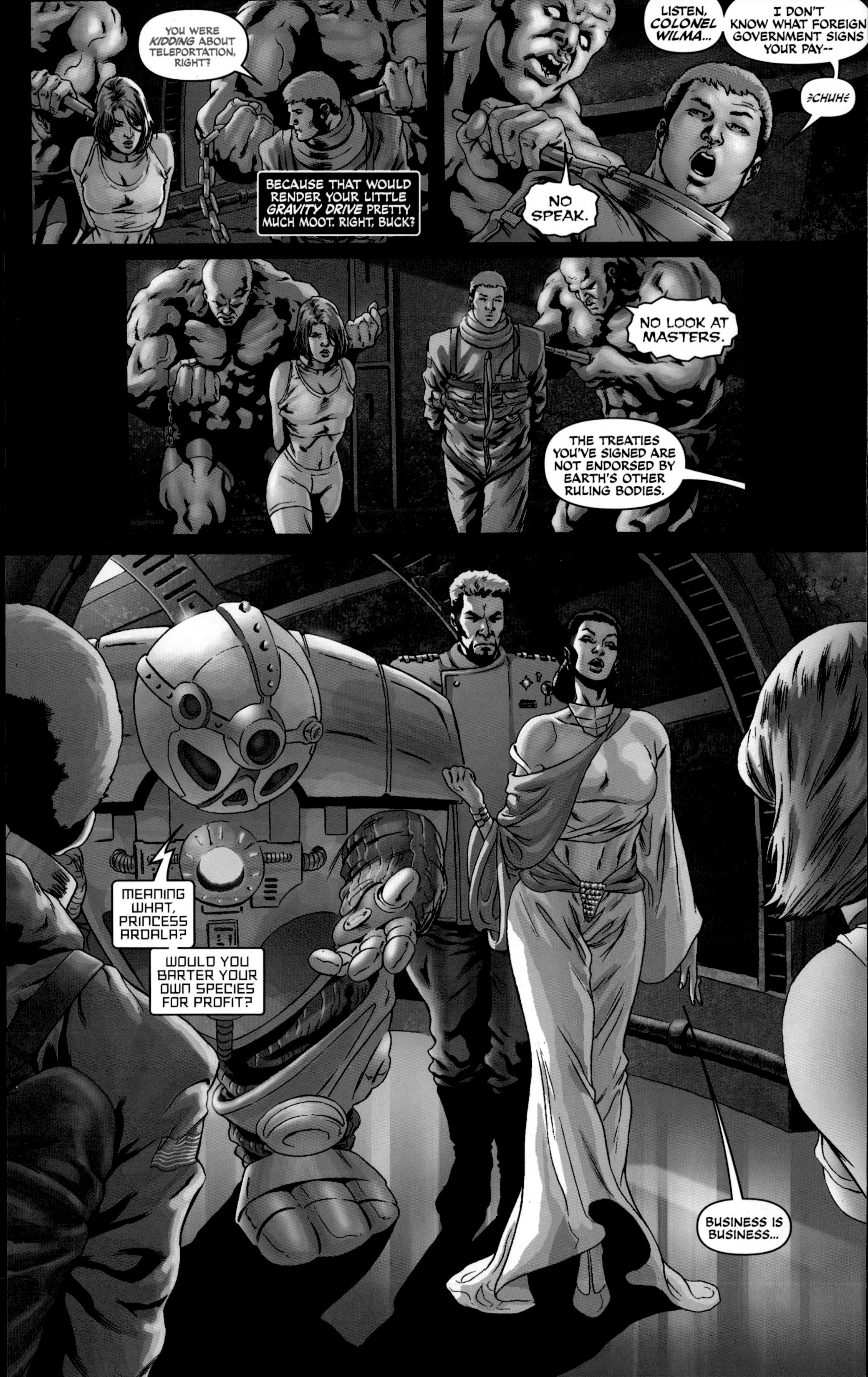
YOU WERE KIDDING ABOUT TELEPORTATION, RIGHT?
BECAUSE THAT WOULD RENDER YOUR LITTLE GRAVITY DRIVE PRETTY MUCH MOOT. RIGHT, BUCK?
LISTEN, COLONEL WILMA...
I DON'T KNOW WHAT FOREIGN GOVERNMENT SIGNS YOUR PAY--
NO SPEAK.
CHUH
NO LOOK AT MASTERS.
THE TREATIES YOU'VE SIGNED ARE NOT ENDORSED BY EARTH'S OTHER RULING BODIES.
MEANING WHAT, PRINCESS ARDALA?
WOULD YOU BARTER YOUR OWN SPECIES FOR PROFIT?
BUSINESS IS BUSINESS...

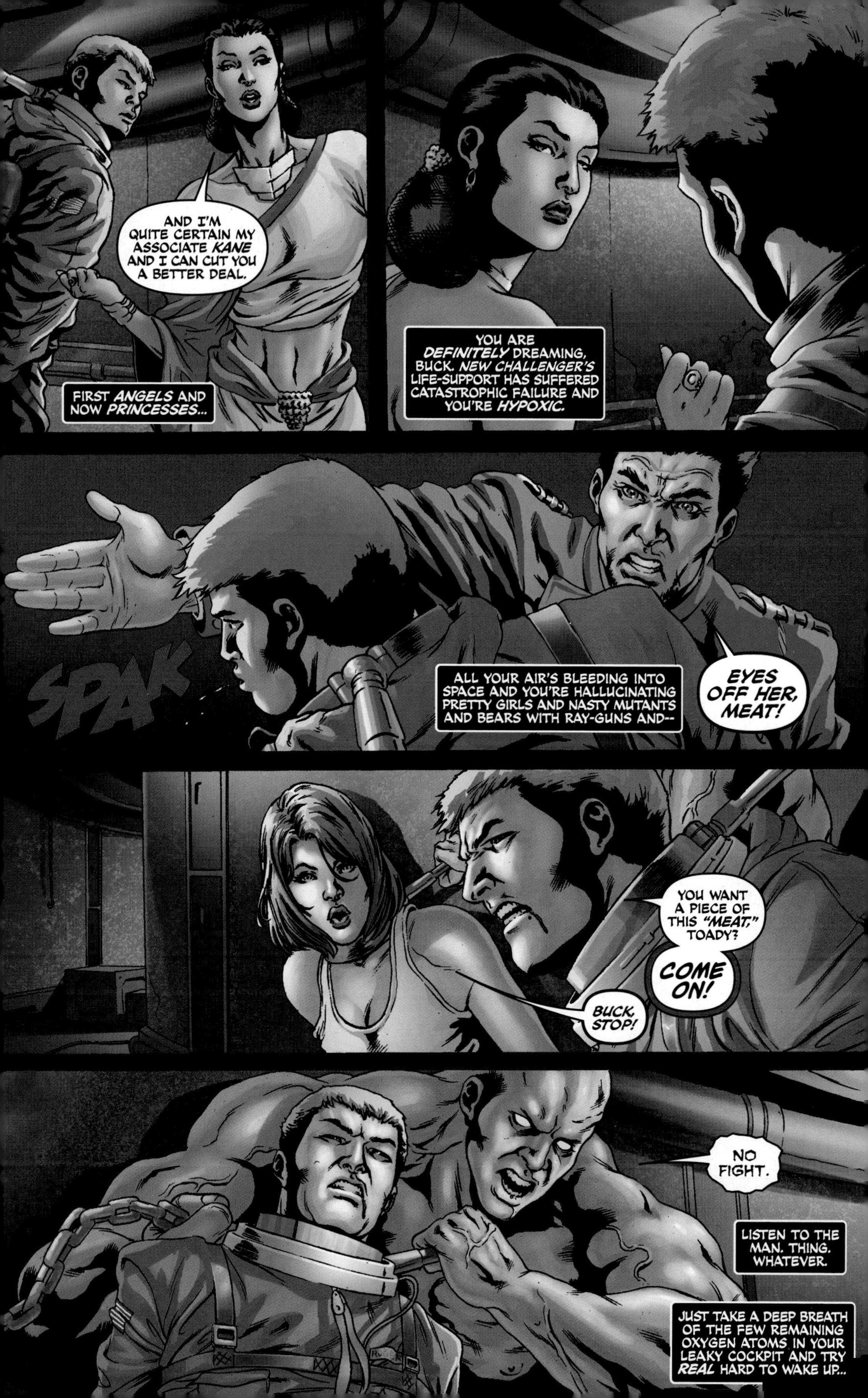
AND I'M QUITE CERTAIN MY ASSOCIATE *KANE* AND I CAN CUT YOU A BETTER DEAL.
FIRST *ANGELS* AND NOW *PRINCESSES*...
YOU ARE *DEFINITELY* DREAMING, BUCK. *NEW CHALLENGER'S* LIFE-SUPPORT HAS SUFFERED CATASTROPHIC FAILURE AND YOU'RE *HYPOXIC.*
SPAK
ALL YOUR AIR'S BLEEDING INTO SPACE AND YOU'RE HALLUCINATING PRETTY GIRLS AND NASTY MUTANTS AND BEARS WITH RAY-GUNS AND--
EYES OFF HER, MEAT!
YOU WANT A PIECE OF THIS *"MEAT,"* TOADY?
COME ON!
BUCK, STOP!
NO FIGHT.
LISTEN TO THE MAN. THING. WHATEVER.
JUST TAKE A DEEP BREATH OF THE FEW REMAINING OXYGEN ATOMS IN YOUR LEAKY COCKPIT AND TRY *REAL* HARD TO WAKE UP...

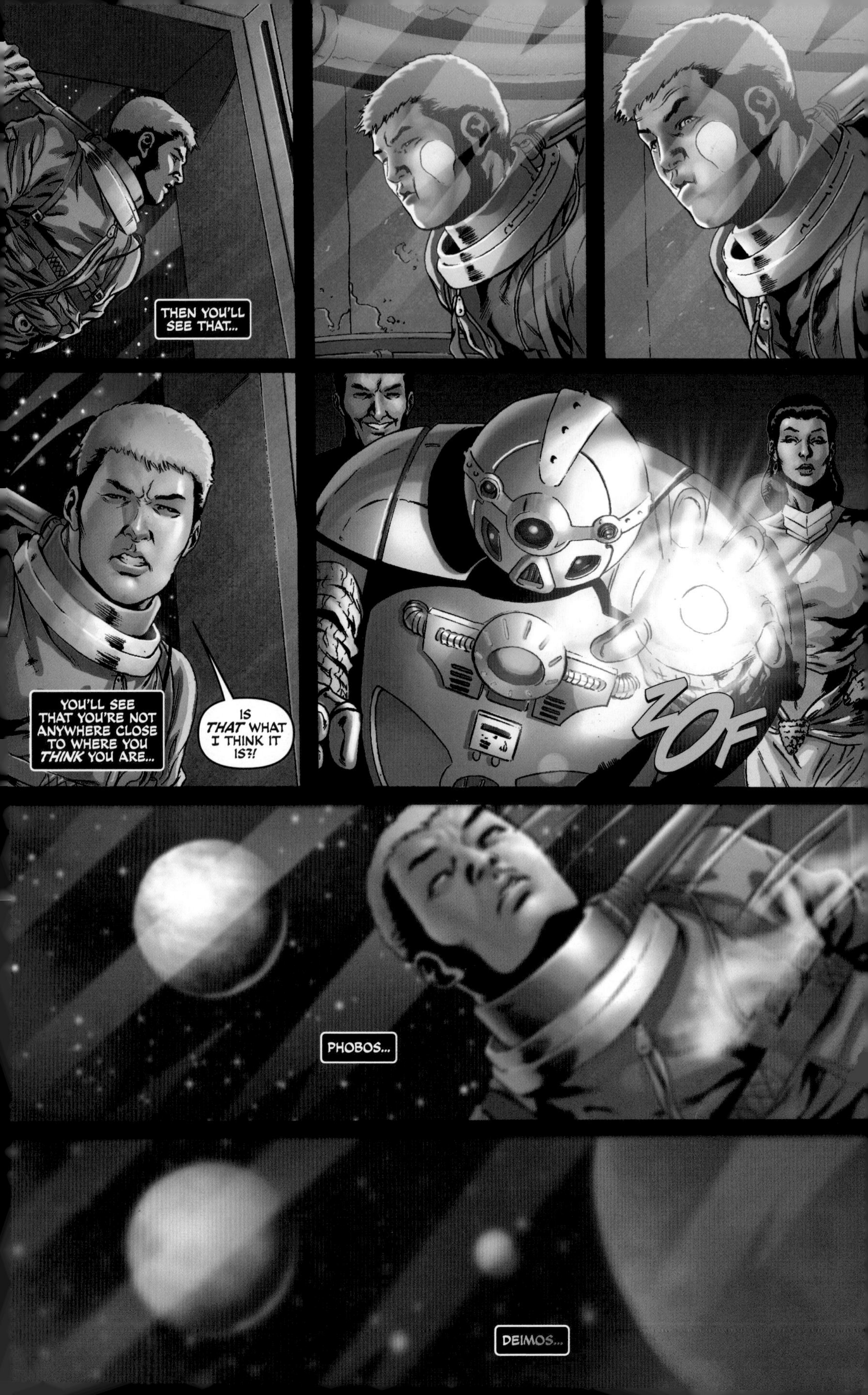
THEN YOU'LL SEE THAT...
YOU'LL SEE THAT YOU'RE NOT ANYWHERE CLOSE TO WHERE YOU *THINK* YOU ARE...
IS *THAT* WHAT I THINK IT IS?!
ZOF
PHOBOS...
DEIMOS...

THIS IS *MARS*, OF COURSE...

BEEN THERE.

BUCK, JUST LISTEN FOR ONCE.

PLEASE *CONTINUE,* CAPTAIN DEERING.

THE FOLLOWING FOOTAGE WAS OBTAINED FROM *HUBBLE II.*

YOU'RE ALL AWARE OF THE *PLAGUE* THAT STRUCK THE COLONISTS AT *FORT HEINLEIN.*

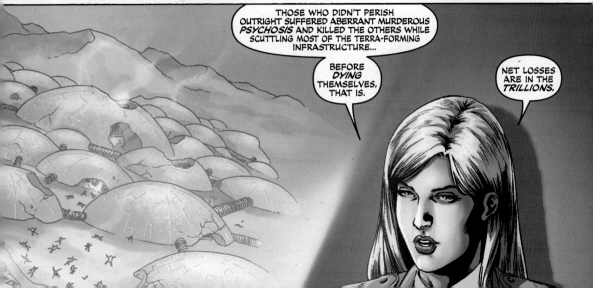

THOSE WHO DIDN'T PERISH OUTRIGHT *SUFFERED* ABERRANT MURDEROUS *PSYCHOSIS* AND KILLED THE OTHERS WHILE SCUTTLING MOST OF THE TERRA-FORMING INFRASTRUCTURE...

BEFORE *DYING* THEMSELVES, THAT IS.

NET LOSSES ARE IN THE *TRILLIONS.*

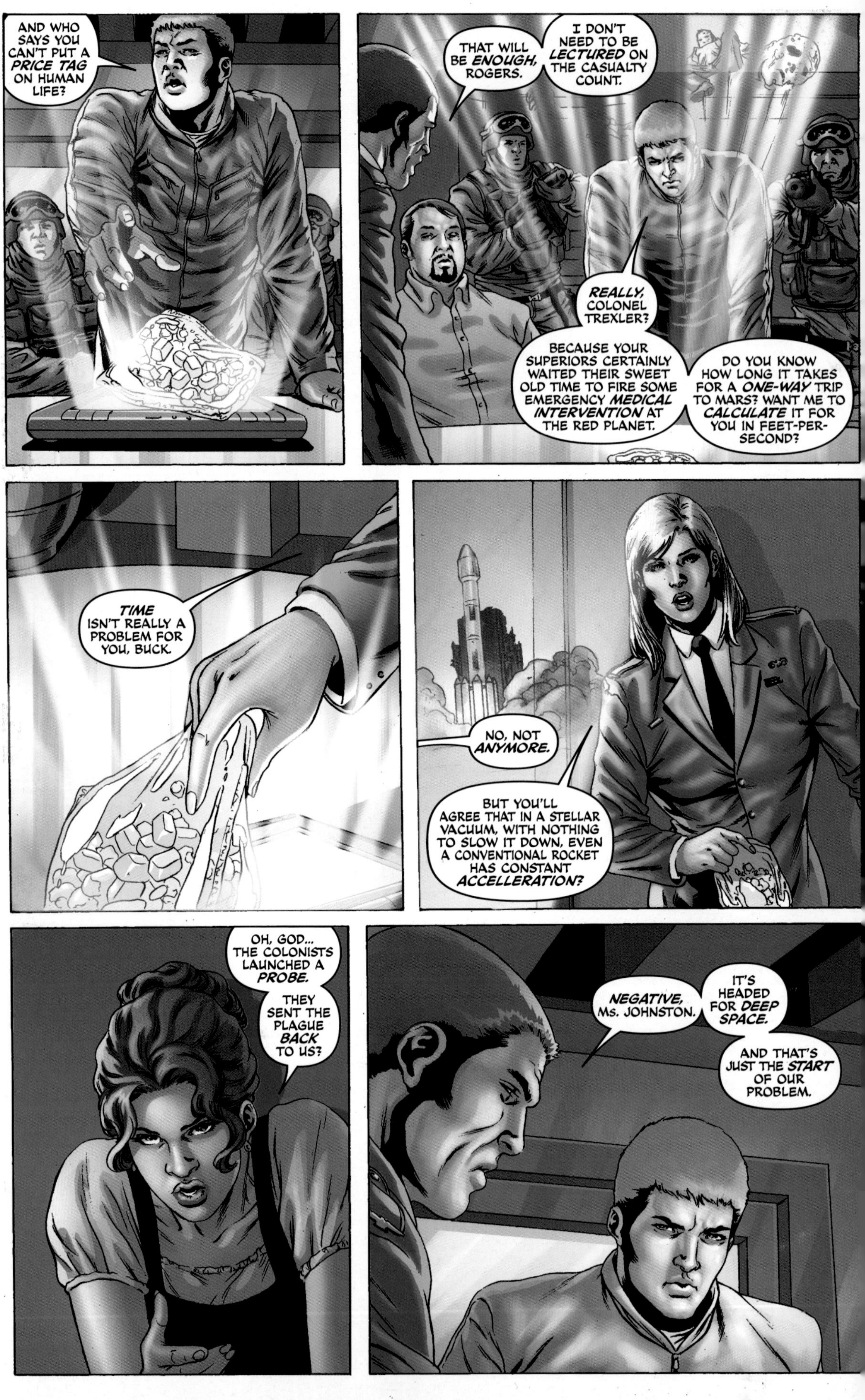
AND WHO SAYS YOU CAN'T PUT A PRICE TAG ON HUMAN LIFE?
THAT WILL BE ENOUGH, ROGERS.
I DON'T NEED TO BE LECTURED ON THE CASUALTY COUNT.
REALLY, COLONEL TREXLER?
BECAUSE YOUR SUPERIORS CERTAINLY WAITED THEIR SWEET OLD TIME TO FIRE SOME EMERGENCY MEDICAL INTERVENTION AT THE RED PLANET.
DO YOU KNOW HOW LONG IT TAKES FOR A ONE-WAY TRIP TO MARS? WANT ME TO CALCULATE IT FOR YOU IN FEET-PER-SECOND?
TIME ISN'T REALLY A PROBLEM FOR YOU, BUCK.
NO, NOT ANYMORE.
BUT YOU'LL AGREE THAT IN A STELLAR VACUUM, WITH NOTHING TO SLOW IT DOWN, EVEN A CONVENTIONAL ROCKET HAS CONSTANT ACCELLERATION?
OH, GOD... THE COLONISTS LAUNCHED A PROBE.
THEY SENT THE PLAGUE BACK TO US?
NEGATIVE, MS. JOHNSTON.
IT'S HEADED FOR DEEP SPACE.
AND THAT'S JUST THE START OF OUR PROBLEM.

ONE OF THE RESEARCHERS--HIS NAME DOESN'T MATTER NOW--DECIDED TO *PRESERVE* HIS WORK.

SPECIFICALLY BY *LAUNCHING* HIS EXPERIMENTS INSIDE ONE OF THE FORT'S MARTIAN CARTOGRAPHY SATELLITES REPROGRAMMED WITH A NEW TRAJECTORY.

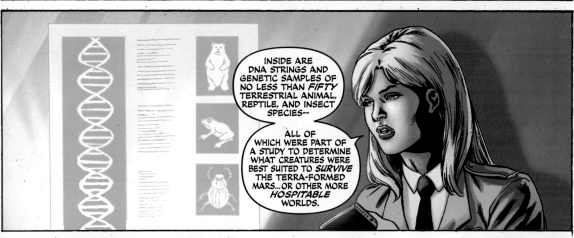

INSIDE ARE DNA STRINGS AND GENETIC SAMPLES OF NO LESS THAN *FIFTY* TERRESTRIAL ANIMAL, REPTILE, AND INSECT SPECIES--

ALL OF WHICH WERE PART OF A STUDY TO DETERMINE WHAT CREATURES WERE BEST SUITED TO *SURVIVE* THE TERRA-FORMED MARS...OR OTHER MORE *HOSPITABLE* WORLDS.

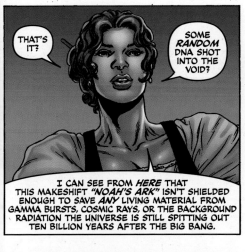

THAT'S IT?

SOME *RANDOM* DNA SHOT INTO THE VOID?

I CAN SEE FROM *HERE* THAT THIS MAKESHIFT *"NOAH'S ARK"* ISN'T SHIELDED ENOUGH TO SAVE *ANY* LIVING MATERIAL FROM GAMMA BURSTS, COSMIC RAYS, OR THE BACKGROUND RADIATION THE UNIVERSE IS STILL SPITTING OUT TEN BILLION YEARS AFTER THE BIG BANG.

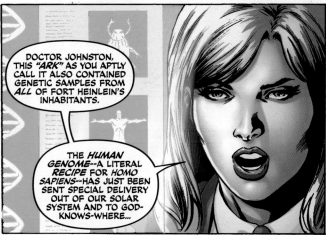

DOCTOR JOHNSTON, THIS *"ARK"* AS YOU APTLY CALL IT ALSO CONTAINED GENETIC SAMPLES FROM *ALL* OF FORT HEINLEIN'S INHABITANTS.

THE *HUMAN GENOME*--A LITERAL *RECIPE* FOR *HOMO SAPIENS*--HAS JUST BEEN SENT SPECIAL DELIVERY OUT OF OUR SOLAR SYSTEM AND TO GOD-KNOWS-WHERE...

NOW *THAT'S* ONE GIANT LEAP FOR MAN--

MAKE LIGHT OF IT ALL YOU WILL, PROFESSOR TANAKA...

SPACE IS MANKIND'S NEXT BATTLEGROUND.

BY PRESIDENTIAL EDICT, THE *STELLAR SECURITY INITIATIVE* HAS GIVEN ME AUTHORITY TO *CONFISCATE* YOUR EXPERIMENTAL SHIP OUT THERE--

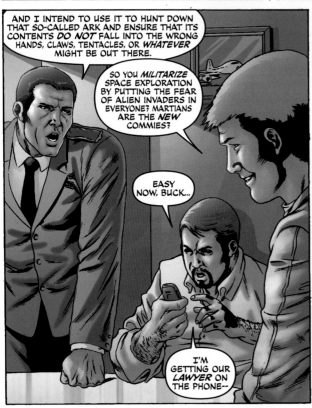

AND I INTEND TO USE IT TO HUNT DOWN THAT SO-CALLED ARK AND ENSURE THAT ITS CONTENTS *DO NOT* FALL INTO THE WRONG HANDS, CLAWS, TENTACLES, OR *WHATEVER* MIGHT BE OUT THERE.

SO YOU *MILITARIZE* SPACE EXPLORATION BY PUTTING THE FEAR OF ALIEN INVADERS IN EVERYONE? MARTIANS ARE THE *NEW* COMMIES?

EASY NOW, BUCK...

I'M GETTING OUR *LAWYER* ON THE PHONE--

HANG UP, CRAIG.

THE COLONEL SHOULD KNOW THAT HE CAN'T HAVE OUR SHIP UNLESS *I'M* PILOTING IT.

NEW CHALLENGER IS SLAVED TO MY VOCAL COMMANDS ALONE.

YOU CAN'T EVEN START THE ENGINES WITHOUT A RETINAL SCAN AND A TEN-POINT PALM PRINT MATCH ON THE JOYSTICK'S SMART-GRIP.

WITHOUT *ME* IN THE SEAT, SHE'LL GO *NOWHERE* FAST.

THEN SUIT UP.

AND IF YOU MAKE IT BACK SUCCESSFUL AND ALIVE--IN THAT ORDER--THEN PERHAPS WE'LL HAVE A MORE FORMAL CONVERSATION ABOUT OUR NEW WORKING RELATIONSHIP.

FINE. BUT I SHOULD WARN YOU--

--MY RELATIONSHIPS NEVER SEEM TO END *WELL*.

THEY'RE AN *ITEM*, YOU KNOW...

ARM DIDN'T WASTE ANY TIME. OR *SHE* DIDN'T.

I'M *WORRIED*, BUCK.

I'M *FINE*, CRAIG. SHE MADE HER CHOICE. *SOLO FLIGHTS* AND ALL--

NO, I MEAN ALL THIS *SCORING* ON *CHALLENGER*. THESE *PITTED* HEAT SHIELDS NEED REPLACING AND WE SHOULD *REALLY* TAKE SOME TIME TO FINE-TUNE THE GRAVITY--

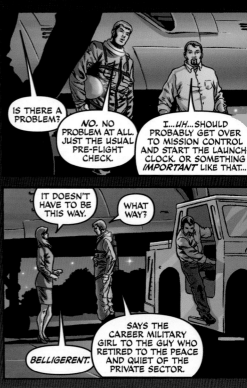

IS THERE A PROBLEM?

NO. NO PROBLEM AT ALL. JUST THE USUAL PRE-FLIGHT CHECK.

I...*UH*...SHOULD PROBABLY GET OVER TO MISSION CONTROL AND START THE LAUNCH-CLOCK. OR SOMETHING *IMPORTANT* LIKE THAT...

IT DOESN'T HAVE TO BE THIS WAY.

WHAT WAY?

BELLIGERENT.

SAYS THE CAREER MILITARY GIRL TO THE GUY WHO RETIRED TO THE PEACE AND QUIET OF THE PRIVATE SECTOR.

BUCK, I NEED TO *TELL* YOU SOMETHING.

CAN IT WAIT, ASH?

SINCE *TIME* ISN'T A PROBLEM FOR ME OR US ANYMORE, IF I MAKE IT BACK SUCCESSFUL AND ALIVE--

THEN MAYBE WE CAN HAVE A MORE FORMAL CONVERSATION ABOUT *ALL* OUR NEW RELATIONSHIPS.

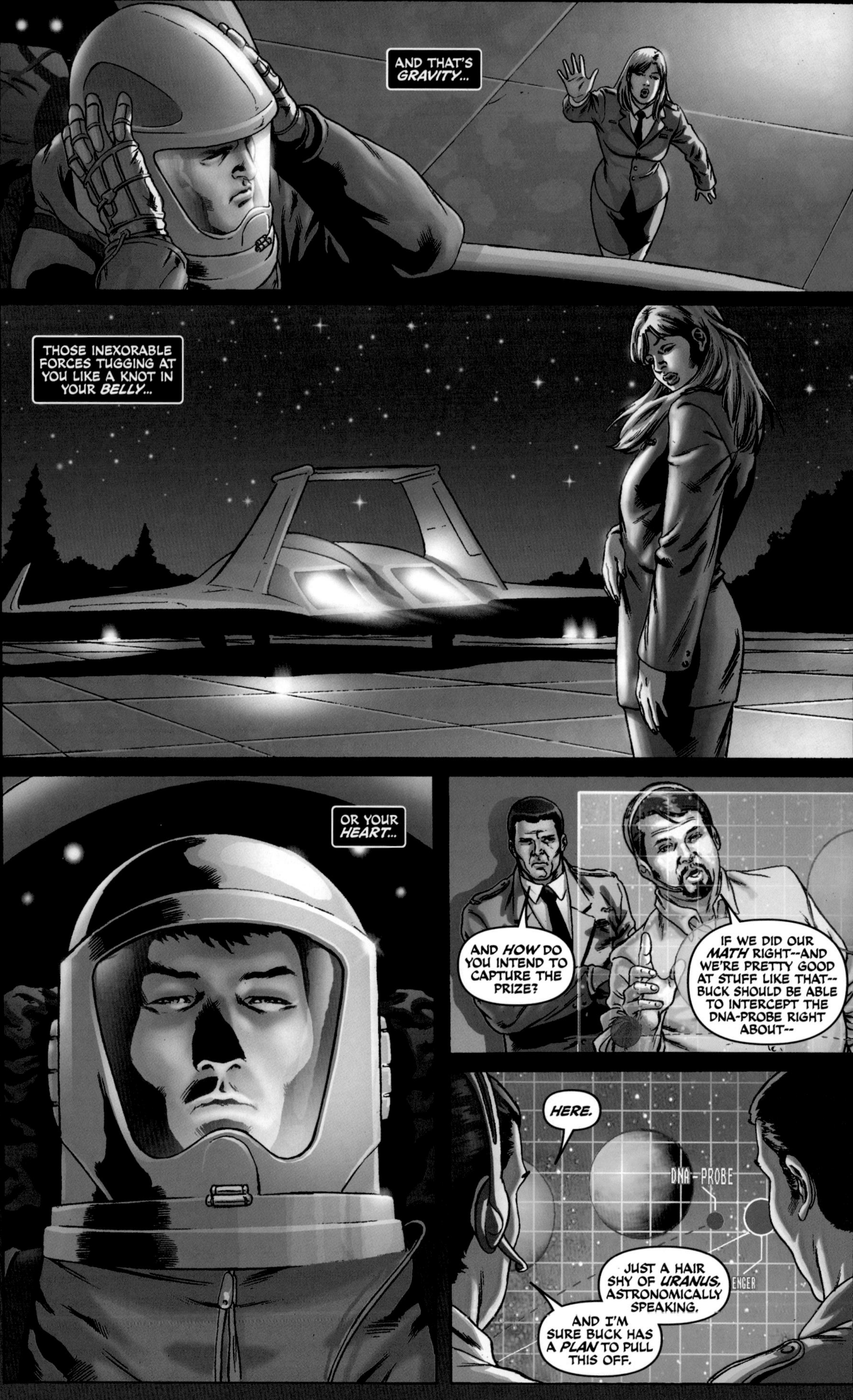
AND THAT'S GRAVITY...
THOSE INEXORABLE FORCES TUGGING AT YOU LIKE A KNOT IN YOUR BELLY...
OR YOUR HEART...
AND HOW DO YOU INTEND TO CAPTURE THE PRIZE?
IF WE DID OUR MATH RIGHT--AND WE'RE PRETTY GOOD AT STUFF LIKE THAT--BUCK SHOULD BE ABLE TO INTERCEPT THE DNA-PROBE RIGHT ABOUT--
HERE.
DNA-PROBE
ENGER
JUST A HAIR SHY OF URANUS, ASTRONOMICALLY SPEAKING.
AND I'M SURE BUCK HAS A PLAN TO PULL THIS OFF.

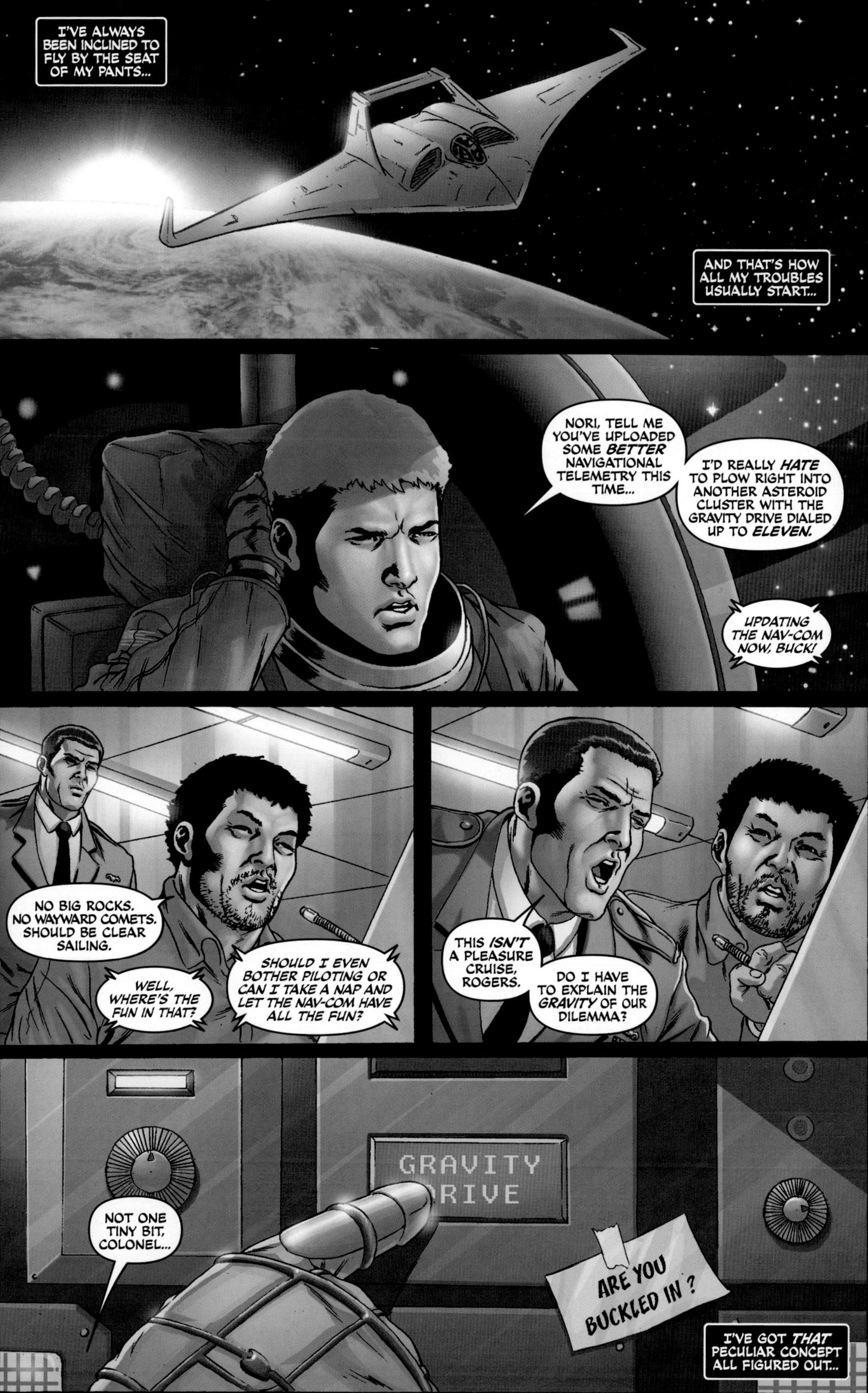
I'VE ALWAYS BEEN INCLINED TO FLY BY THE SEAT OF MY PANTS...
AND THAT'S HOW ALL MY TROUBLES USUALLY START...
NORI, TELL ME YOU'VE UPLOADED SOME *BETTER* NAVIGATIONAL TELEMETRY THIS TIME...
I'D REALLY *HATE* TO PLOW RIGHT INTO ANOTHER ASTEROID CLUSTER WITH THE GRAVITY DRIVE DIALED UP TO *ELEVEN.*
UPDATING THE NAV-COM NOW, BUCK!
NO BIG ROCKS. NO WAYWARD COMETS. SHOULD BE CLEAR SAILING.
WELL, WHERE'S THE FUN IN THAT?
SHOULD I EVEN BOTHER PILOTING OR CAN I TAKE A NAP AND LET THE NAV-COM HAVE ALL THE FUN?
THIS *ISN'T* A PLEASURE CRUISE, ROGERS.
DO I HAVE TO EXPLAIN THE *GRAVITY* OF OUR DILEMMA?
GRAVITY DRIVE
NOT ONE TINY BIT, COLONEL...
ARE YOU BUCKLED IN ?
I'VE GOT *THAT* PECULIAR CONCEPT ALL FIGURED OUT...

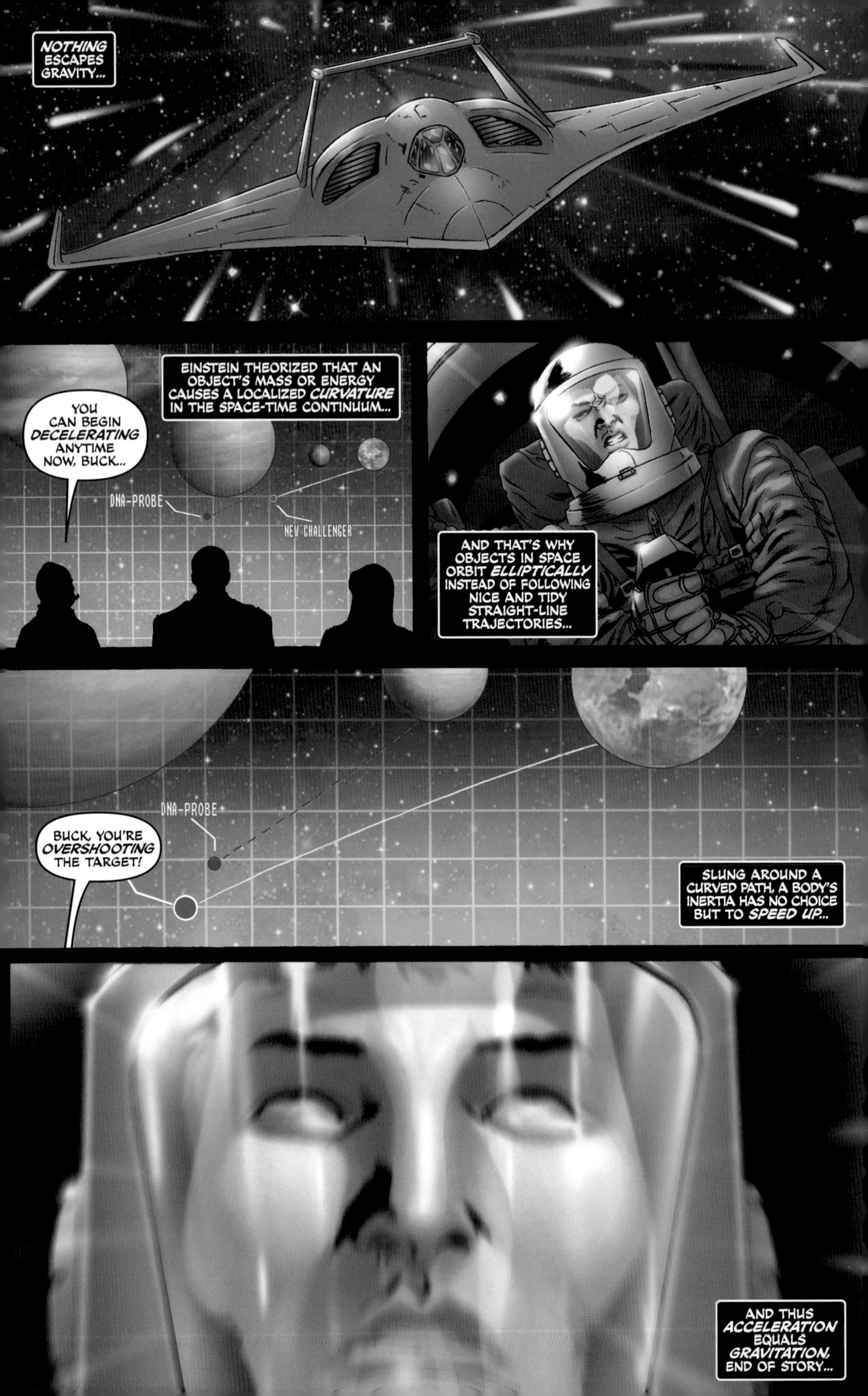
NOTHING ESCAPES GRAVITY...
EINSTEIN THEORIZED THAT AN OBJECT'S MASS OR ENERGY CAUSES A LOCALIZED CURVATURE IN THE SPACE-TIME CONTINUUM...
YOU CAN BEGIN DECELERATING ANYTIME NOW, BUCK...
DNA-PROBE
NEW CHALLENGER
AND THAT'S WHY OBJECTS IN SPACE ORBIT ELLIPTICALLY INSTEAD OF FOLLOWING NICE AND TIDY STRAIGHT-LINE TRAJECTORIES...
DNA-PROBE
BUCK, YOU'RE OVERSHOOTING THE TARGET!
SLUNG AROUND A CURVED PATH, A BODY'S INERTIA HAS NO CHOICE BUT TO SPEED UP...
AND THUS ACCELERATION EQUALS GRAVITATION, END OF STORY...

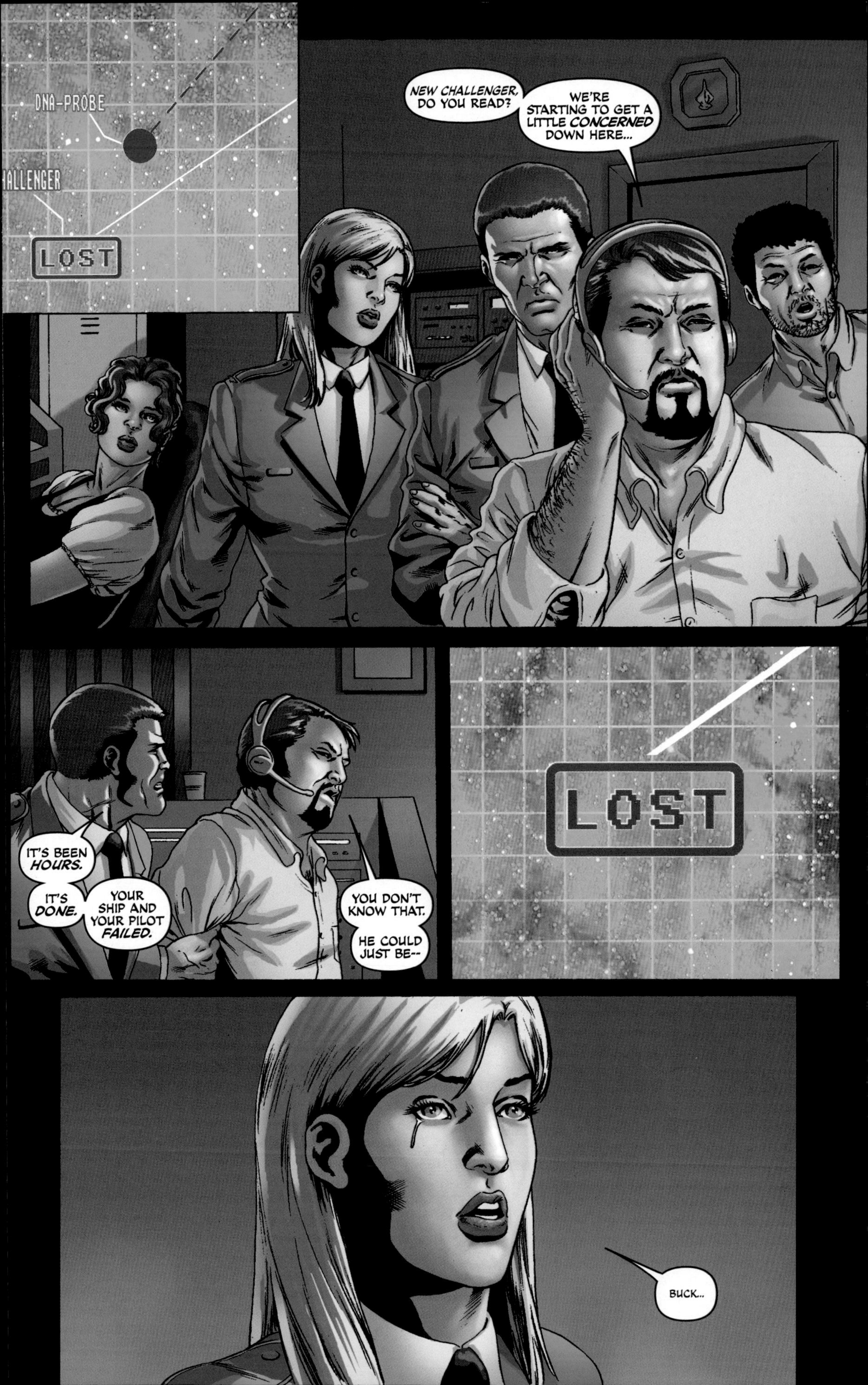
DNA-PROBE
HALLENGER
LOST
NEW CHALLENGER, DO YOU READ?
WE'RE STARTING TO GET A LITTLE *CONCERNED* DOWN HERE...
IT'S BEEN *HOURS.*
IT'S *DONE.*
YOUR SHIP AND YOUR PILOT *FAILED.*
YOU DON'T KNOW THAT.
HE COULD JUST BE--
LOST
BUCK...

"...WHERE ARE YOU?"

NO...

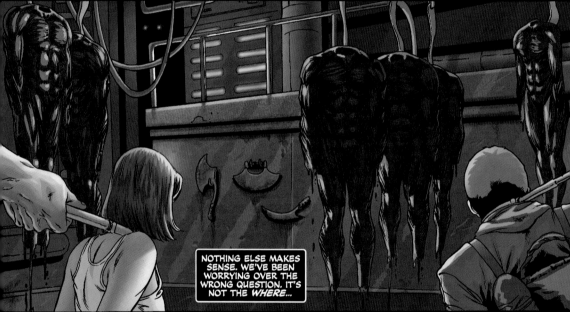

NOTHING ELSE MAKES SENSE. WE'VE BEEN WORRYING OVER THE WRONG QUESTION. IT'S NOT THE *WHERE*...

IT'S THE *WHEN*.

WHAT *YEAR* IS THIS?

2519 BY THE OLD-CIV CALENDAR...

WHAT YEAR WOULD YOU *LIKE* IT TO BE?

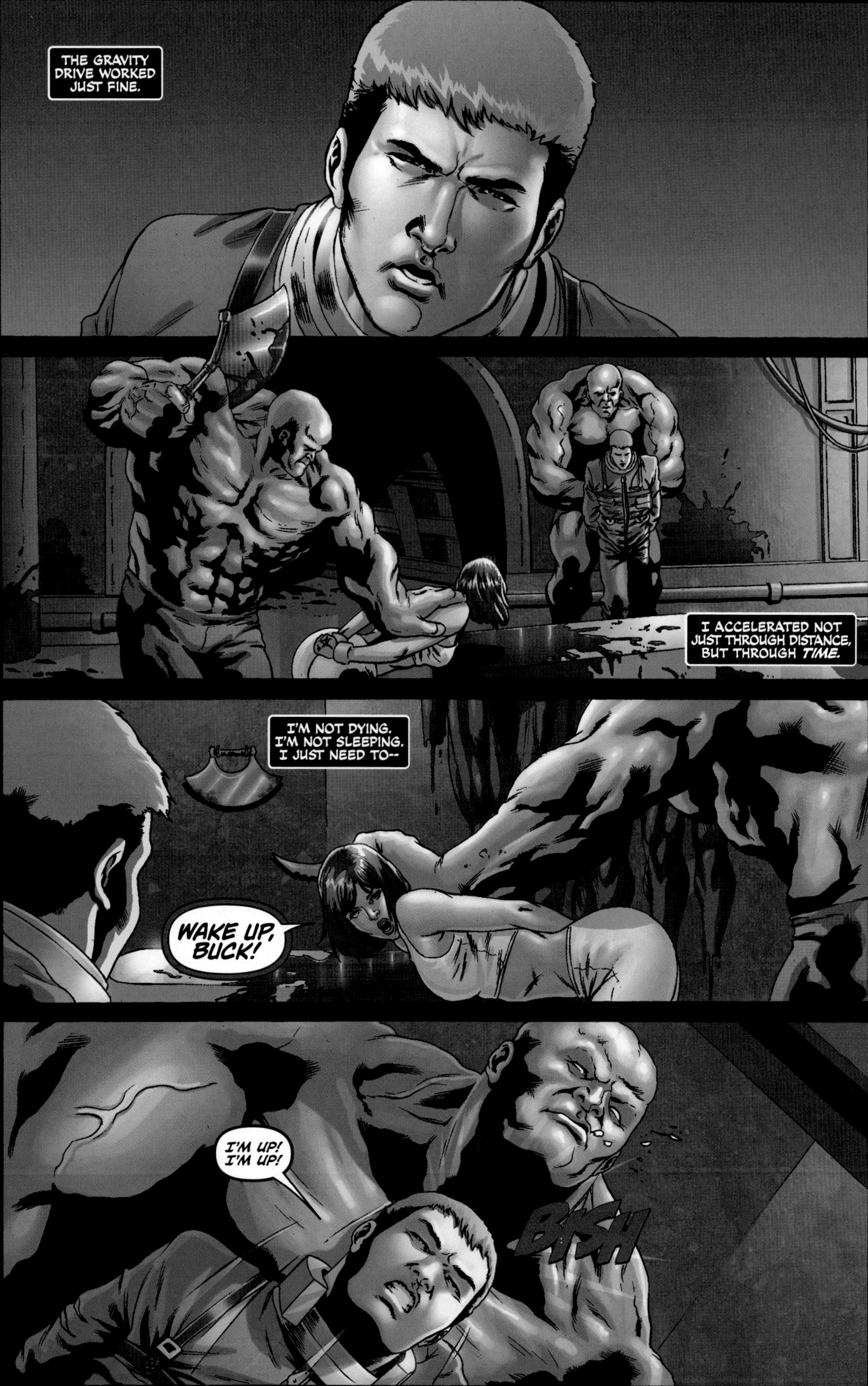
THE GRAVITY DRIVE WORKED JUST FINE.
I ACCELERATED NOT JUST THROUGH DISTANCE, BUT THROUGH *TIME.*
I'M NOT DYING. I'M NOT SLEEPING. I JUST NEED TO--
WAKE UP, BUCK!
I'M UP! I'M UP!
BASH

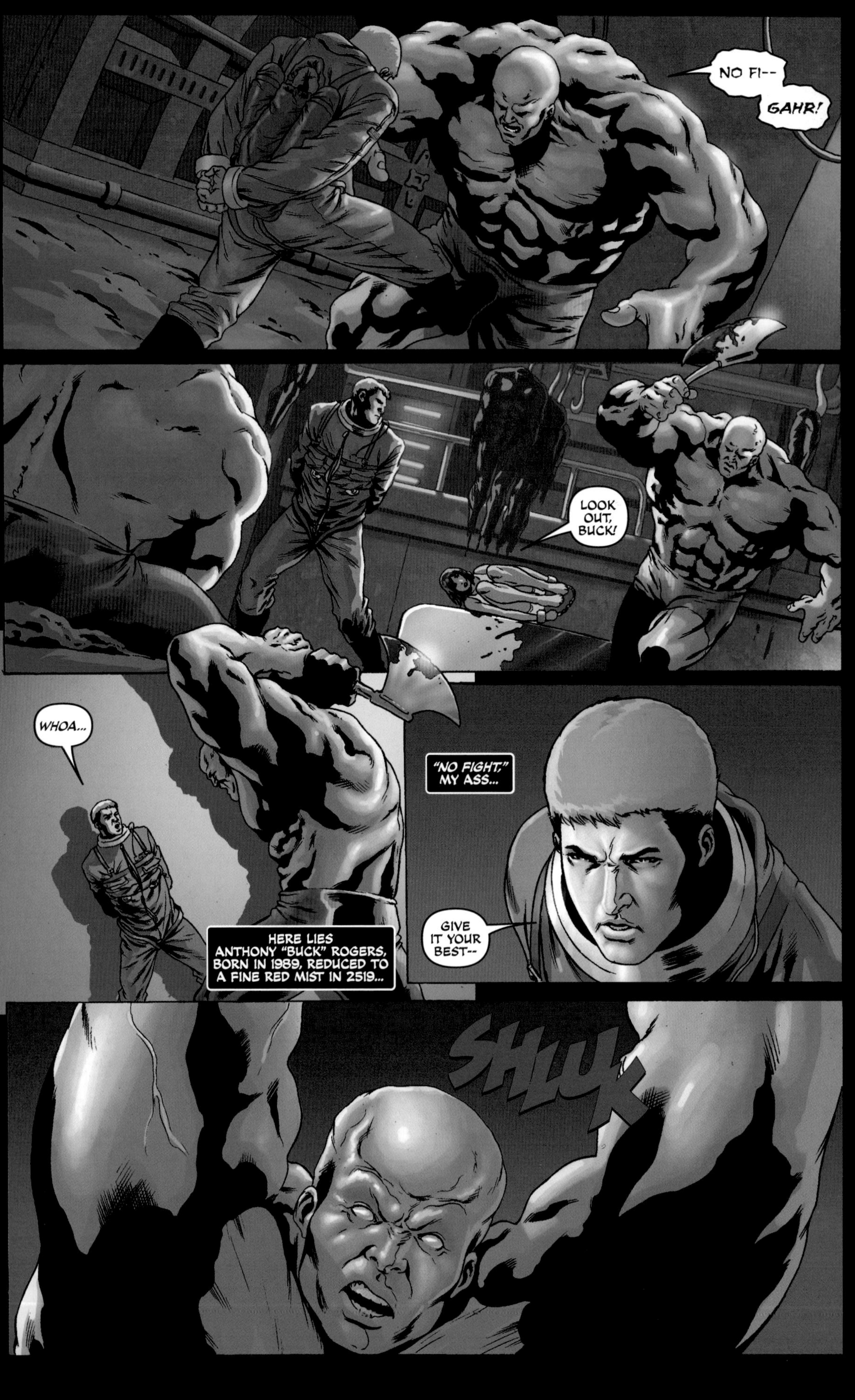
NO FI--
GAHR!
LOOK OUT, BUCK!
WHOA...
HERE LIES ANTHONY "BUCK" ROGERS, BORN IN 1989, REDUCED TO A FINE RED MIST IN 2519...
"NO FIGHT," MY ASS...
GIVE IT YOUR BEST--
SHUK

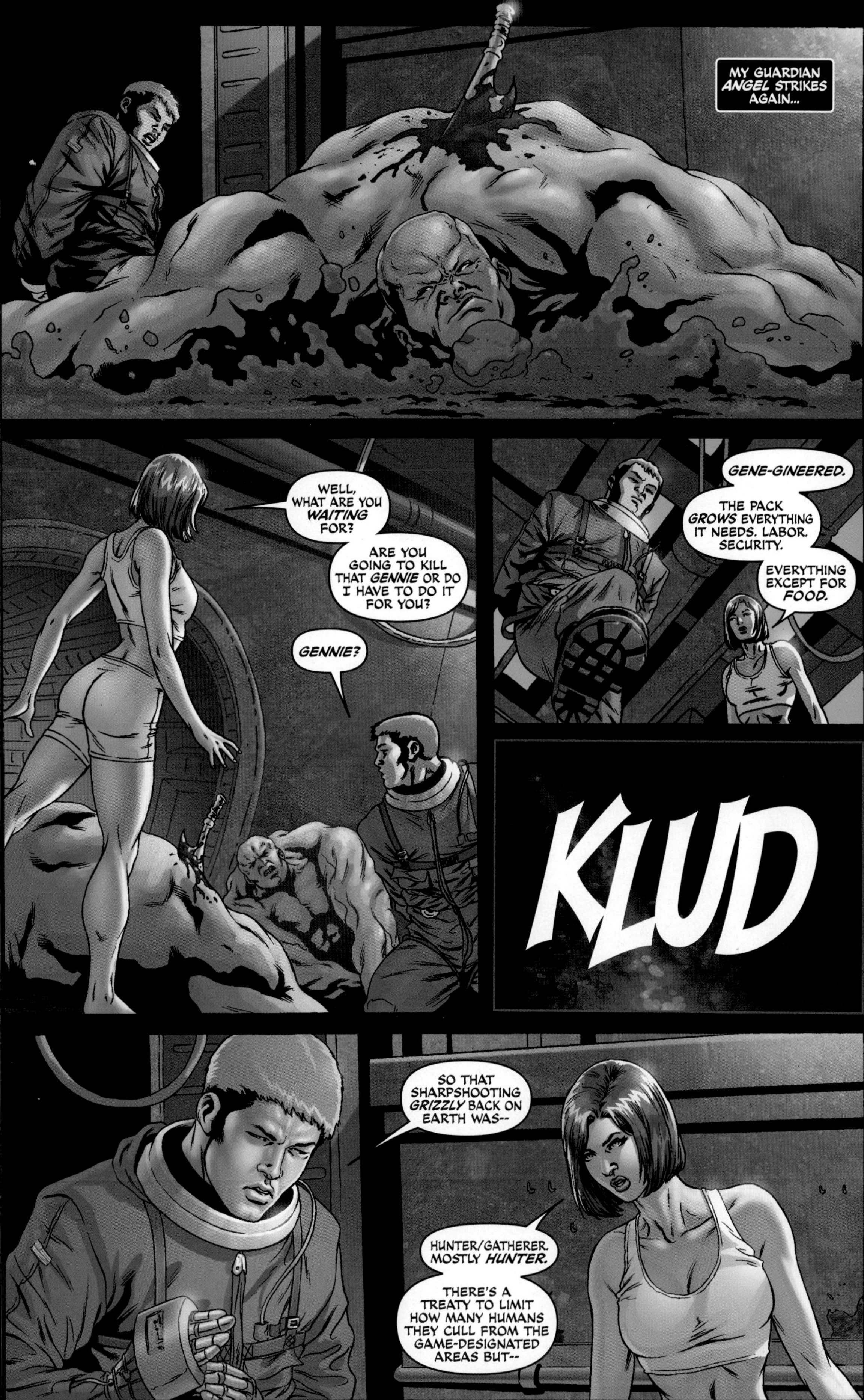
MY GUARDIAN ANGEL STRIKES AGAIN...
WELL, WHAT ARE YOU WAITING FOR?
ARE YOU GOING TO KILL THAT GENNIE OR DO I HAVE TO DO IT FOR YOU?
GENNIE?
GENE-GINEERED.
THE PACK GROWS EVERYTHING IT NEEDS. LABOR. SECURITY.
EVERYTHING EXCEPT FOR FOOD.
KLUD
SO THAT SHARPSHOOTING GRIZZLY BACK ON EARTH WAS--
HUNTER/GATHERER. MOSTLY HUNTER.
THERE'S A TREATY TO LIMIT HOW MANY HUMANS THEY CULL FROM THE GAME-DESIGNATED AREAS BUT--

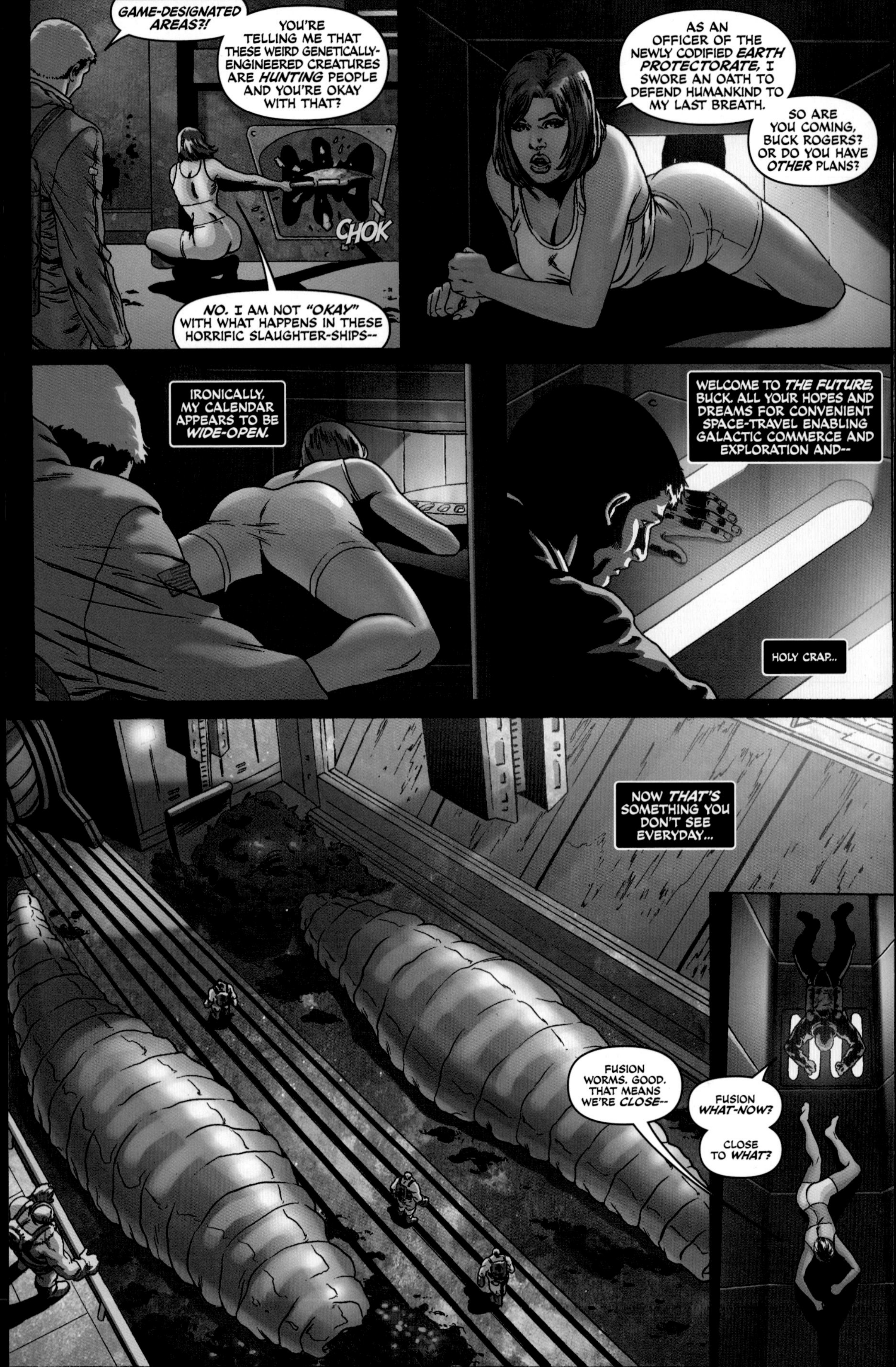
GAME-DESIGNATED AREAS?!
YOU'RE TELLING ME THAT THESE WEIRD GENETICALLY-ENGINEERED CREATURES ARE HUNTING PEOPLE AND YOU'RE OKAY WITH THAT?
CHOK
NO. I AM NOT "OKAY" WITH WHAT HAPPENS IN THESE HORRIFIC SLAUGHTER-SHIPS--
AS AN OFFICER OF THE NEWLY CODIFIED EARTH PROTECTORATE, I SWORE AN OATH TO DEFEND HUMANKIND TO MY LAST BREATH.
SO ARE YOU COMING, BUCK ROGERS? OR DO YOU HAVE OTHER PLANS?
IRONICALLY, MY CALENDAR APPEARS TO BE WIDE-OPEN.
WELCOME TO THE FUTURE, BUCK. ALL YOUR HOPES AND DREAMS FOR CONVENIENT SPACE-TRAVEL ENABLING GALACTIC COMMERCE AND EXPLORATION AND--
HOLY CRAP...
NOW THAT'S SOMETHING YOU DON'T SEE EVERYDAY...
FUSION WORMS. GOOD. THAT MEANS WE'RE CLOSE--
FUSION WHAT-NOW?
CLOSE TO WHAT?

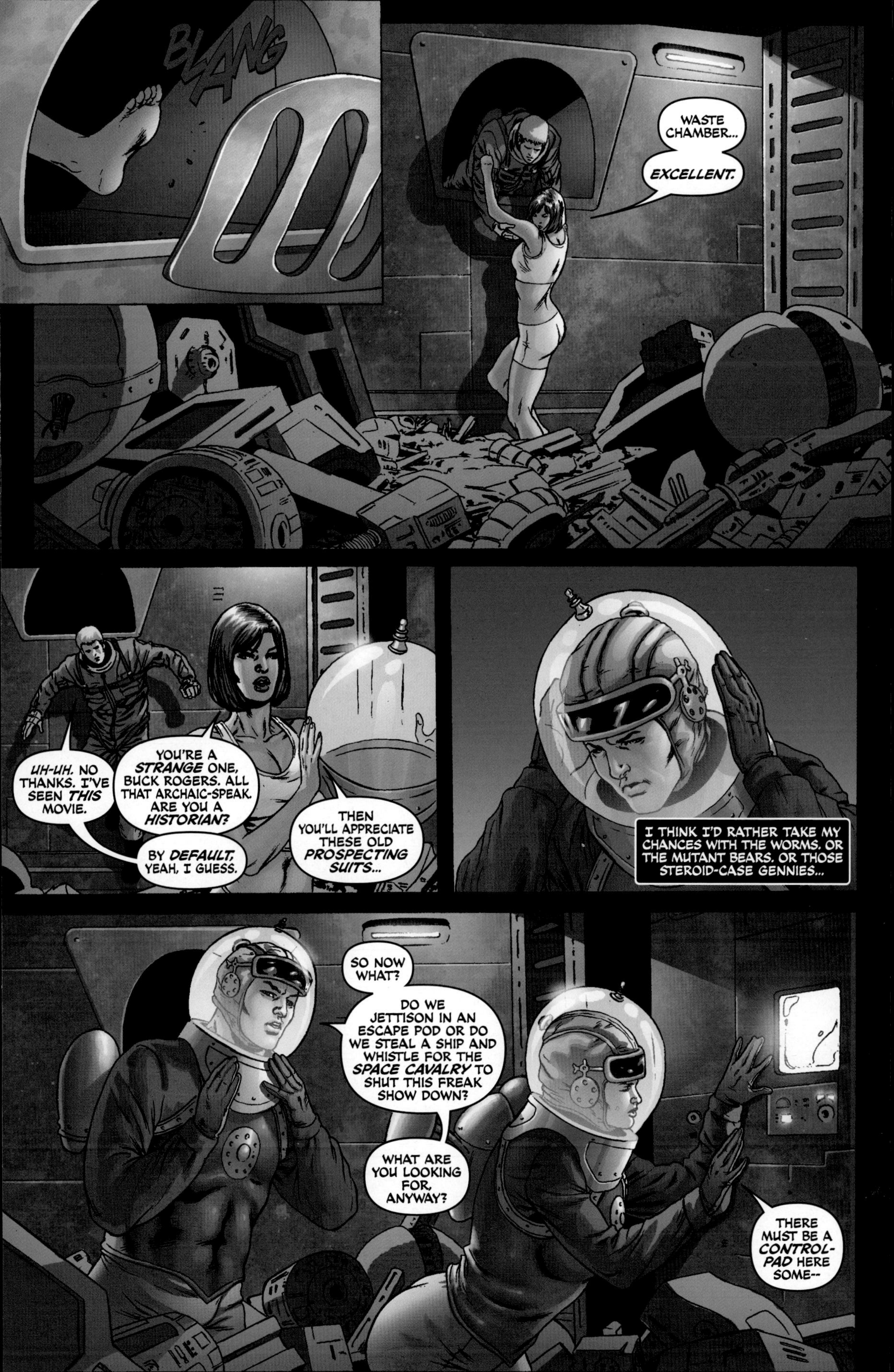
BLANG
WASTE CHAMBER...
EXCELLENT.
UH-UH. NO THANKS. I'VE SEEN THIS MOVIE.
YOU'RE A STRANGE ONE, BUCK ROGERS. ALL THAT ARCHAIC-SPEAK. ARE YOU A HISTORIAN?
BY DEFAULT, YEAH, I GUESS.
THEN YOU'LL APPRECIATE THESE OLD PROSPECTING SUITS...
I THINK I'D RATHER TAKE MY CHANCES WITH THE WORMS. OR THE MUTANT BEARS. OR THOSE STEROID-CASE GENNIES...
SO NOW WHAT?
DO WE JETTISON IN AN ESCAPE POD OR DO WE STEAL A SHIP AND WHISTLE FOR THE SPACE CAVALRY TO SHUT THIS FREAK SHOW DOWN?
WHAT ARE YOU LOOKING FOR, ANYWAY?
THERE MUST BE A CONTROL-PAD HERE SOME--

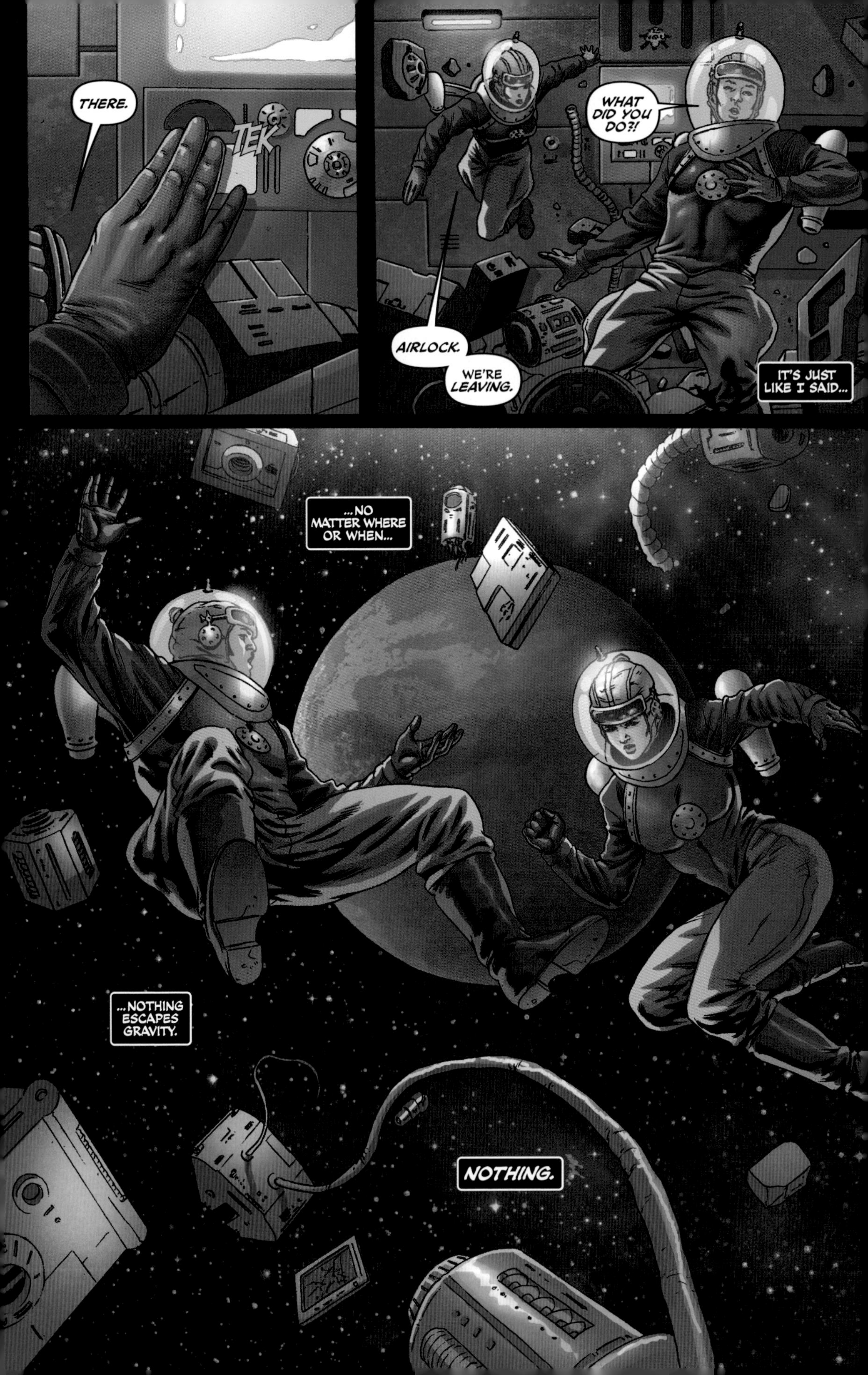
THERE.
TEK
WHAT DID YOU DO?!
AIRLOCK.
WE'RE LEAVING.
IT'S JUST LIKE I SAID...
...NO MATTER WHERE OR WHEN...
...NOTHING ESCAPES GRAVITY.
NOTHING.

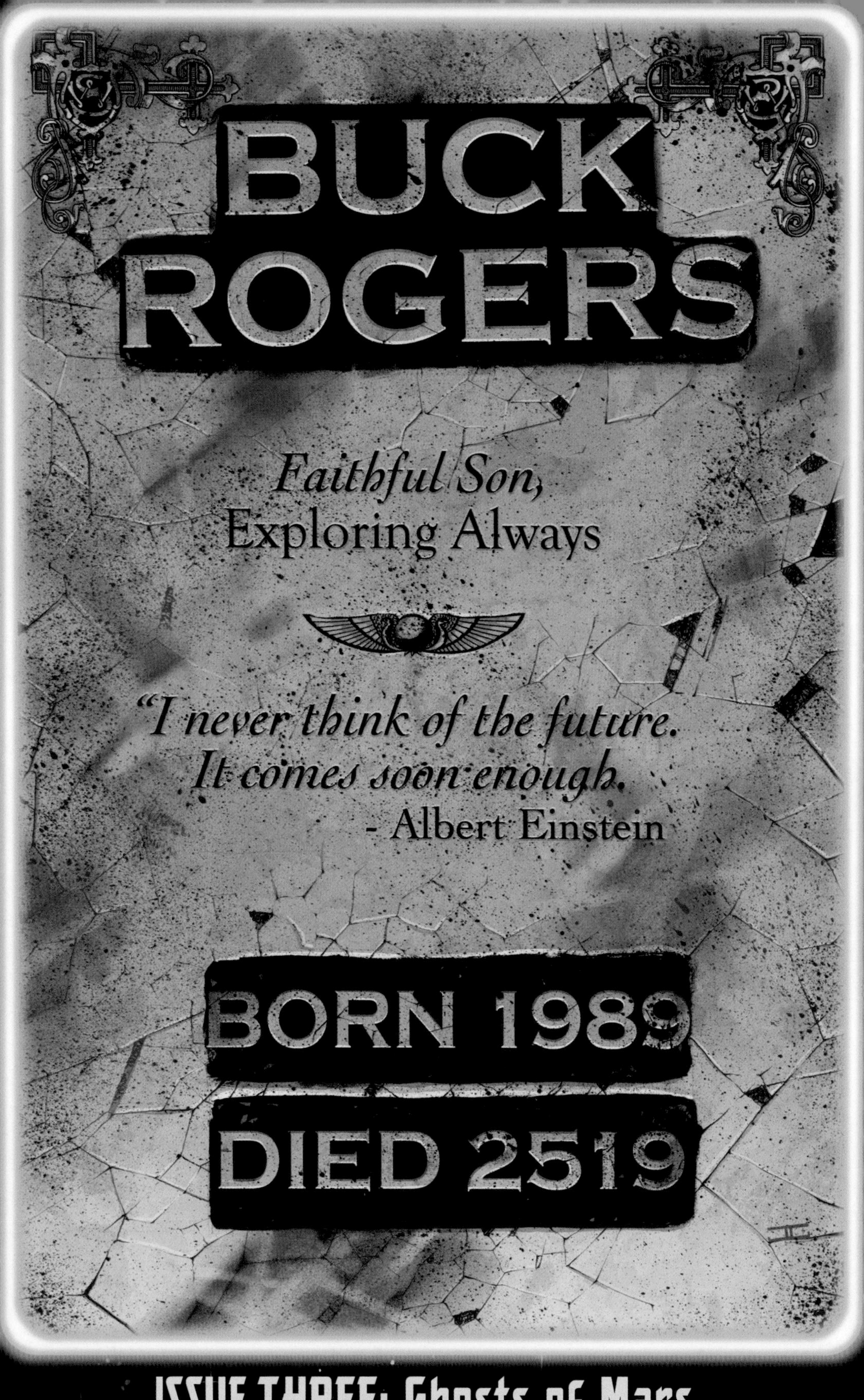
BUCK ROGERS
Faithful Son,
Exploring Always
"I never think of the future.
It comes soon enough.
- Albert Einstein
BORN 1989
DIED 2519

ISSUE THREE: Ghosts of Mars

COVER BY JOHN CASSADAY

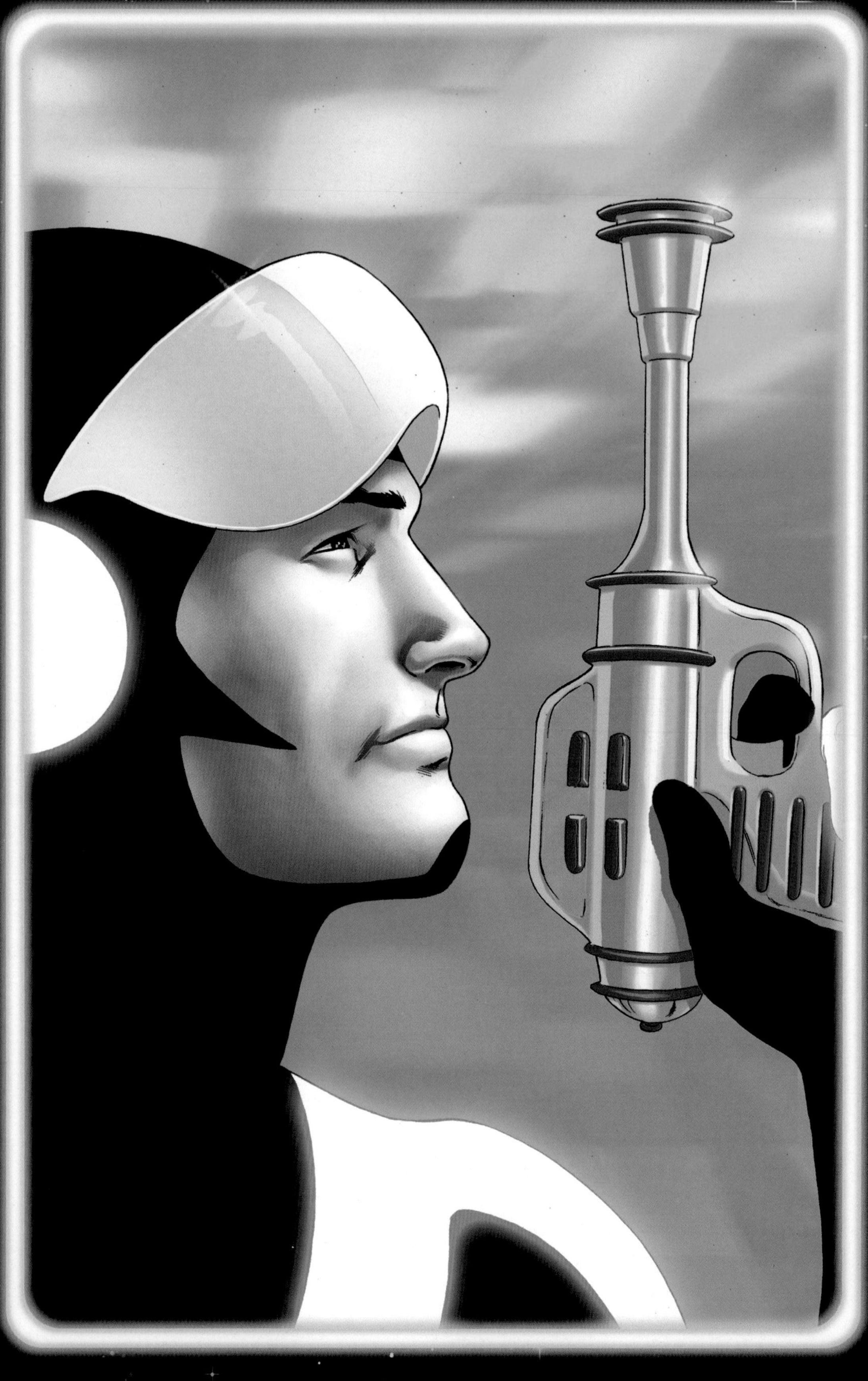

ALTERNATE COVER BY CARLOS RAFAEL

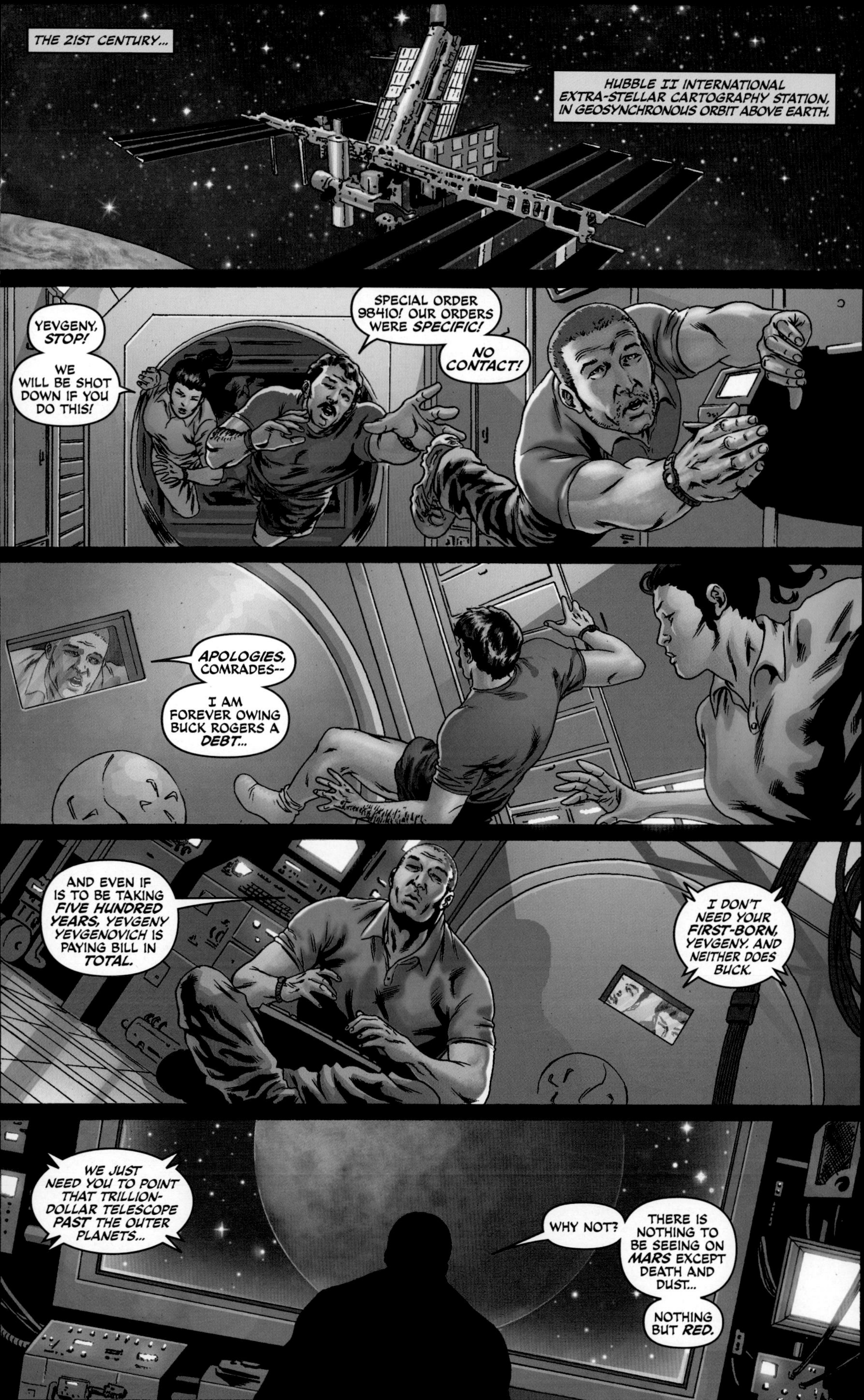

THE 21ST CENTURY...
HUBBLE II INTERNATIONAL EXTRA-STELLAR CARTOGRAPHY STATION, IN GEOSYNCHRONOUS ORBIT ABOVE EARTH.
YEVGENY, *STOP!*
WE WILL BE SHOT DOWN IF YOU DO THIS!
SPECIAL ORDER 98410! OUR ORDERS WERE *SPECIFIC!*
NO CONTACT!
APOLOGIES, COMRADES--
I AM FOREVER OWING BUCK ROGERS A *DEBT...*
AND EVEN IF IS TO BE TAKING *FIVE HUNDRED YEARS,* YEVGENY YEVGENOVICH IS PAYING BILL IN *TOTAL.*
I DON'T NEED YOUR *FIRST-BORN,* YEVGENY. AND NEITHER DOES BUCK.
WE JUST NEED YOU TO POINT THAT TRILLION-DOLLAR TELESCOPE *PAST* THE OUTER PLANETS...
WHY NOT?
THERE IS NOTHING TO BE SEEING ON *MARS* EXCEPT DEATH AND DUST...
NOTHING BUT *RED.*

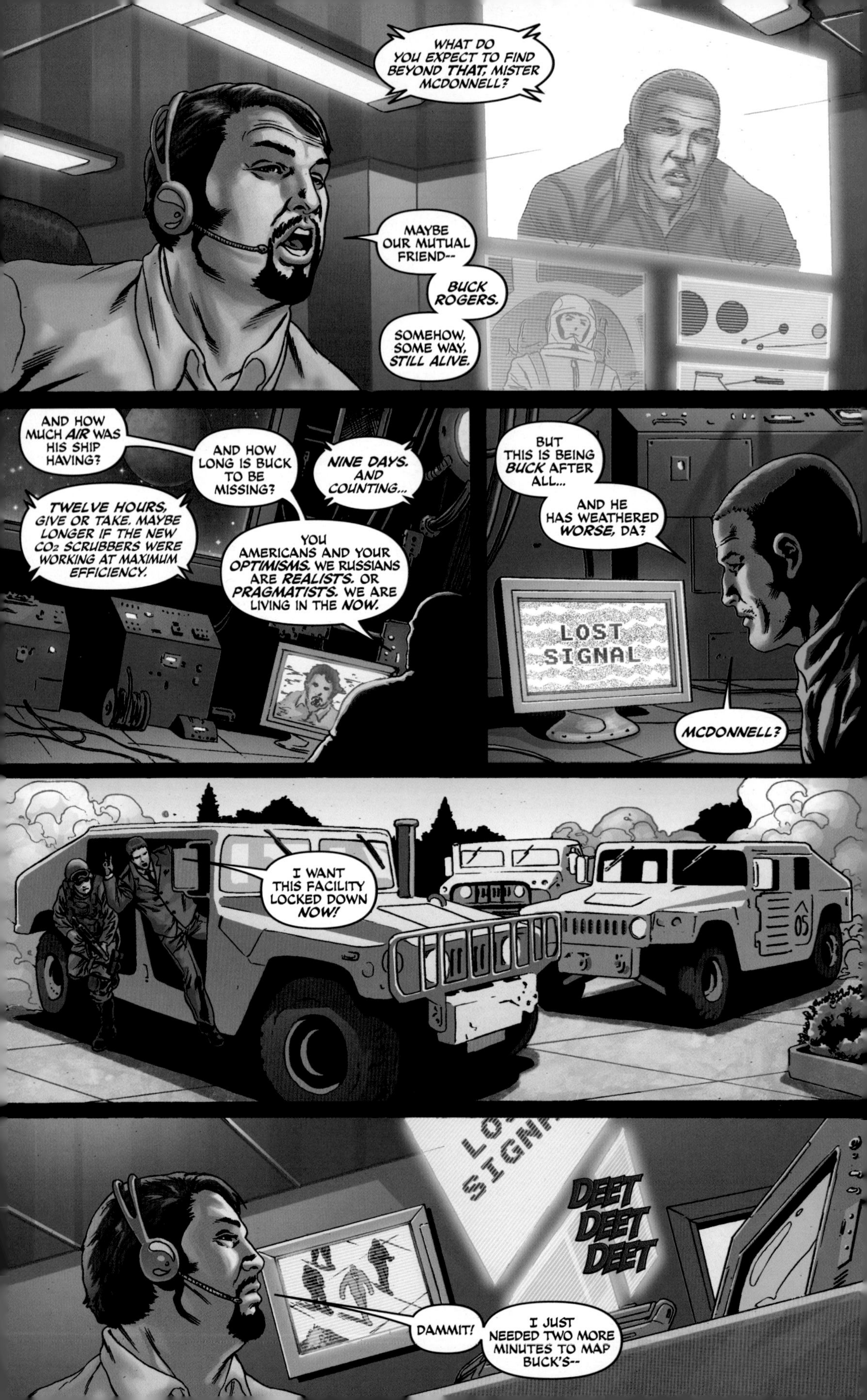
WHAT DO YOU EXPECT TO FIND BEYOND THAT, MISTER MCDONNELL?
MAYBE OUR MUTUAL FRIEND--
BUCK ROGERS.
SOMEHOW, SOME WAY, STILL ALIVE.
AND HOW MUCH AIR WAS HIS SHIP HAVING?
TWELVE HOURS, GIVE OR TAKE. MAYBE LONGER IF THE NEW CO2 SCRUBBERS WERE WORKING AT MAXIMUM EFFICIENCY.
AND HOW LONG IS BUCK TO BE MISSING?
NINE DAYS. AND COUNTING...
YOU AMERICANS AND YOUR OPTIMISMS. WE RUSSIANS ARE REALISTS. OR PRAGMATISTS. WE ARE LIVING IN THE NOW.
BUT THIS IS BEING BUCK AFTER ALL...
AND HE HAS WEATHERED WORSE, DA?
LOST SIGNAL
MCDONNELL?
I WANT THIS FACILITY LOCKED DOWN NOW!
05
LOST SIGNAL
DEET DEET DEET
DAMMIT!
I JUST NEEDED TWO MORE MINUTES TO MAP BUCK'S--

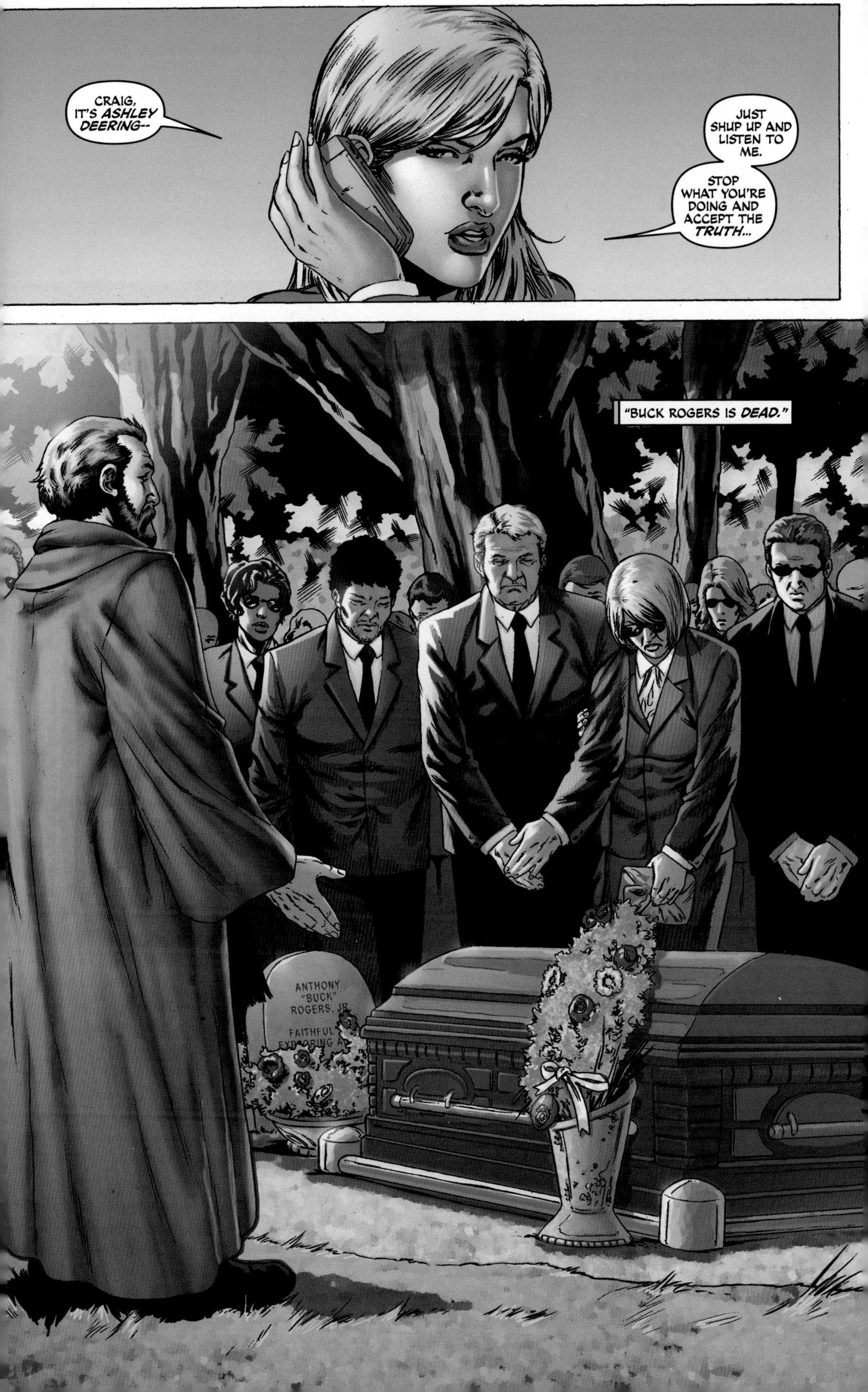
CRAIG, IT'S *ASHLEY DEERING--*
JUST SHUP UP AND LISTEN TO ME.
STOP WHAT YOU'RE DOING AND ACCEPT THE *TRUTH...*
"BUCK ROGERS IS *DEAD.*"
ANTHONY "BUCK" ROGERS, JR.
FAITHFUL

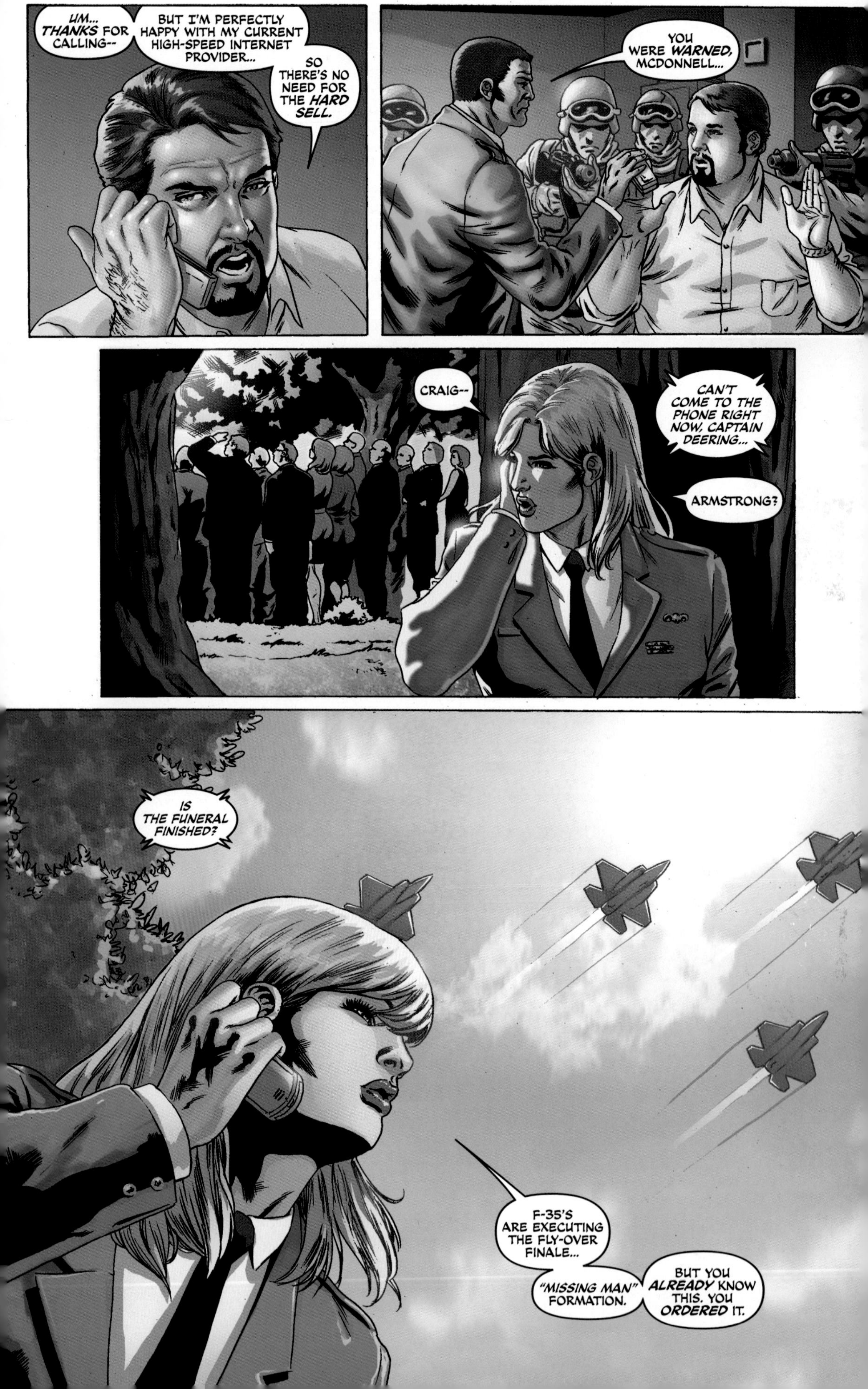
UM... THANKS FOR CALLING--
BUT I'M PERFECTLY HAPPY WITH MY CURRENT HIGH-SPEED INTERNET PROVIDER...
SO THERE'S NO NEED FOR THE HARD SELL.
YOU WERE WARNED, MCDONNELL...
CRAIG--
CAN'T COME TO THE PHONE RIGHT NOW, CAPTAIN DEERING...
ARMSTRONG?
IS THE FUNERAL FINISHED?
F-35'S ARE EXECUTING THE FLY-OVER FINALE...
"MISSING MAN" FORMATION.
BUT YOU ALREADY KNOW THIS. YOU ORDERED IT.

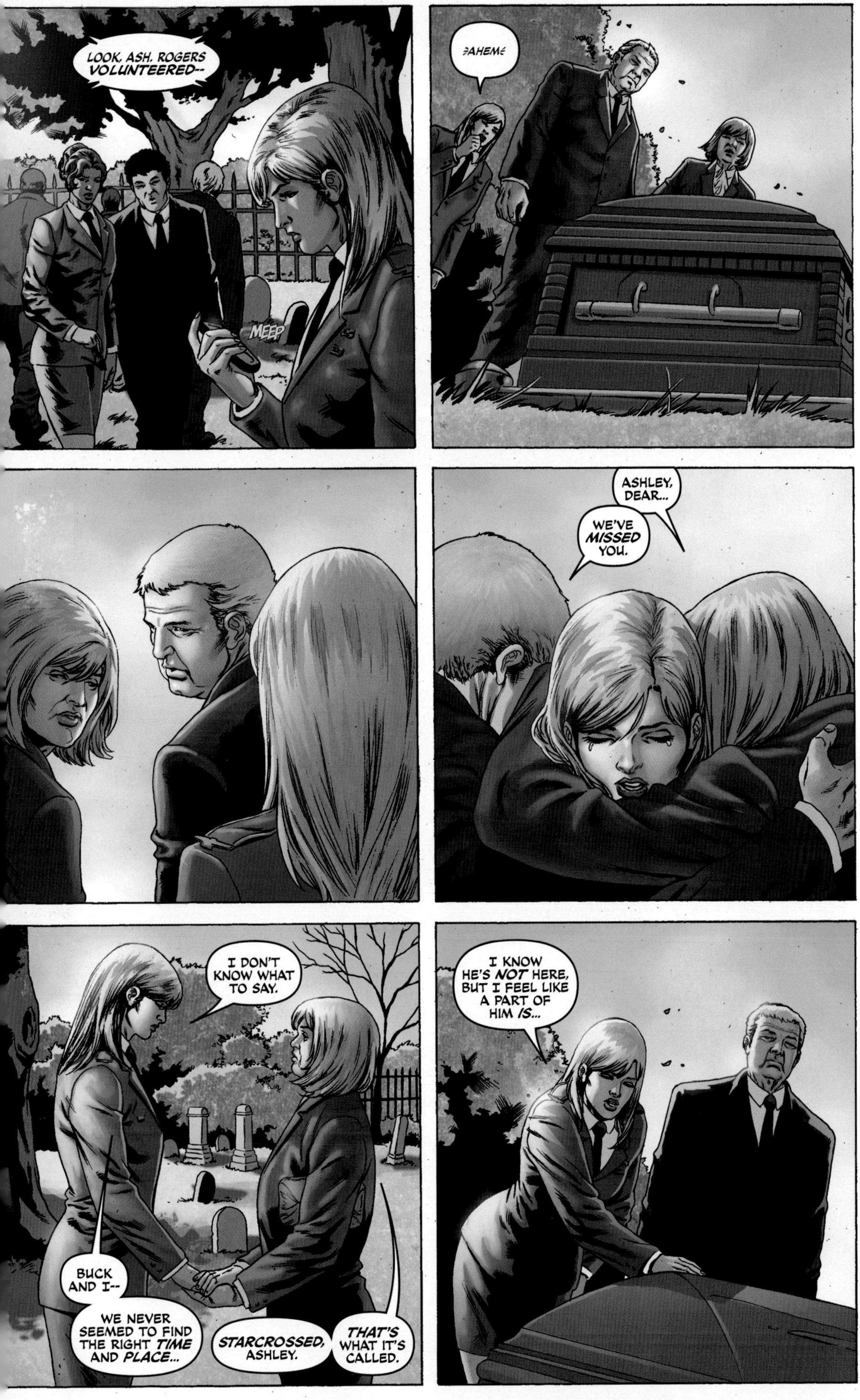
LOOK, ASH. ROGERS VOLUNTEERED--
MEEP
AHEM
ASHLEY, DEAR...
WE'VE MISSED YOU.
I DON'T KNOW WHAT TO SAY.
BUCK AND I--
WE NEVER SEEMED TO FIND THE RIGHT TIME AND PLACE...
STARCROSSED, ASHLEY.
THAT'S WHAT IT'S CALLED.
I KNOW HE'S NOT HERE, BUT I FEEL LIKE A PART OF HIM IS...

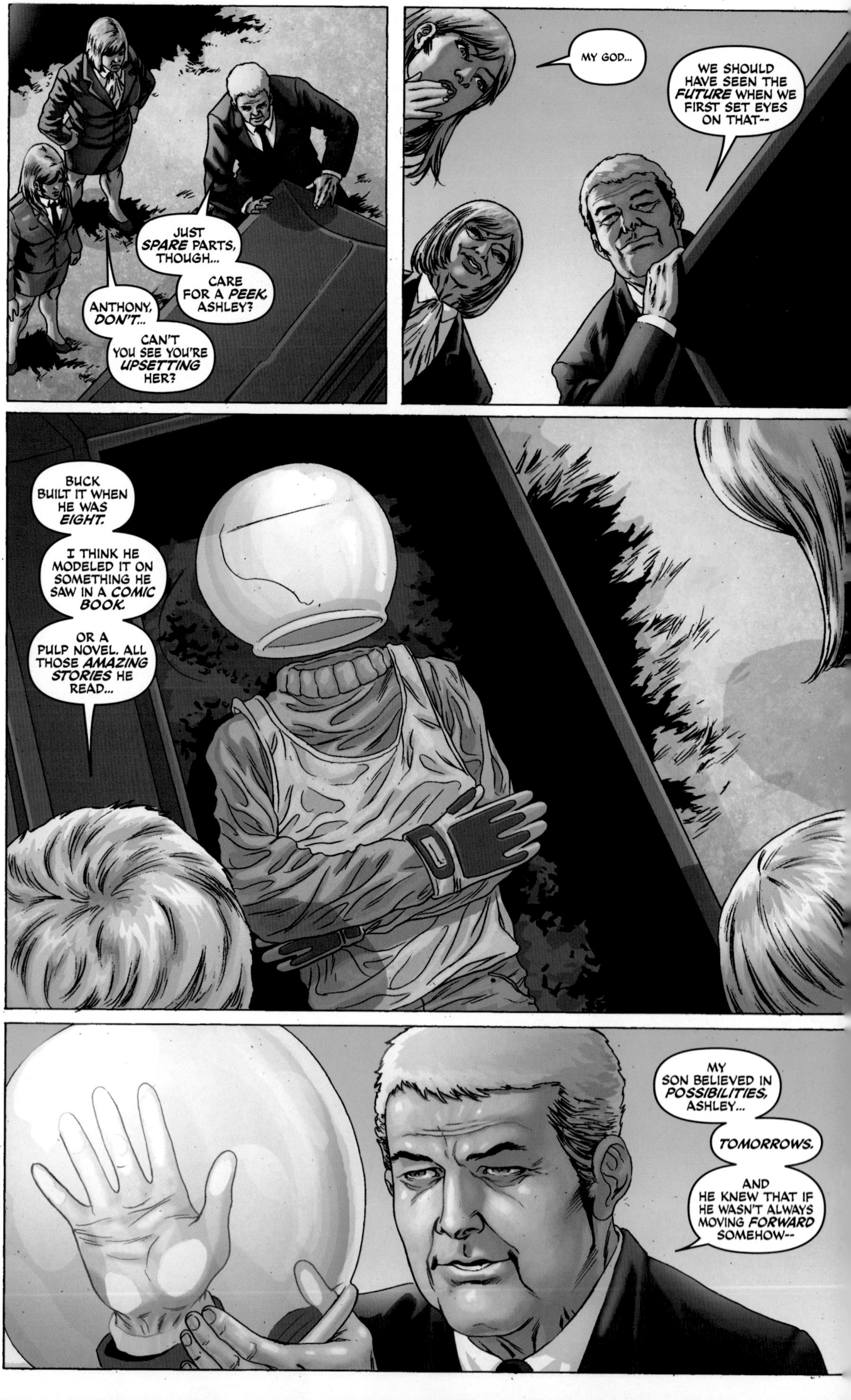
JUST SPARE PARTS, THOUGH...
CARE FOR A PEEK, ASHLEY?
ANTHONY, DON'T...
CAN'T YOU SEE YOU'RE UPSETTING HER?
MY GOD...
WE SHOULD HAVE SEEN THE FUTURE WHEN WE FIRST SET EYES ON THAT--
BUCK BUILT IT WHEN HE WAS EIGHT.
I THINK HE MODELED IT ON SOMETHING HE SAW IN A COMIC BOOK.
OR A PULP NOVEL. ALL THOSE AMAZING STORIES HE READ...
MY SON BELIEVED IN POSSIBILITIES, ASHLEY...
TOMORROWS.
AND HE KNEW THAT IF HE WASN'T ALWAYS MOVING FORWARD SOMEHOW--

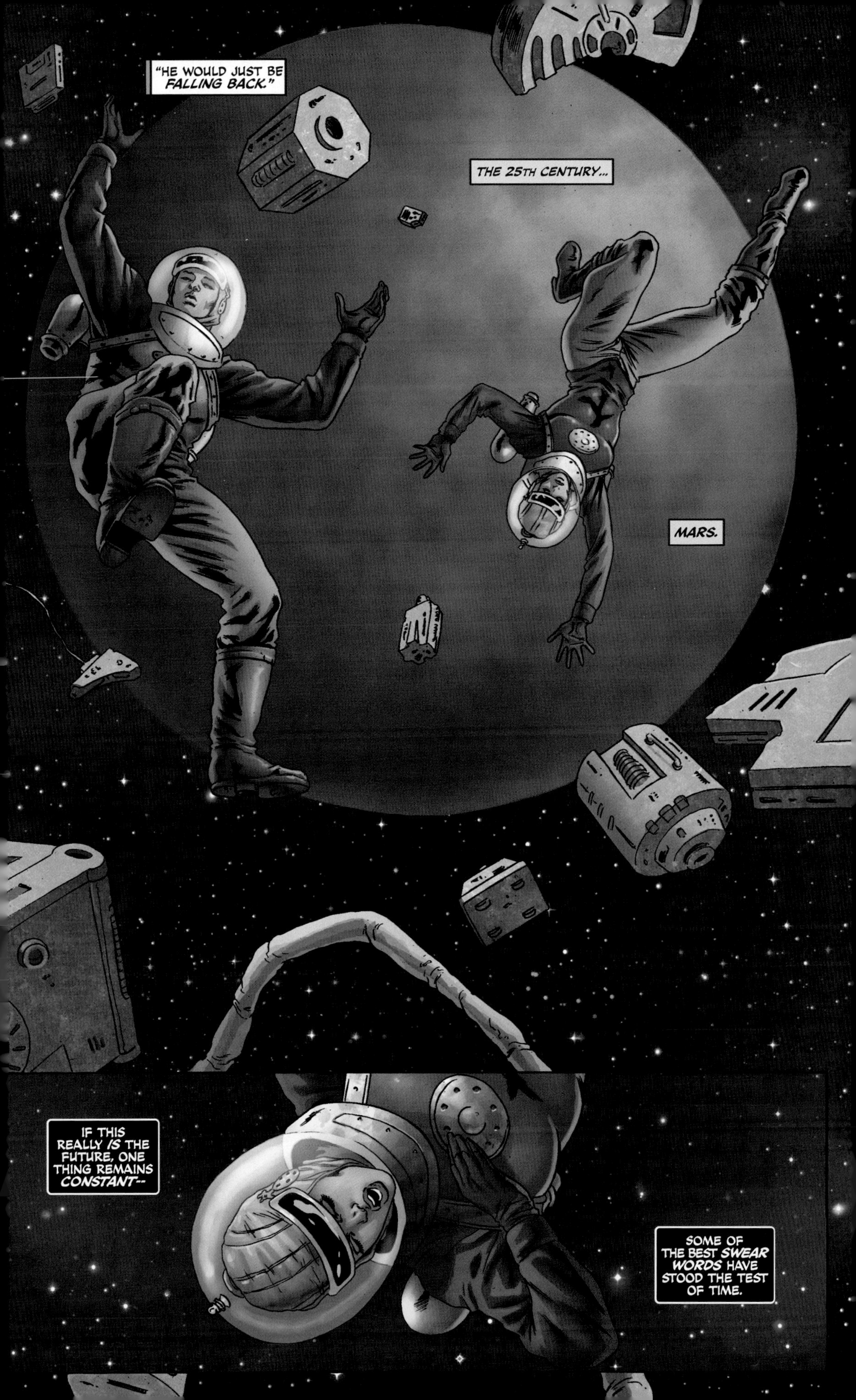
"HE WOULD JUST BE FALLING BACK."
THE 25TH CENTURY...
MARS.
IF THIS REALLY IS THE FUTURE, ONE THING REMAINS CONSTANT--
SOME OF THE BEST SWEAR WORDS HAVE STOOD THE TEST OF TIME.

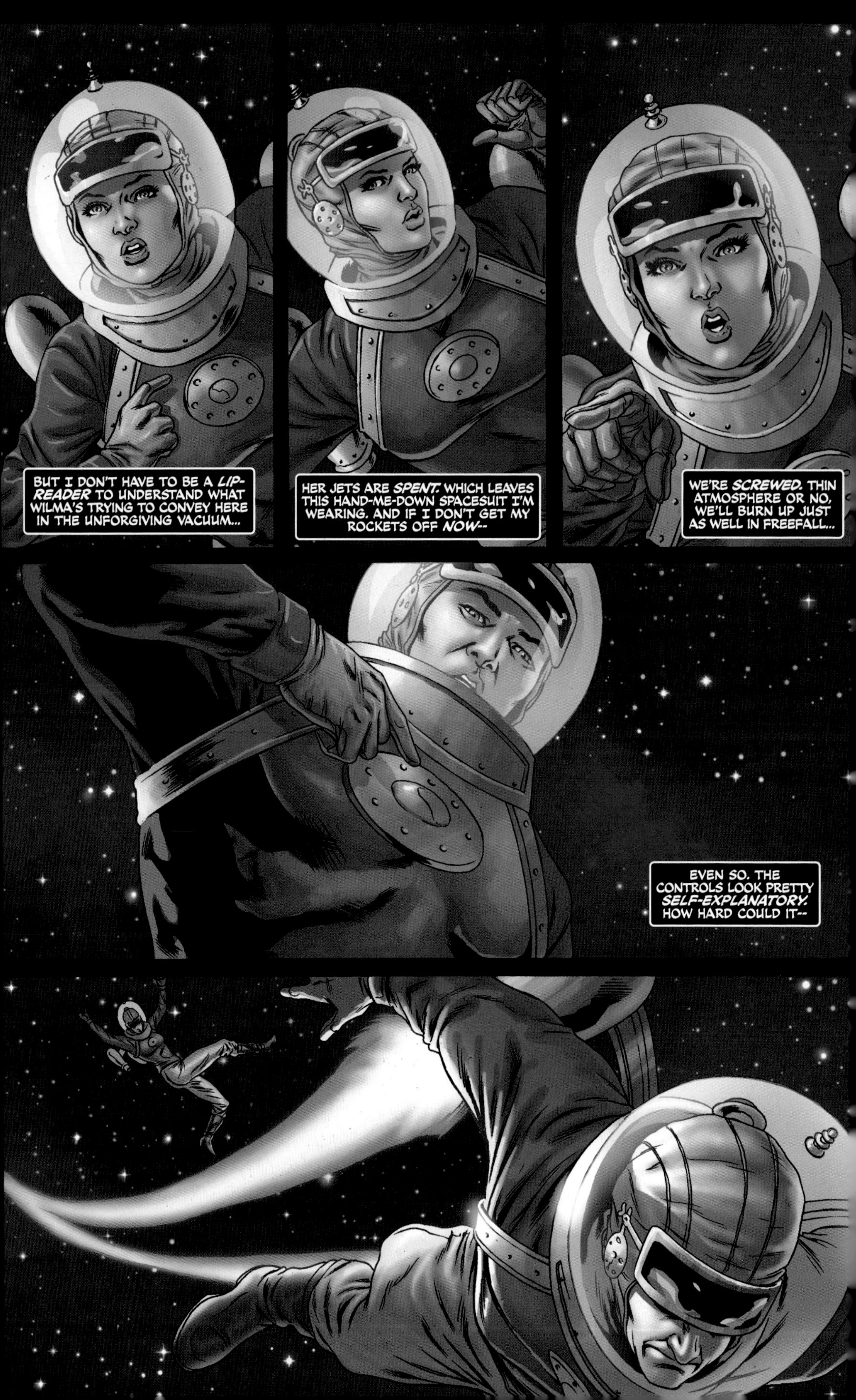

BUT I DON'T HAVE TO BE A *LIP-READER* TO UNDERSTAND WHAT WILMA'S TRYING TO CONVEY HERE IN THE UNFORGIVING VACUUM...
HER JETS ARE *SPENT.* WHICH LEAVES THIS HAND-ME-DOWN SPACESUIT I'M WEARING. AND IF I DON'T GET MY ROCKETS OFF *NOW*--
WE'RE *SCREWED.* THIN ATMOSPHERE OR NO, WE'LL BURN UP JUST AS WELL IN FREEFALL...
EVEN SO. THE CONTROLS LOOK PRETTY *SELF-EXPLANATORY.* HOW HARD COULD IT--

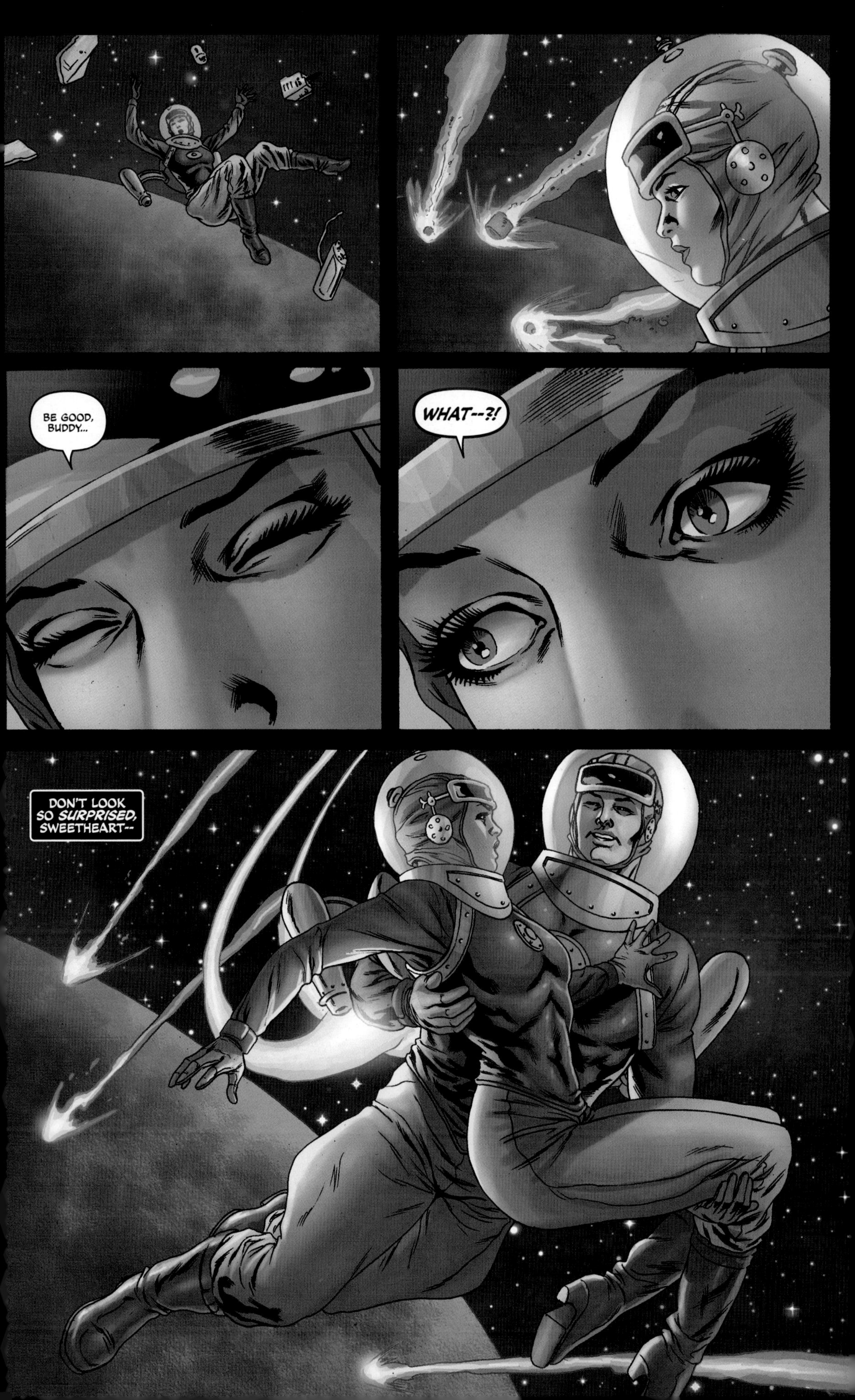
BE GOOD, BUDDY...
WHAT--?!
DON'T LOOK SO *SURPRISED,* SWEETHEART--

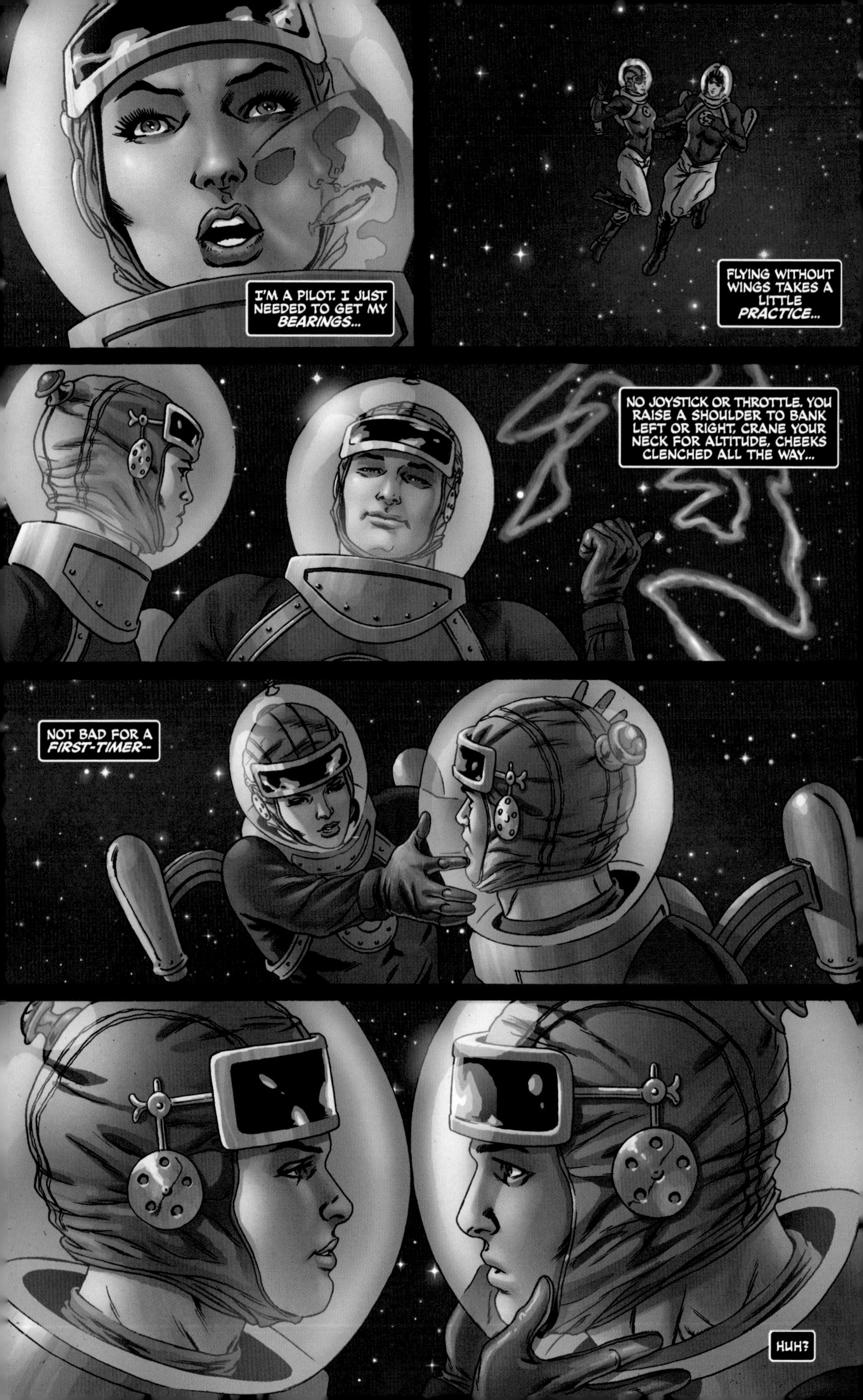
I'M A PILOT. I JUST NEEDED TO GET MY *BEARINGS...*
FLYING WITHOUT WINGS TAKES A LITTLE *PRACTICE...*
NO JOYSTICK OR THROTTLE. YOU RAISE A SHOULDER TO BANK LEFT OR RIGHT, CRANE YOUR NECK FOR ALTITUDE, CHEEKS CLENCHED ALL THE WAY...
NOT BAD FOR A *FIRST-TIMER--*
HUH?

ARE YOU THROUGH FOOLING AROUND?!

WHO SAYS NO ONE CAN HEAR YOU *SCREAM* IN SPACE?

THE COMMS ON THESE PROSPECTING SUITS ARE *DEAD*--

SO OUR FISHBOWL HELMETS HAVE TO BE IN CONTACT JUST TO MAKE *SMALL TALK*...

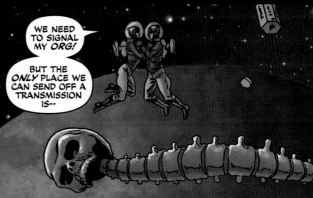

WE NEED TO SIGNAL MY *ORG*!

BUT THE *ONLY* PLACE WE CAN SEND OFF A TRANSMISSION IS--

THERE! THE PACK SLAUGHTER-SHIP!

WHERE WE WILL BE *KILLED*, *FLAYED*, AND *EATEN*--NOT NECESSARILY IN THAT ORDER--IF WE TRY TO REBOARD!

PERFECT!

IT'LL BE THE *LAST THING* THEY EXPECT US TO DO...

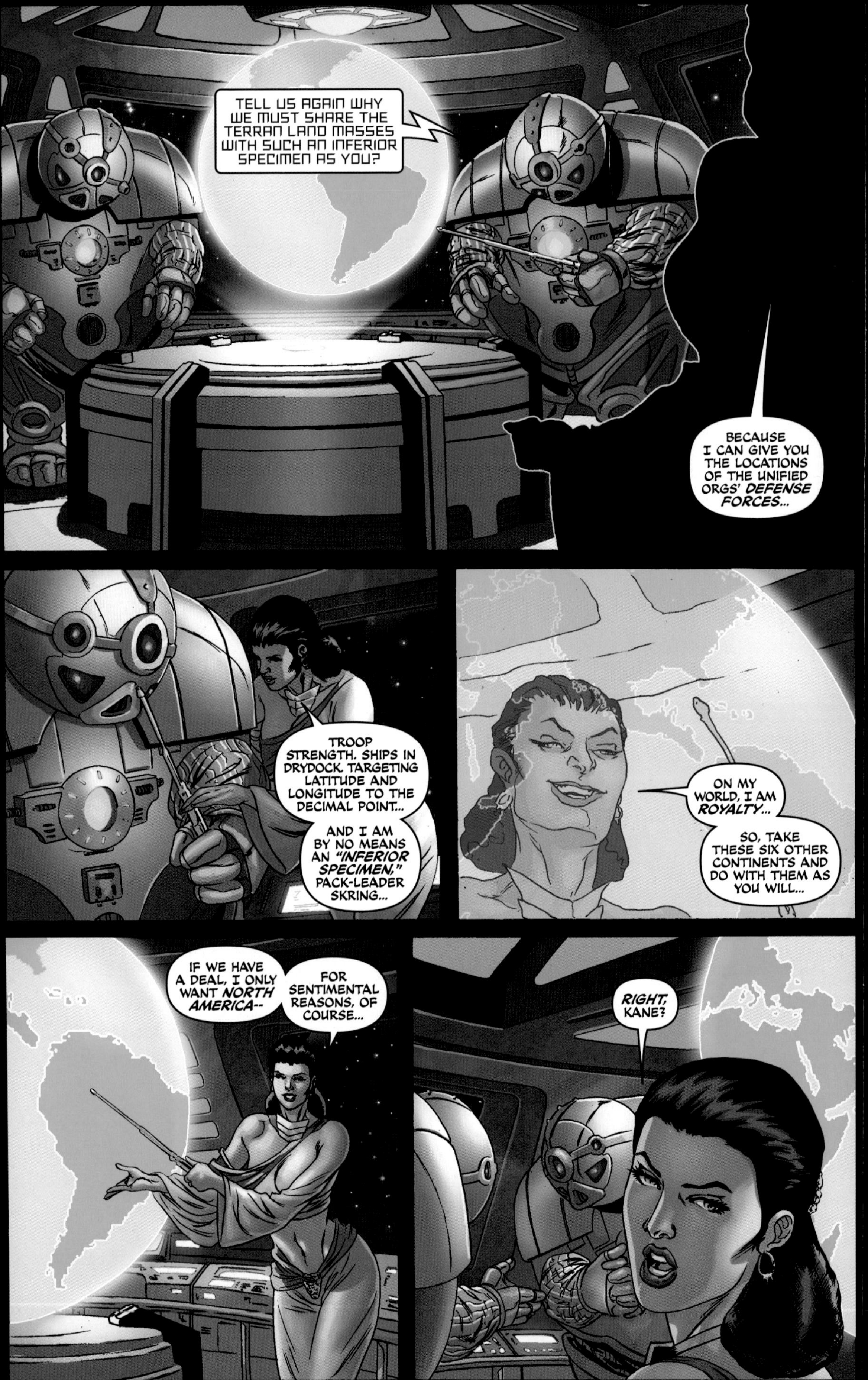
TELL US AGAIN WHY WE MUST SHARE THE TERRAN LAND MASSES WITH SUCH AN INFERIOR SPECIMEN AS YOU?
BECAUSE I CAN GIVE YOU THE LOCATIONS OF THE UNIFIED ORGS' *DEFENSE FORCES*...
TROOP STRENGTH. SHIPS IN DRYDOCK. TARGETING LATITUDE AND LONGITUDE TO THE DECIMAL POINT...
AND I AM BY NO MEANS AN *"INFERIOR SPECIMEN,"* PACK-LEADER SKRING...
ON MY WORLD, I AM *ROYALTY*...
SO, TAKE THESE SIX OTHER CONTINENTS AND DO WITH THEM AS YOU WILL...
IF WE HAVE A DEAL, I ONLY WANT *NORTH AMERICA*--
FOR SENTIMENTAL REASONS, OF COURSE...
RIGHT, KANE?

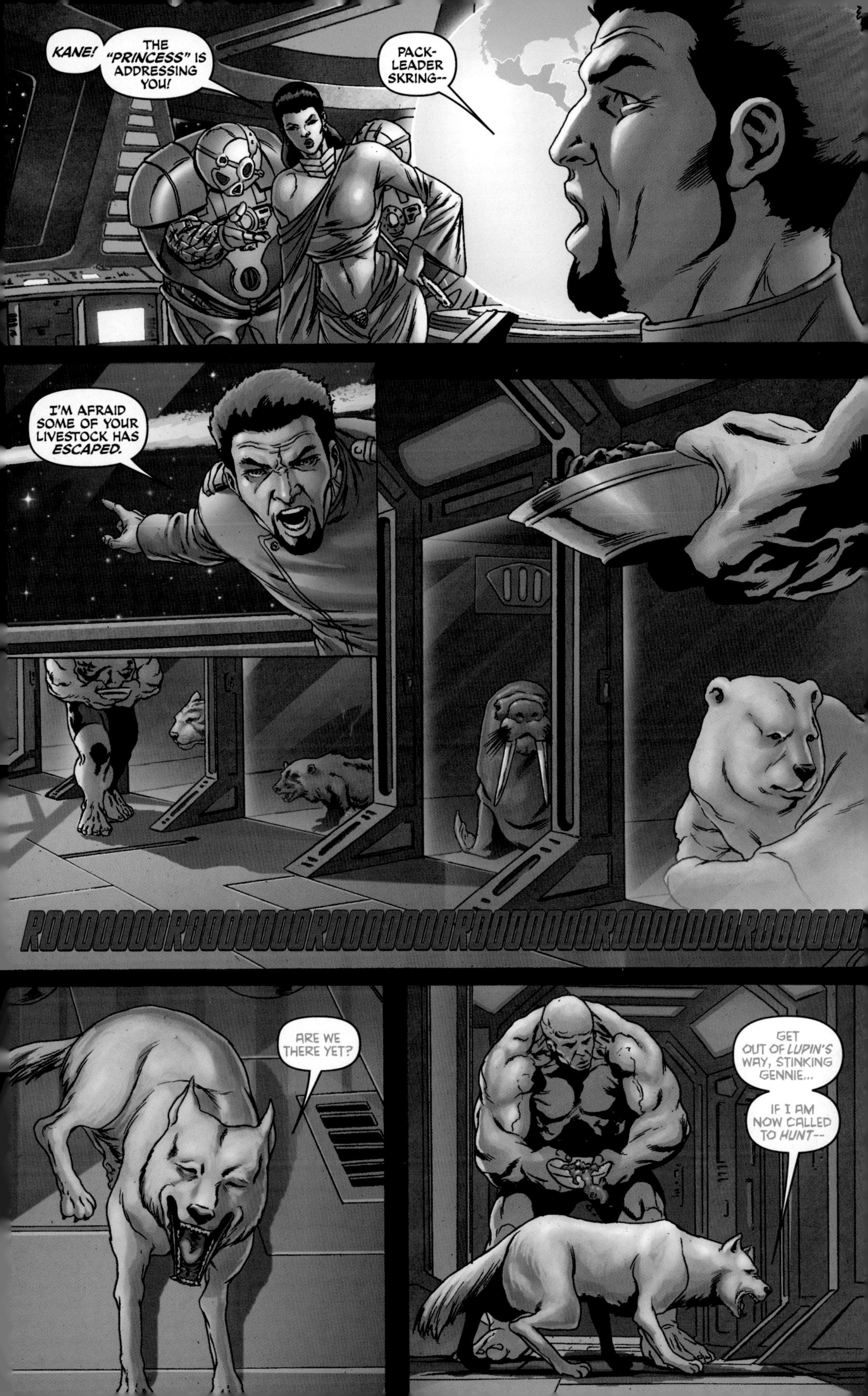
KANE!
THE "PRINCESS" IS ADDRESSING YOU!
PACK-LEADER SKRING--
I'M AFRAID SOME OF YOUR LIVESTOCK HAS ESCAPED.
ROOOOOOOROOOOOOOOROOOOOOOOROOOOOOOOROOOOOOOOOROOOOOO
ARE WE THERE YET?
GET OUT OF LUPIN'S WAY, STINKING GENNIE...
IF I AM NOW CALLED TO HUNT--

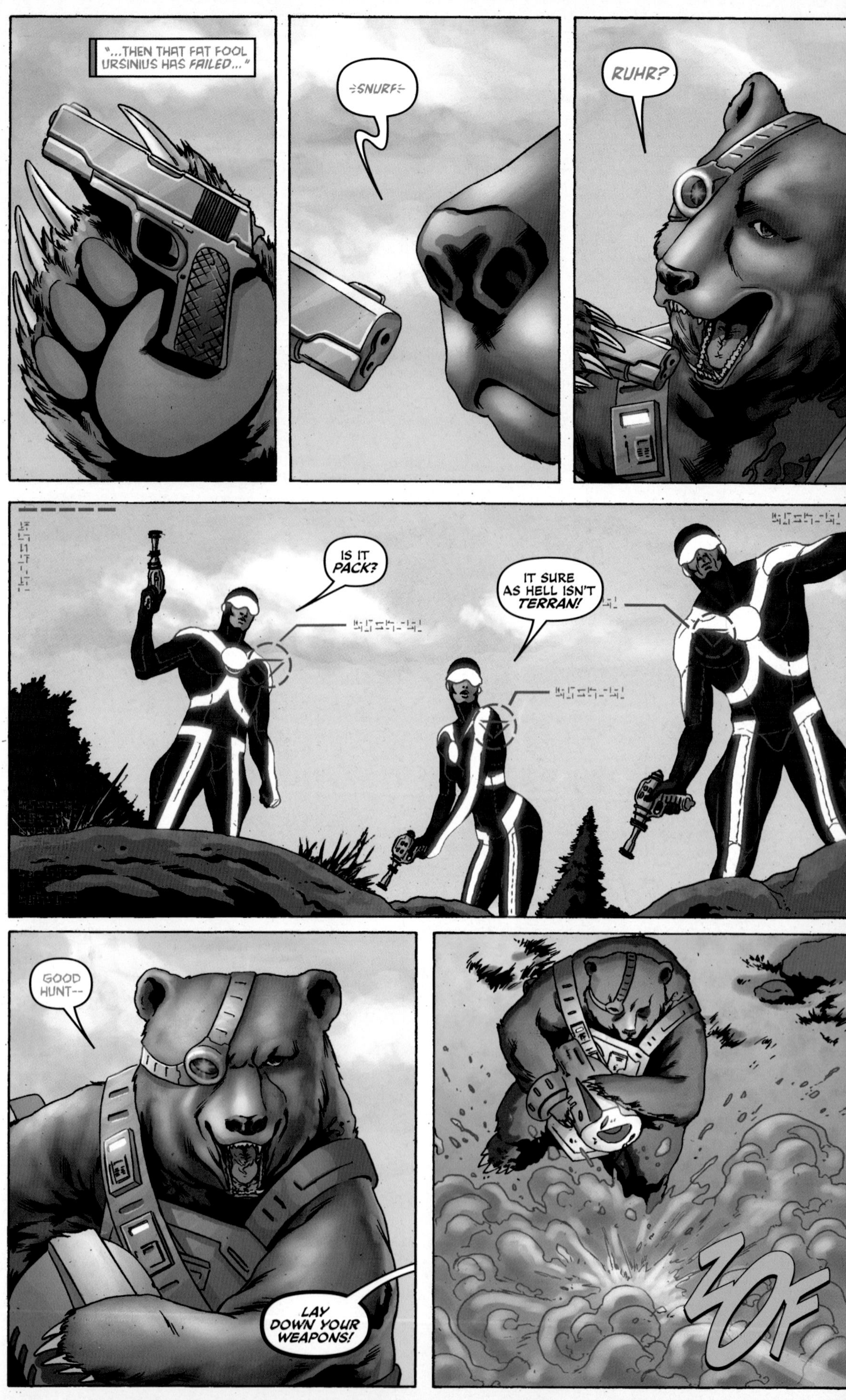
"...THEN THAT FAT FOOL URSINIUS HAS FAILED..."
SNURF
RUHR?
IS IT PACK?
IT SURE AS HELL ISN'T TERRAN!
GOOD HUNT--
LAY DOWN YOUR WEAPONS!
ZOF

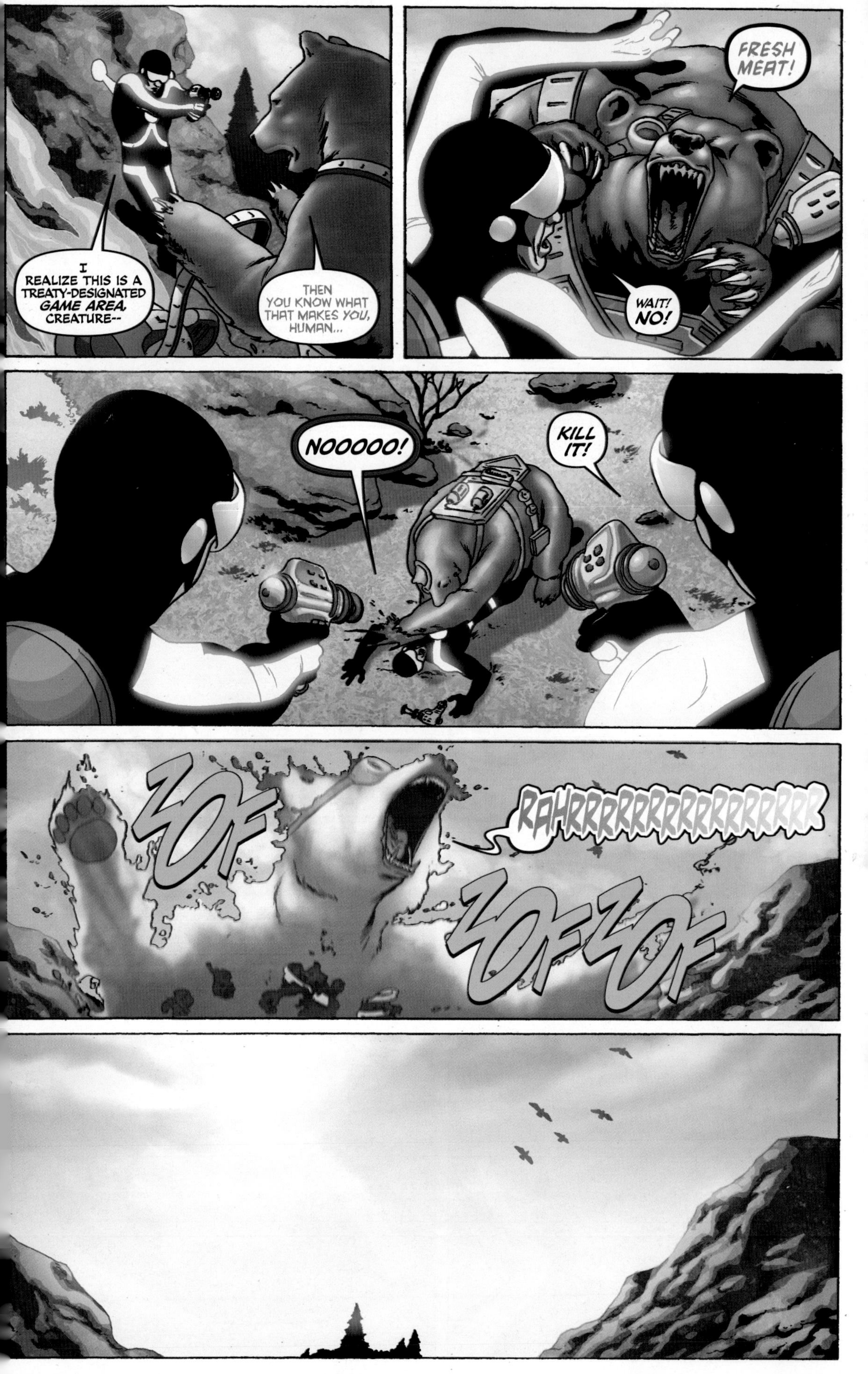

I REALIZE THIS IS A TREATY-DESIGNATED *GAME AREA,* CREATURE--
THEN YOU KNOW WHAT THAT MAKES *YOU,* HUMAN...
FRESH MEAT!
WAIT! **NO!**
NOOOOO!
KILL IT!
ZOF
RAHRRRRRRRRRRRRRRR
ZOF ZOF

SANDOVAL?

GONE. IT RIPPED HIS THROAT OUT. *CRUSHED* HIS CHEST.

THERE COULD BE *OTHER* PACK-HUNTERS...

NEGATIVE. JUST THE LOCAL WILDLIFE. WE'RE CLEAR FOR MILES IN EVERY DIRECTION.

IS THAT--?

COLONEL DEERING'S *ATOMIZER.*

THE REST I'M NOT SURE...

MAYBE IT'S SURVIVAL GEAR FROM THAT *CRASHDOWN* SHE WAS INVESTIGATING.

SO WHAT DO WE HAVE HERE?

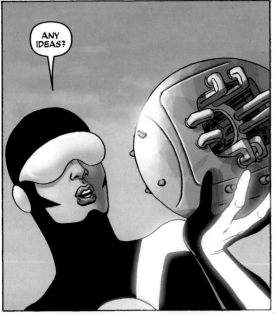

ANY IDEAS?

I'M TRAINED FOR ZERO-GRAV COMBAT AND PRECISION ATOMIZING, MERILEE.

YOU WANT *BIG* IDEAS--

YOU GO TO *DOCTOR HUER.*

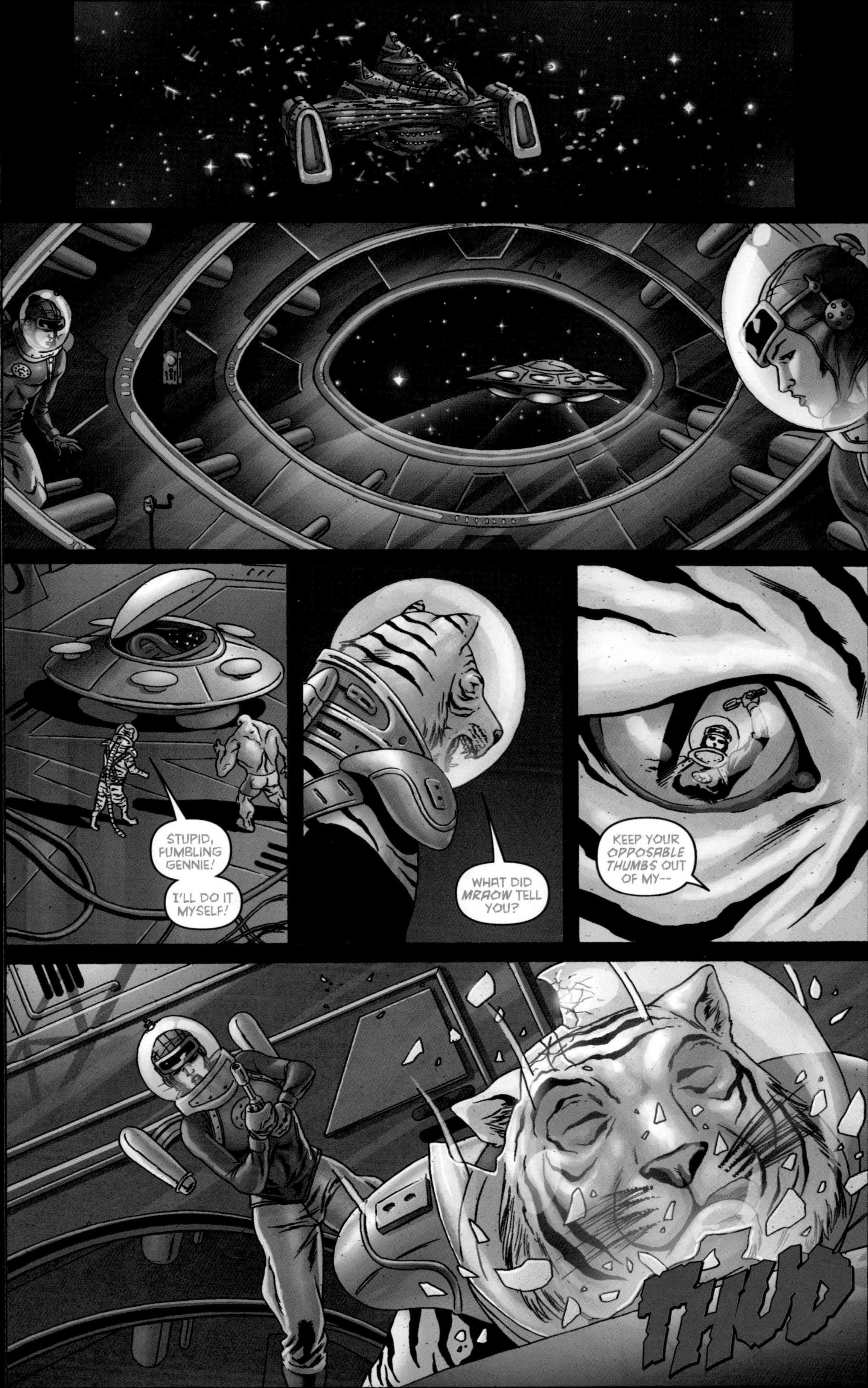
STUPID, FUMBLING GENNIE!
I'LL DO IT MYSELF!
WHAT DID MRAOW TELL YOU?
KEEP YOUR OPPOSABLE THUMBS OUT OF MY--
THUD

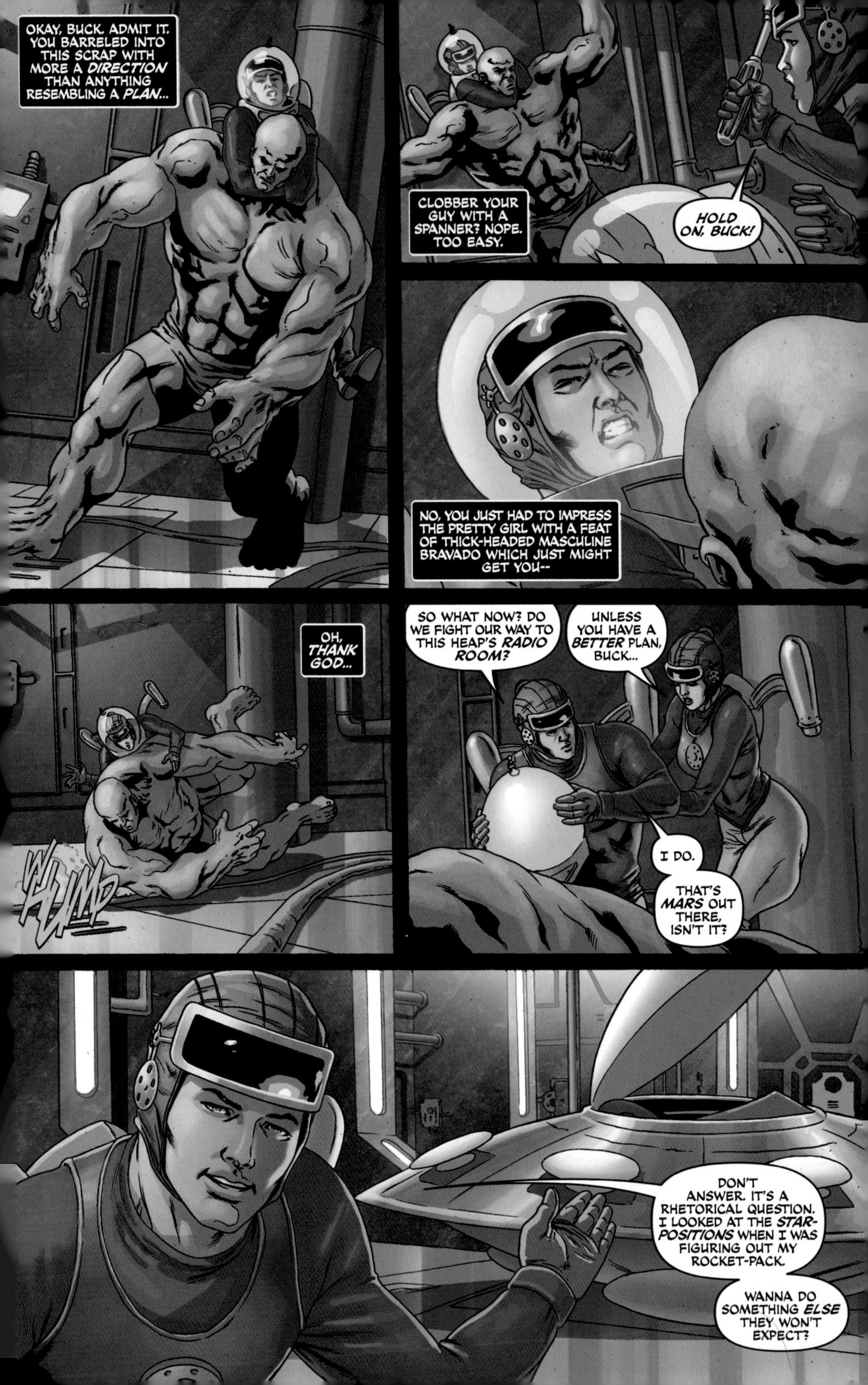
OKAY, BUCK. ADMIT IT. YOU BARRELED INTO THIS SCRAP WITH MORE A *DIRECTION* THAN ANYTHING RESEMBLING A *PLAN*...
CLOBBER YOUR GUY WITH A SPANNER? NOPE. TOO EASY.
HOLD ON, BUCK!
NO, YOU JUST HAD TO IMPRESS THE PRETTY GIRL WITH A FEAT OF THICK-HEADED MASCULINE BRAVADO WHICH JUST MIGHT GET YOU--
OH, *THANK* GOD...
WHUMP
SO WHAT NOW? DO WE FIGHT OUR WAY TO THIS HEAP'S *RADIO ROOM?*
UNLESS YOU HAVE A *BETTER* PLAN, BUCK...
I DO.
THAT'S *MARS* OUT THERE, ISN'T IT?
DON'T ANSWER. IT'S A RHETORICAL QUESTION. I LOOKED AT THE *STAR-POSITIONS* WHEN I WAS FIGURING OUT MY ROCKET-PACK.
WANNA DO SOMETHING *ELSE* THEY WON'T EXPECT?

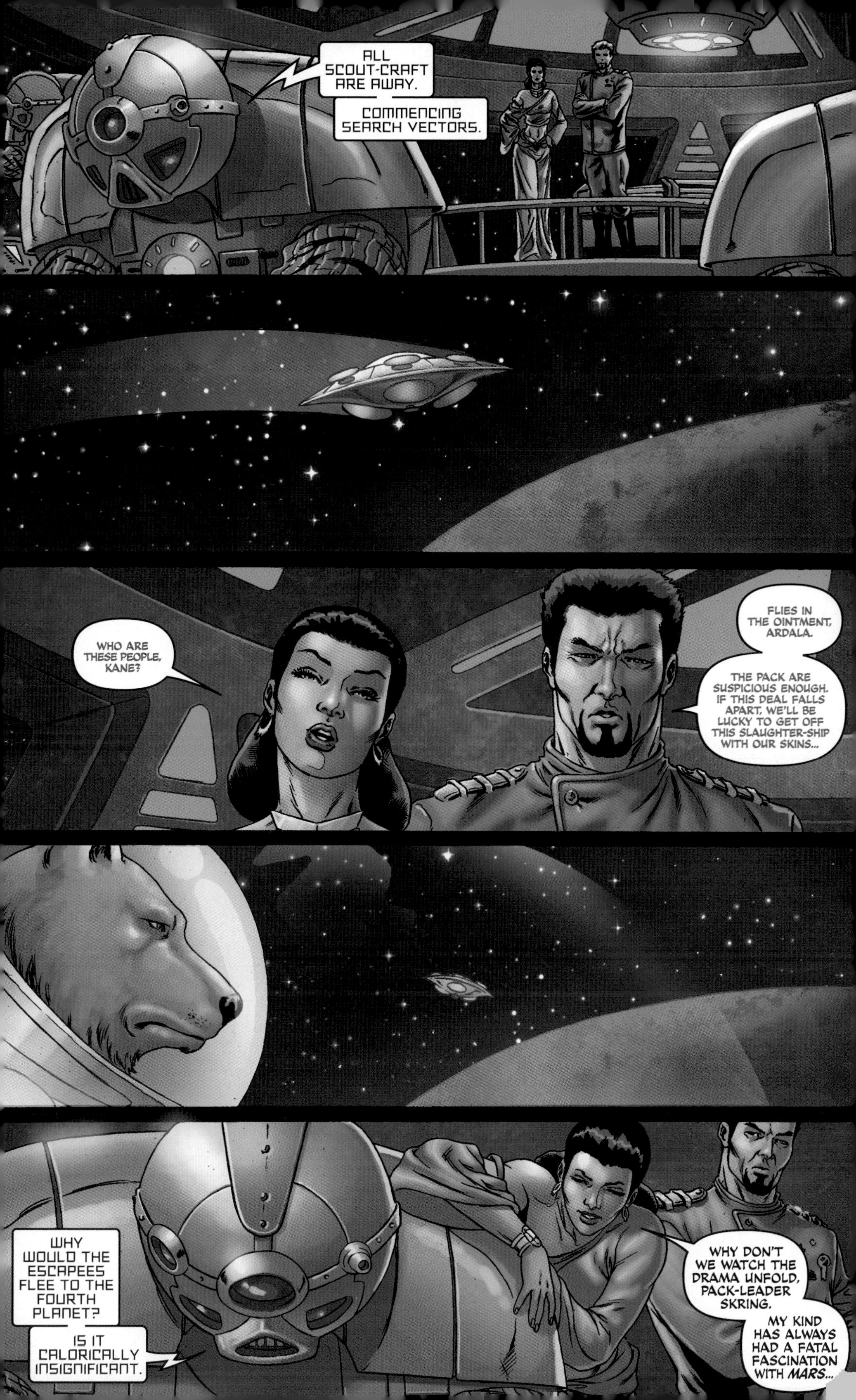
ALL SCOUT-CRAFT ARE AWAY.
COMMENCING SEARCH VECTORS.
WHO ARE THESE PEOPLE, KANE?
FLIES IN THE OINTMENT, ARDALA.
THE PACK ARE SUSPICIOUS ENOUGH. IF THIS DEAL FALLS APART, WE'LL BE LUCKY TO GET OFF THIS SLAUGHTER-SHIP WITH OUR SKINS...
WHY WOULD THE ESCAPEES FLEE TO THE FOURTH PLANET?
IS IT CALORICALLY INSIGNIFICANT.
WHY DON'T WE WATCH THE DRAMA UNFOLD, PACK-LEADER SKRING.
MY KIND HAS ALWAYS HAD A FATAL FASCINATION WITH *MARS*...

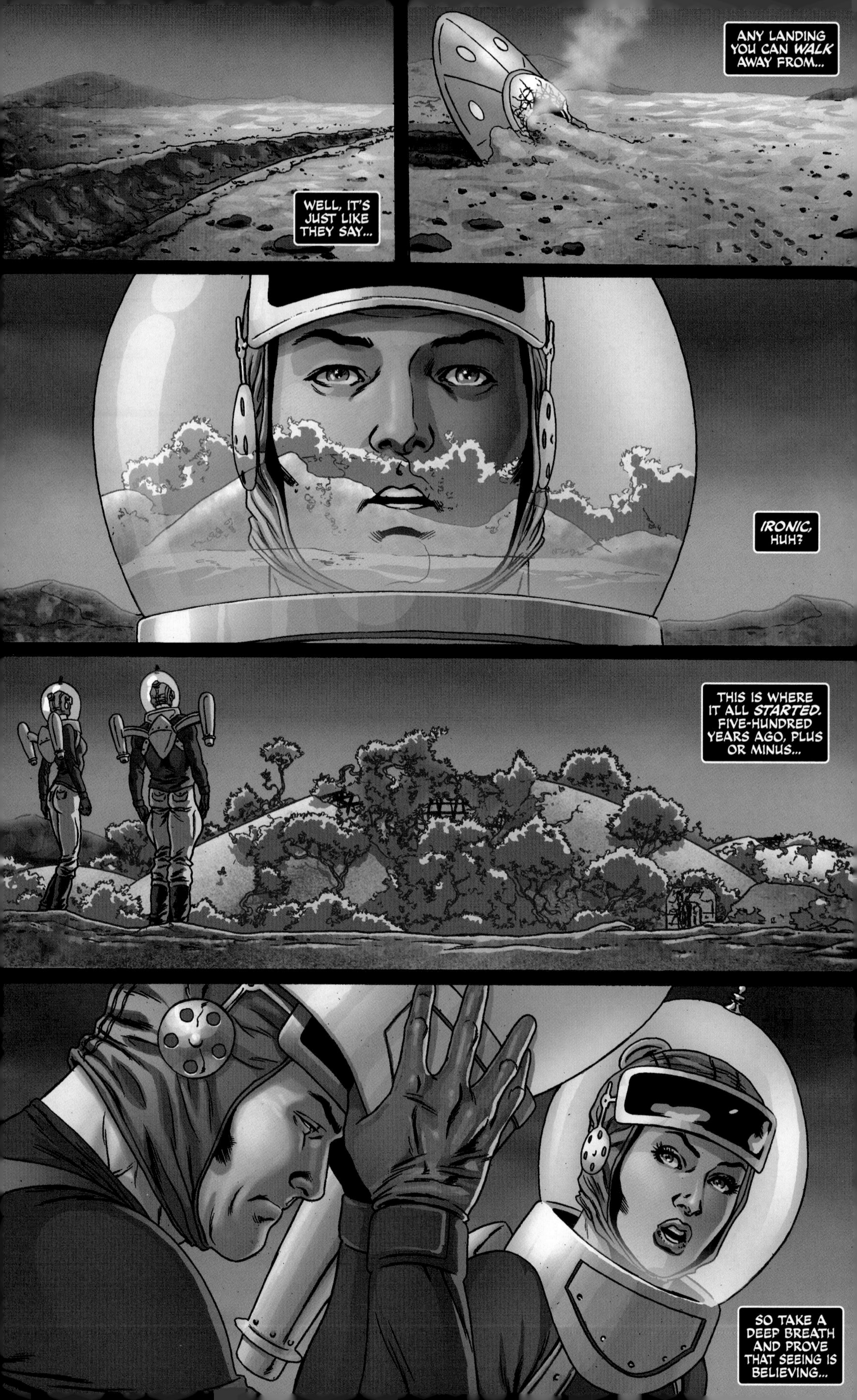
WELL, IT'S JUST LIKE THEY SAY...
ANY LANDING YOU CAN WALK AWAY FROM...
IRONIC, HUH?
THIS IS WHERE IT ALL STARTED. FIVE-HUNDRED YEARS AGO, PLUS OR MINUS...
SO TAKE A DEEP BREATH AND PROVE THAT SEEING IS BELIEVING...

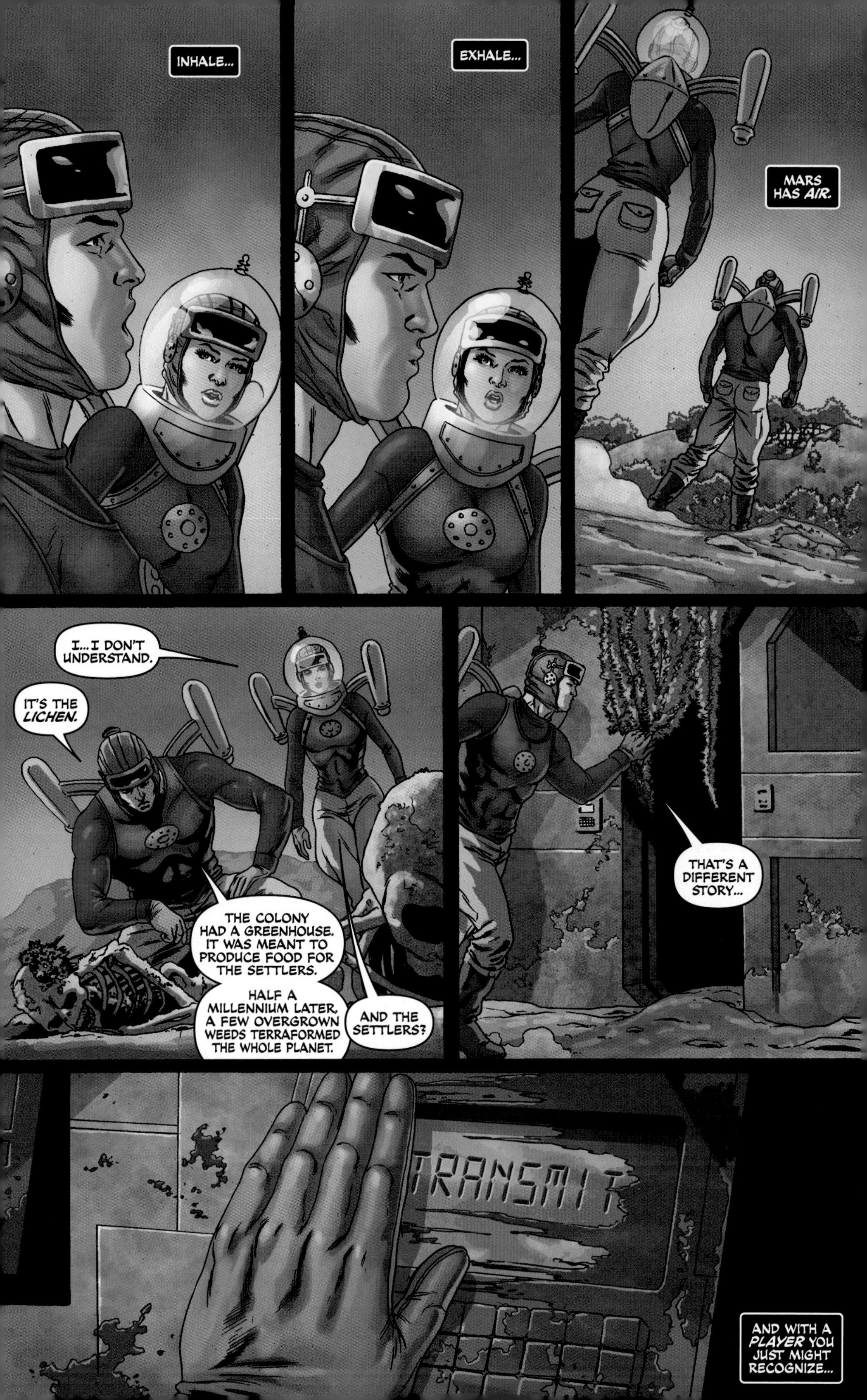
INHALE...
EXHALE...
MARS HAS *AIR.*
I... I DON'T UNDERSTAND.
IT'S THE *LICHEN.*
THE COLONY HAD A GREENHOUSE. IT WAS MEANT TO PRODUCE FOOD FOR THE SETTLERS.
HALF A MILLENNIUM LATER, A FEW OVERGROWN WEEDS TERRAFORMED THE WHOLE PLANET.
AND THE SETTLERS?
THAT'S A DIFFERENT STORY...
TRANSMIT
AND WITH A *PLAYER* YOU JUST MIGHT RECOGNIZE...

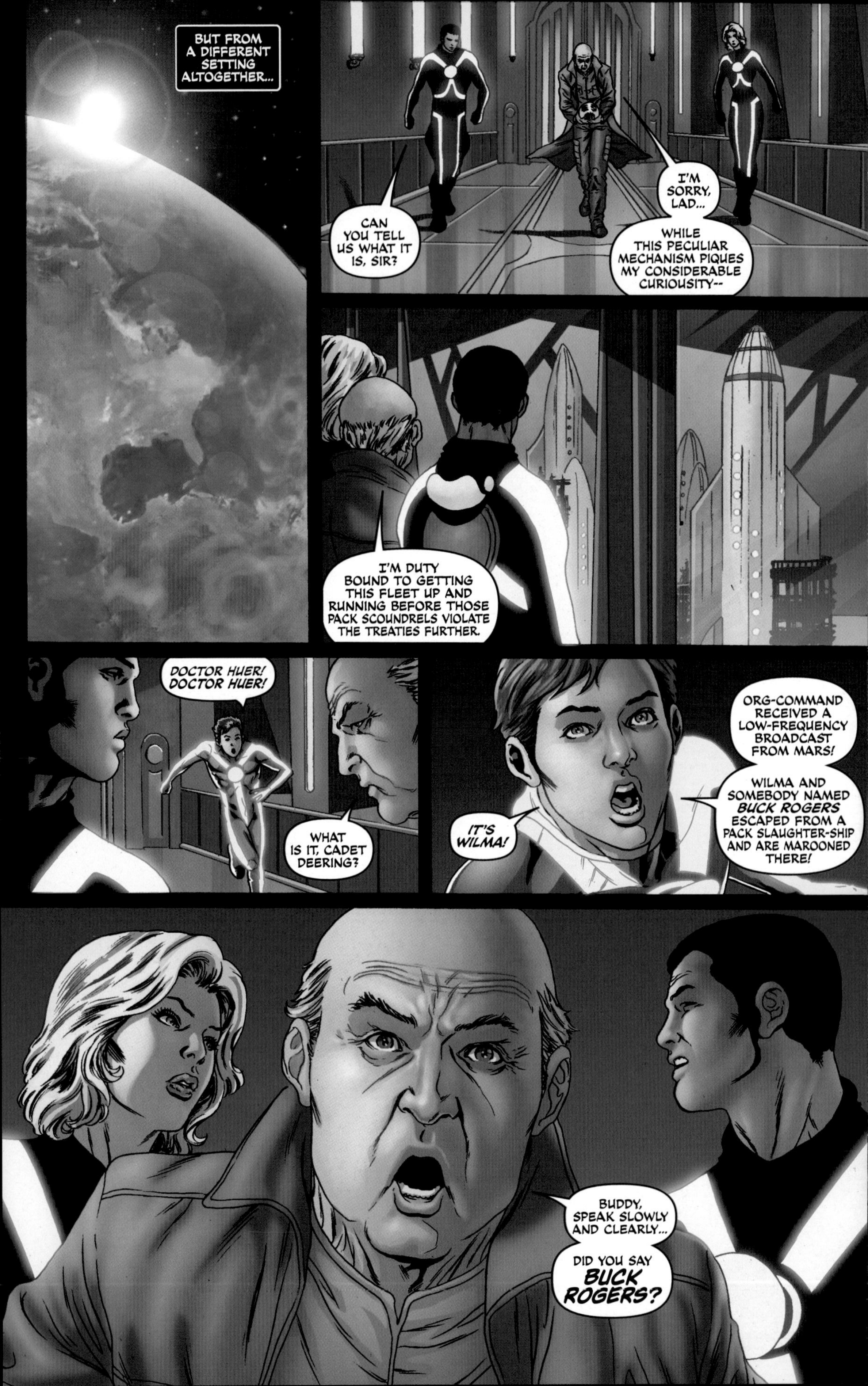
BUT FROM A DIFFERENT SETTING ALTOGETHER...
CAN YOU TELL US WHAT IT IS, SIR?
I'M SORRY, LAD...
WHILE THIS PECULIAR MECHANISM PIQUES MY CONSIDERABLE CURIOUSITY--
I'M DUTY BOUND TO GETTING THIS FLEET UP AND RUNNING BEFORE THOSE PACK SCOUNDRELS VIOLATE THE TREATIES FURTHER.
DOCTOR HUER! DOCTOR HUER!
WHAT IS IT, CADET DEERING?
IT'S WILMA!
ORG-COMMAND RECEIVED A LOW-FREQUENCY BROADCAST FROM MARS!
WILMA AND SOMEBODY NAMED BUCK ROGERS ESCAPED FROM A PACK SLAUGHTER-SHIP AND ARE MAROONED THERE!
BUDDY, SPEAK SLOWLY AND CLEARLY...
DID YOU SAY BUCK ROGERS?

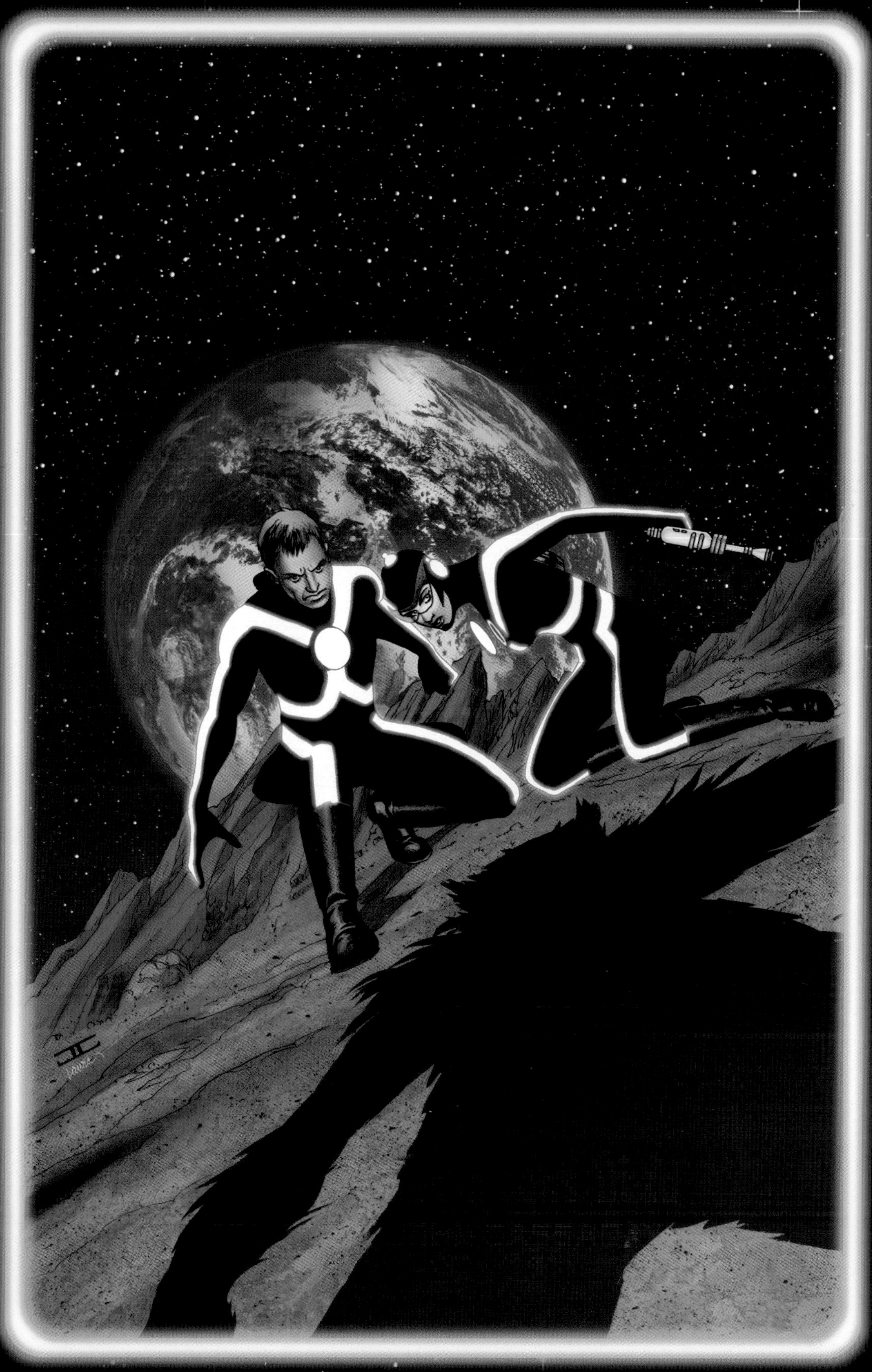

ISSUE FOUR: Red means Dead

COVER BY JOHN CASSADAY

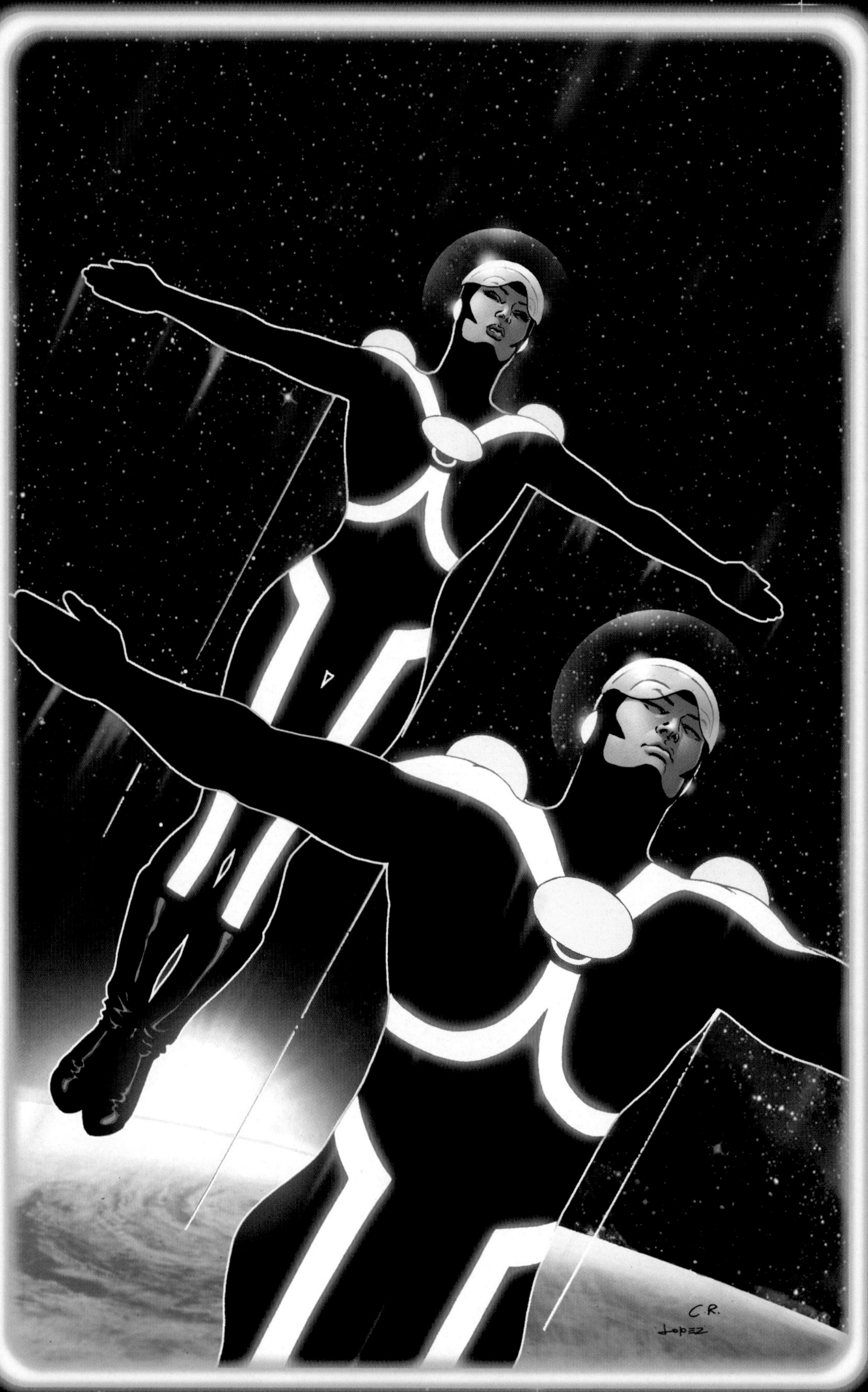
C.R.
Lopez

ALTERNATE COVER BY CARLOS RAFAEL

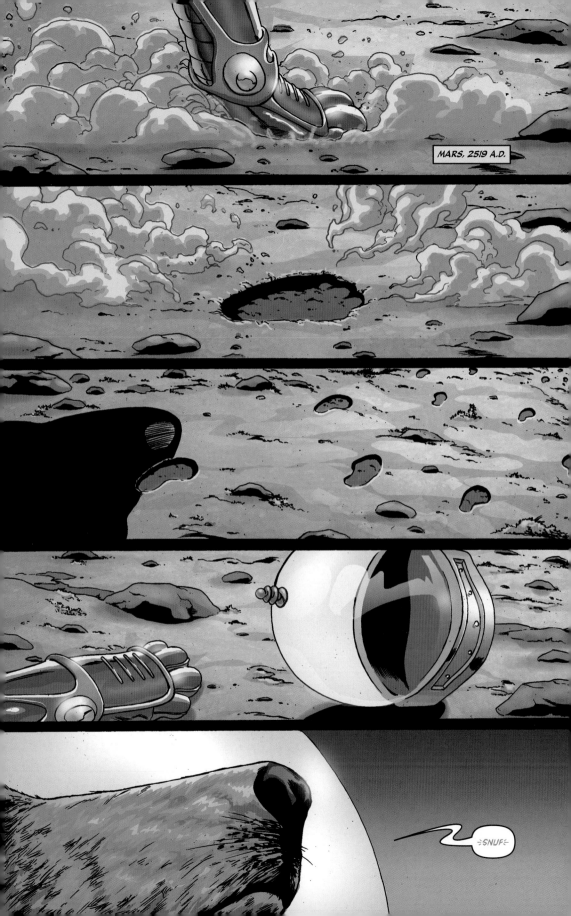

MARS, 2519 A.D.

⇥SNUF⇤

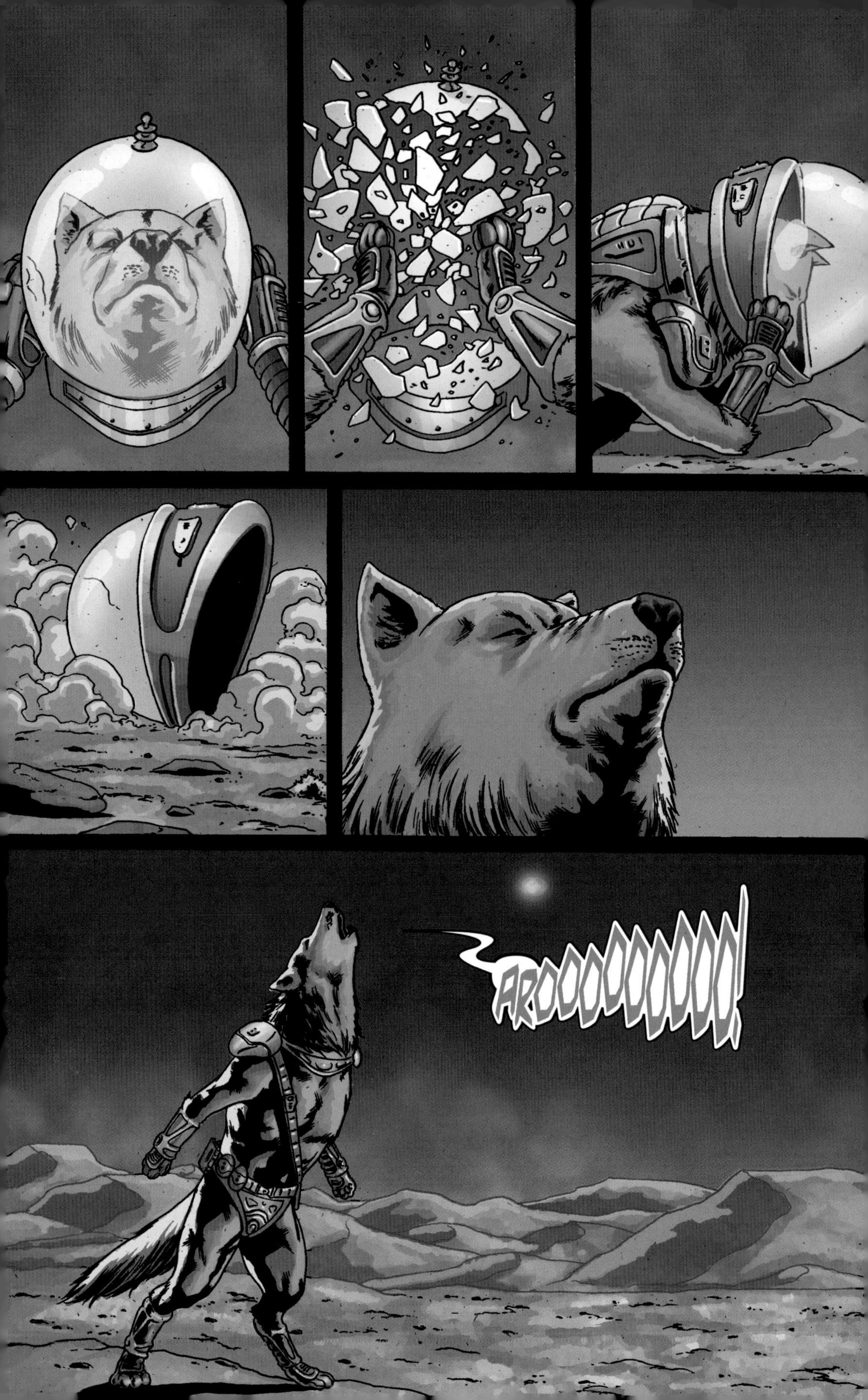
AROOOOOOOOOO!

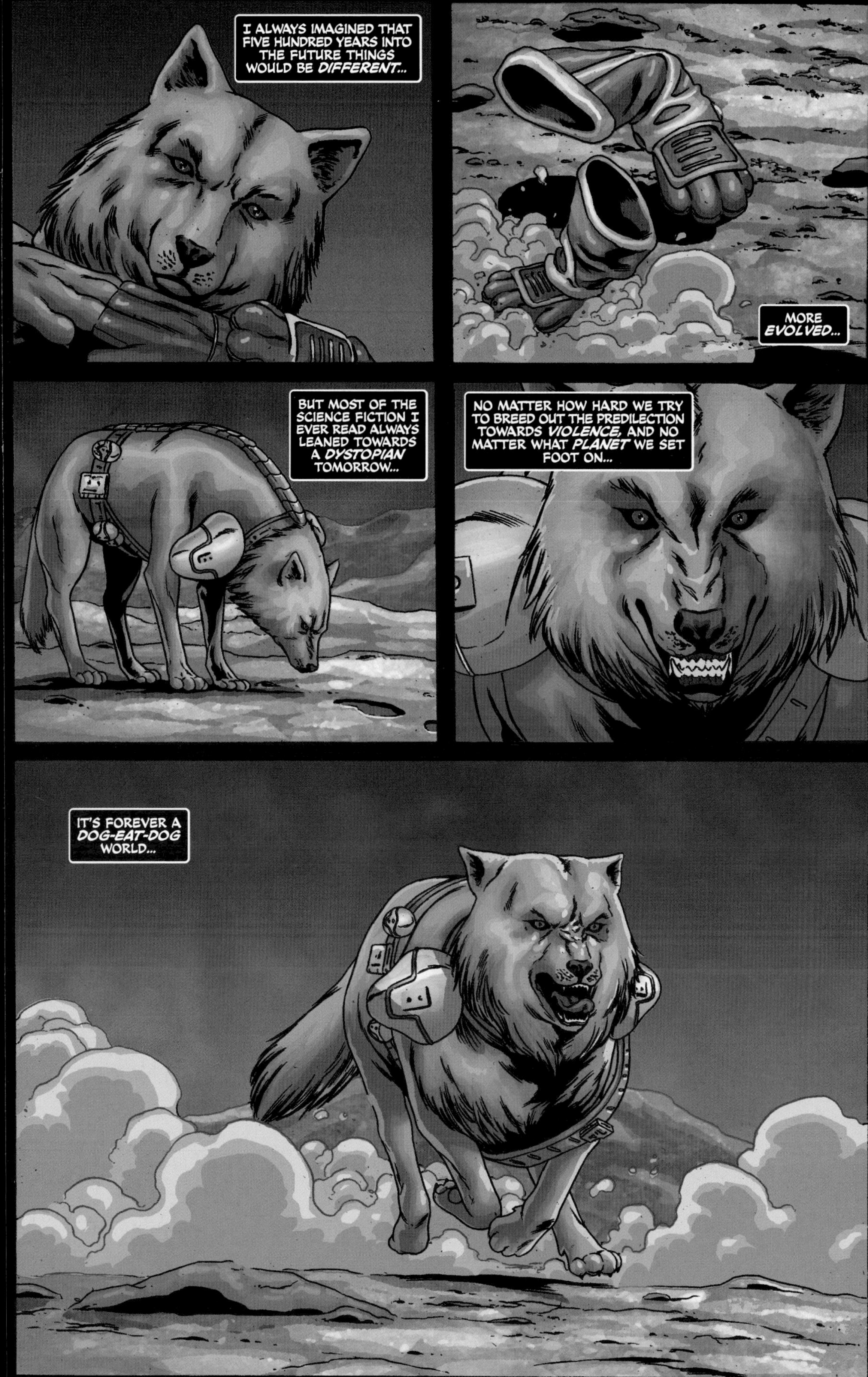
I ALWAYS IMAGINED THAT FIVE HUNDRED YEARS INTO THE FUTURE THINGS WOULD BE *DIFFERENT*...
MORE *EVOLVED*...
BUT MOST OF THE SCIENCE FICTION I EVER READ ALWAYS LEANED TOWARDS A *DYSTOPIAN* TOMORROW...
NO MATTER HOW HARD WE TRY TO BREED OUT THE PREDILECTION TOWARDS *VIOLENCE*, AND NO MATTER WHAT *PLANET* WE SET FOOT ON...
IT'S FOREVER A *DOG-EAT-DOG* WORLD...

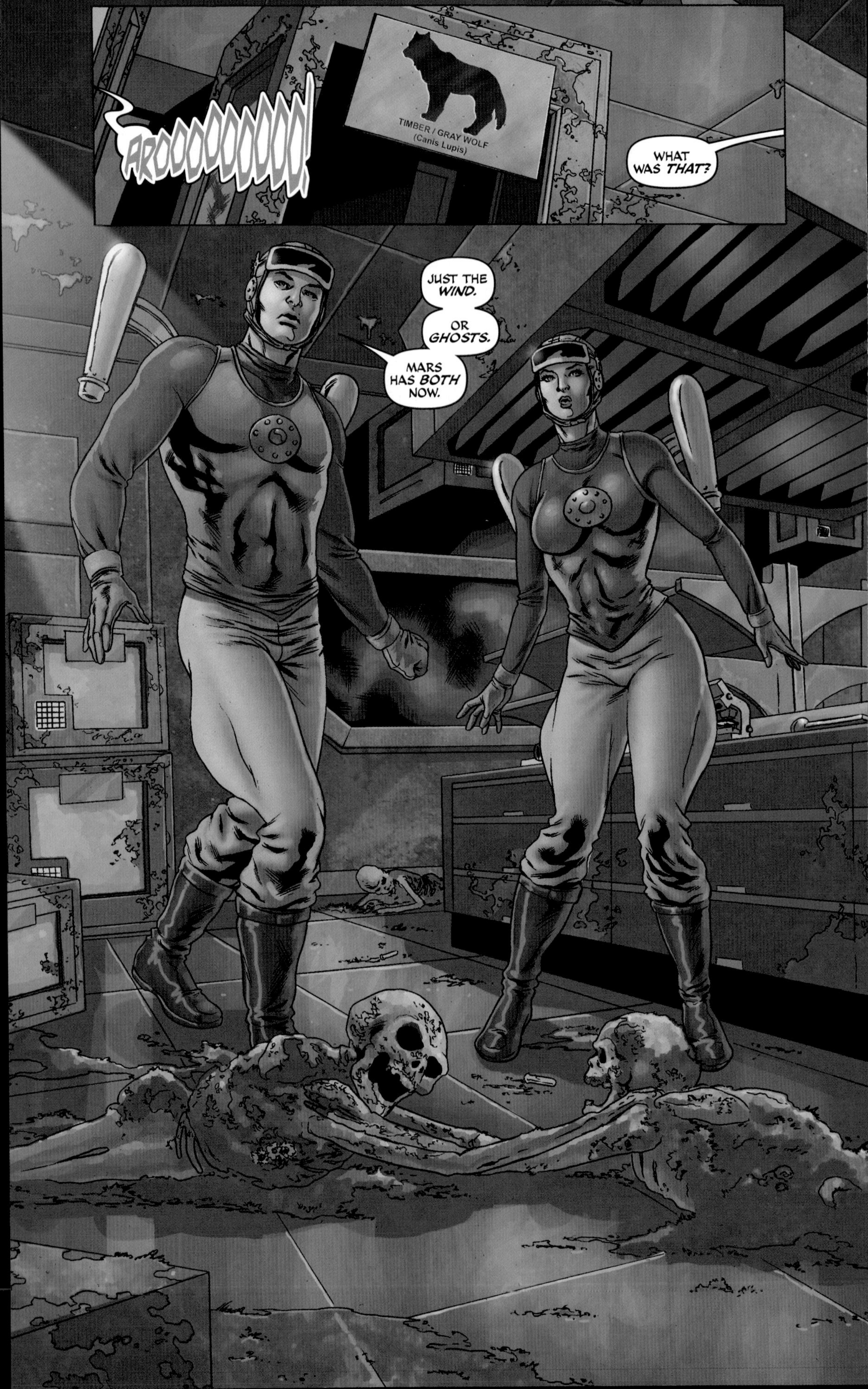
TIMBER / GRAY WOLF
(Canis Lupis)
AROOOOOOOOO!
WHAT WAS THAT?
JUST THE WIND.
OR GHOSTS.
MARS HAS BOTH NOW.

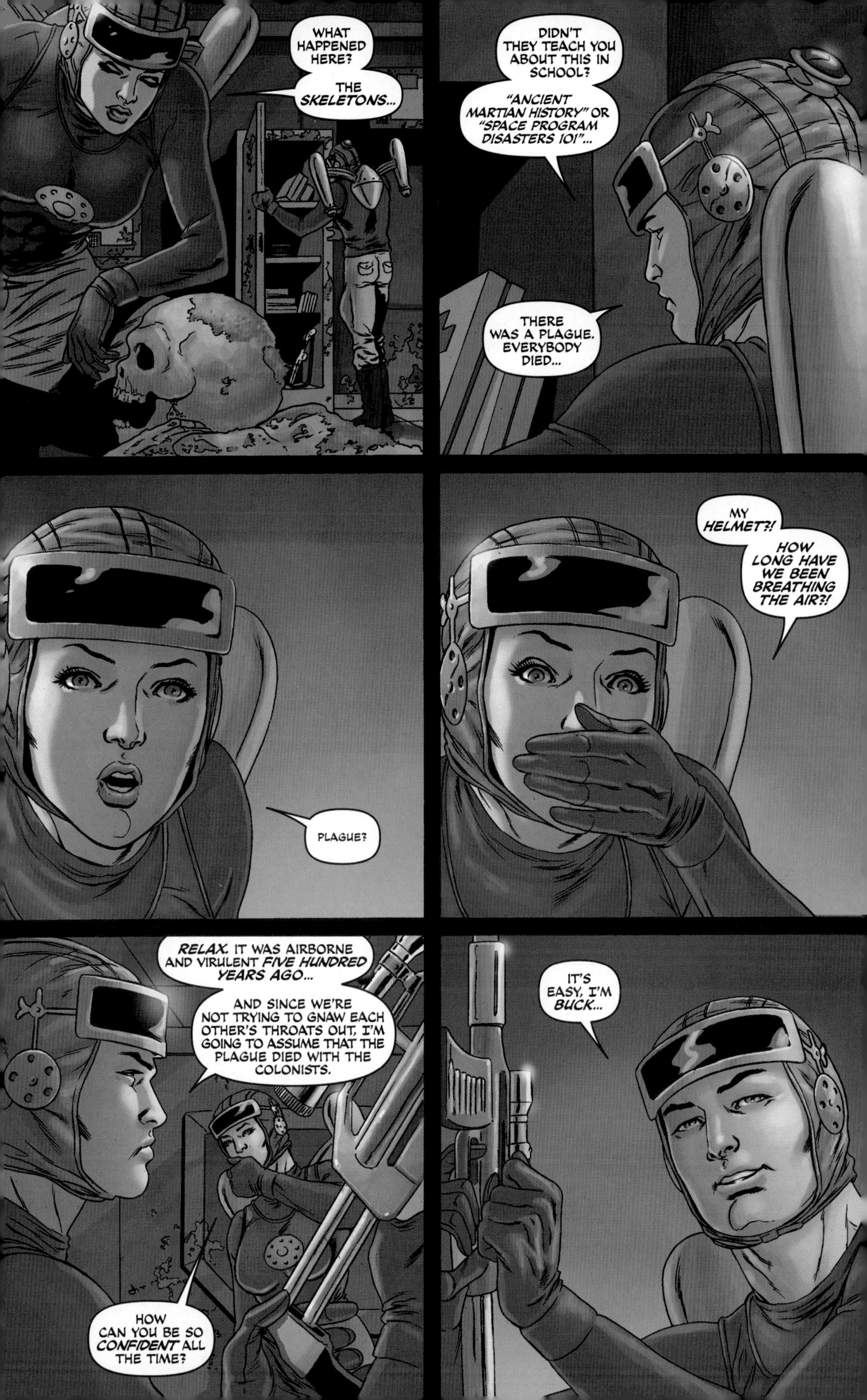
WHAT HAPPENED HERE?
THE SKELETONS...
DIDN'T THEY TEACH YOU ABOUT THIS IN SCHOOL?
"ANCIENT MARTIAN HISTORY" OR "SPACE PROGRAM DISASTERS 101"...
THERE WAS A PLAGUE. EVERYBODY DIED...
PLAGUE?
MY HELMET?!
HOW LONG HAVE WE BEEN BREATHING THE AIR?!
RELAX. IT WAS AIRBORNE AND VIRULENT FIVE HUNDRED YEARS AGO...
AND SINCE WE'RE NOT TRYING TO GNAW EACH OTHER'S THROATS OUT, I'M GOING TO ASSUME THAT THE PLAGUE DIED WITH THE COLONISTS.
HOW CAN YOU BE SO CONFIDENT ALL THE TIME?
IT'S EASY, I'M BUCK...

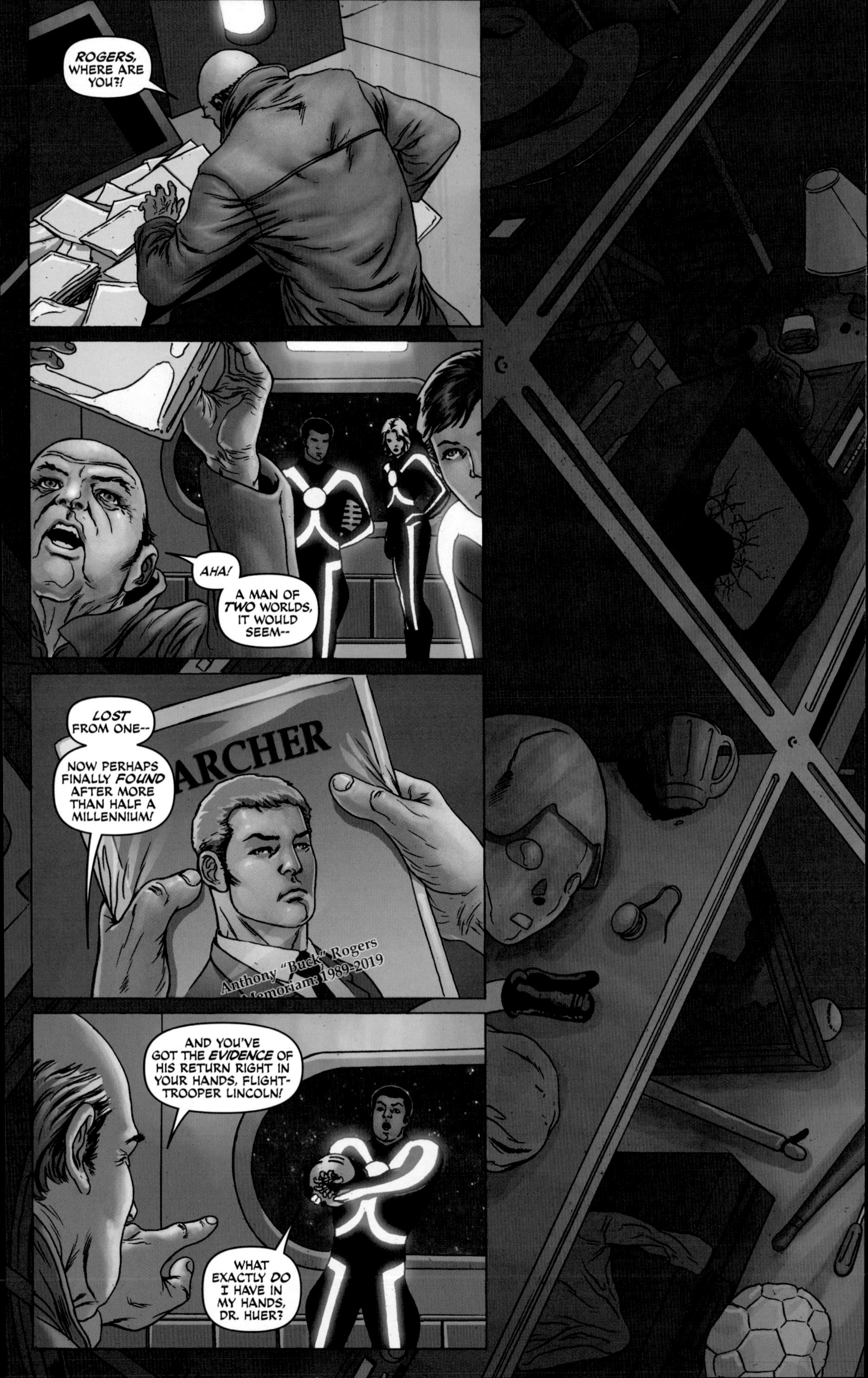
ROGERS, WHERE ARE YOU?!
AHA!
A MAN OF TWO WORLDS, IT WOULD SEEM--
LOST FROM ONE--
NOW PERHAPS FINALLY FOUND AFTER MORE THAN HALF A MILLENNIUM!
ARCHER
Anthony "Buck" Rogers
Memoriam: 1989-2019
AND YOU'VE GOT THE EVIDENCE OF HIS RETURN RIGHT IN YOUR HANDS, FLIGHT-TROOPER LINCOLN!
WHAT EXACTLY DO I HAVE IN MY HANDS, DR. HUER?

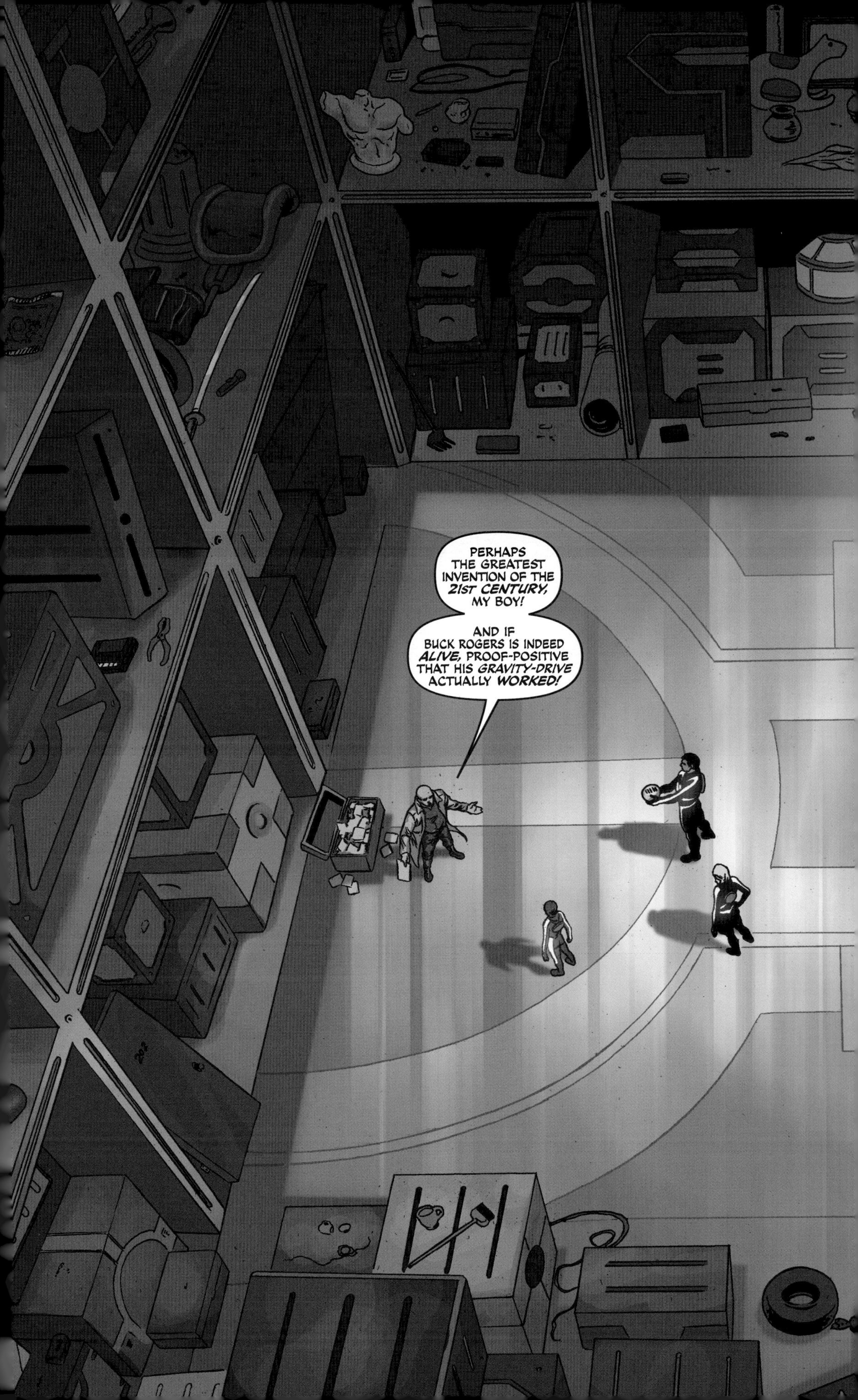
PERHAPS THE GREATEST INVENTION OF THE *21ST CENTURY,* MY BOY!
AND IF BUCK ROGERS IS INDEED *ALIVE,* PROOF-POSITIVE THAT HIS *GRAVITY-DRIVE* ACTUALLY *WORKED!*

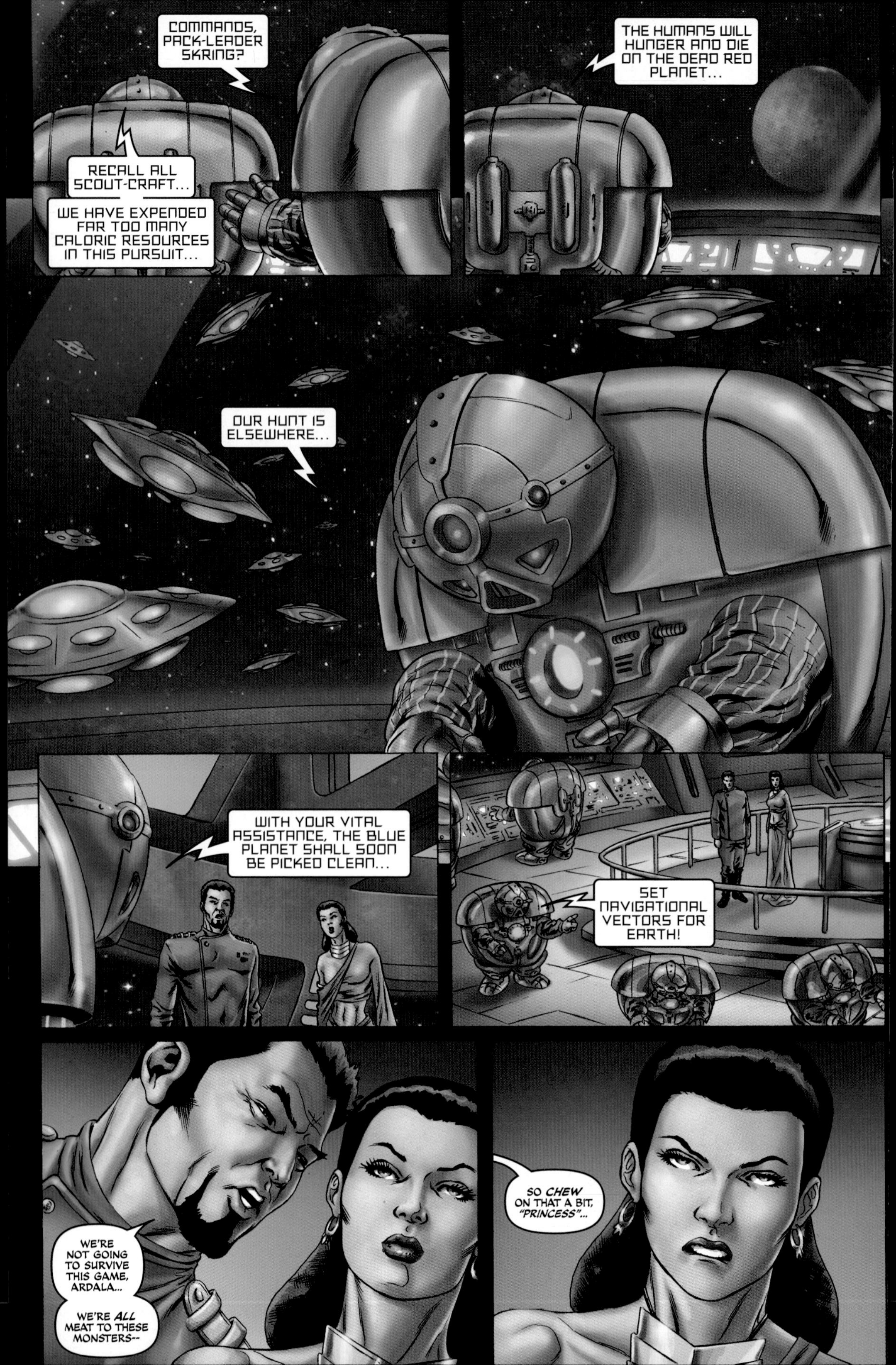
COMMANDS, PACK-LEADER SKRING?
RECALL ALL SCOUT-CRAFT...
WE HAVE EXPENDED FAR TOO MANY CALORIC RESOURCES IN THIS PURSUIT...
THE HUMANS WILL HUNGER AND DIE ON THE DEAD RED PLANET...
OUR HUNT IS ELSEWHERE...
WITH YOUR VITAL ASSISTANCE, THE BLUE PLANET SHALL SOON BE PICKED CLEAN...
SET NAVIGATIONAL VECTORS FOR EARTH!
WE'RE NOT GOING TO SURVIVE THIS GAME, ARDALA...
WE'RE *ALL* MEAT TO THESE MONSTERS--
SO *CHEW* ON THAT A BIT, "PRINCESS"...

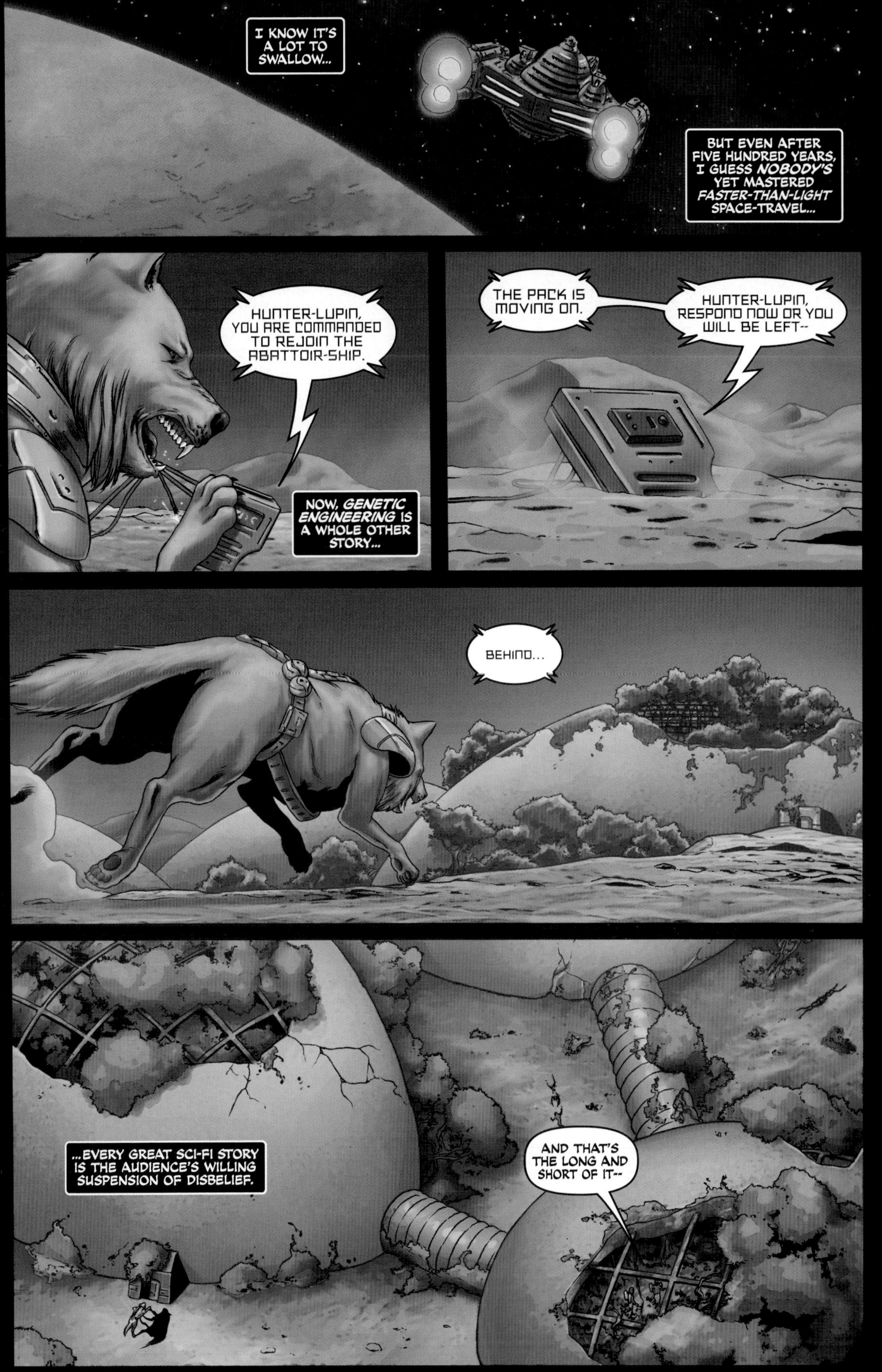
I KNOW IT'S A LOT TO SWALLOW...
BUT EVEN AFTER FIVE HUNDRED YEARS, I GUESS *NOBODY'S* YET MASTERED *FASTER-THAN-LIGHT* SPACE-TRAVEL...
HUNTER-LUPIN, YOU ARE COMMANDED TO REJOIN THE ABATTOIR-SHIP.
NOW, *GENETIC ENGINEERING* IS A WHOLE OTHER STORY...
THE PACK IS MOVING ON.
HUNTER-LUPIN, RESPOND NOW OR YOU WILL BE LEFT--
BEHIND...
...EVERY GREAT SCI-FI STORY IS THE AUDIENCE'S WILLING SUSPENSION OF DISBELIEF.
AND THAT'S THE LONG AND SHORT OF IT--

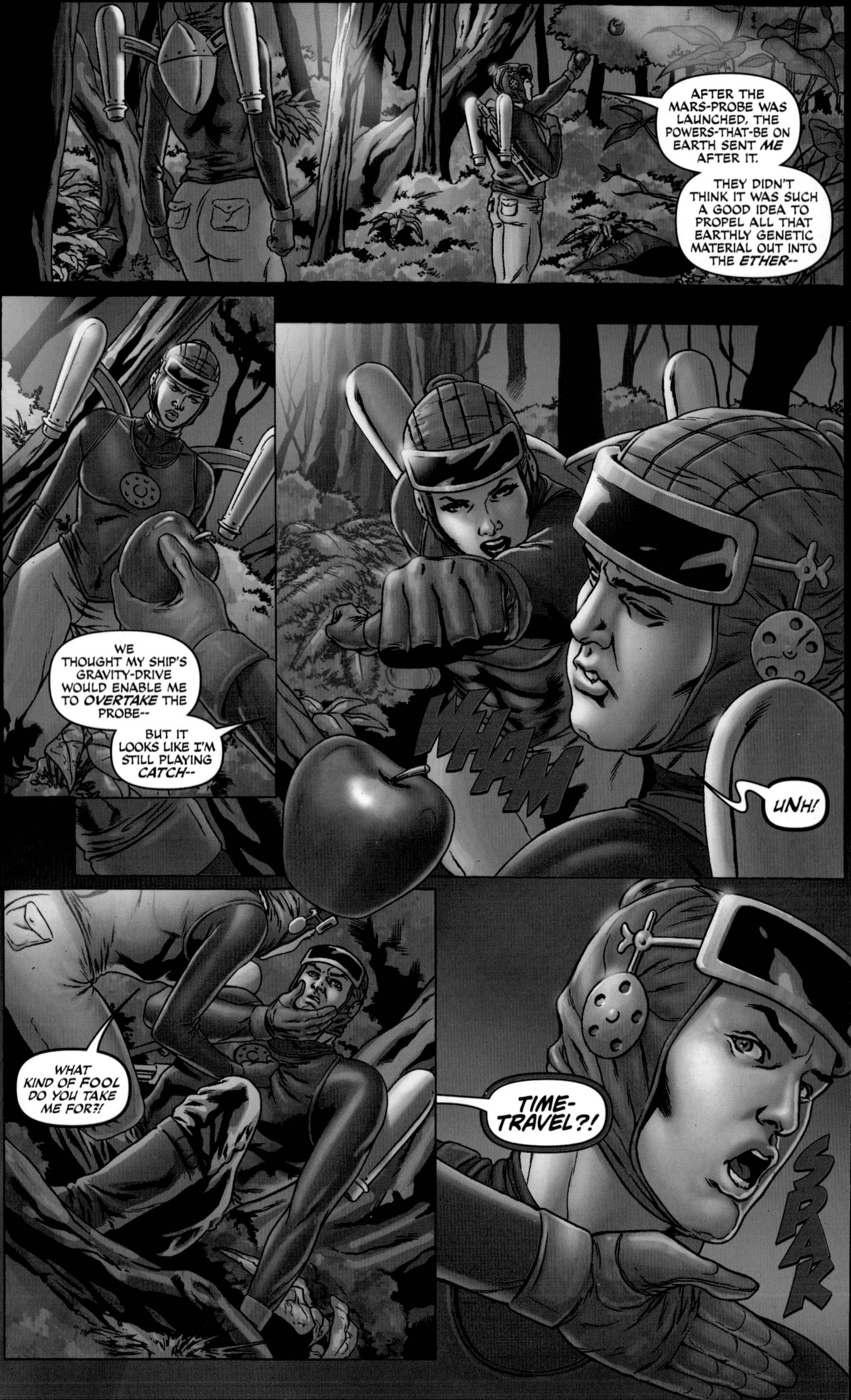
AFTER THE MARS-PROBE WAS LAUNCHED, THE POWERS-THAT-BE ON EARTH SENT *ME* AFTER IT.
THEY DIDN'T THINK IT WAS SUCH A GOOD IDEA TO PROPEL ALL THAT EARTHLY GENETIC MATERIAL OUT INTO THE *ETHER*--
WE THOUGHT MY SHIP'S GRAVITY-DRIVE WOULD ENABLE ME TO *OVERTAKE* THE PROBE--
BUT IT LOOKS LIKE I'M STILL PLAYING *CATCH*--
WHAM
UNH!
WHAT KIND OF FOOL DO YOU TAKE ME FOR?!
TIME-TRAVEL?!
SPAK

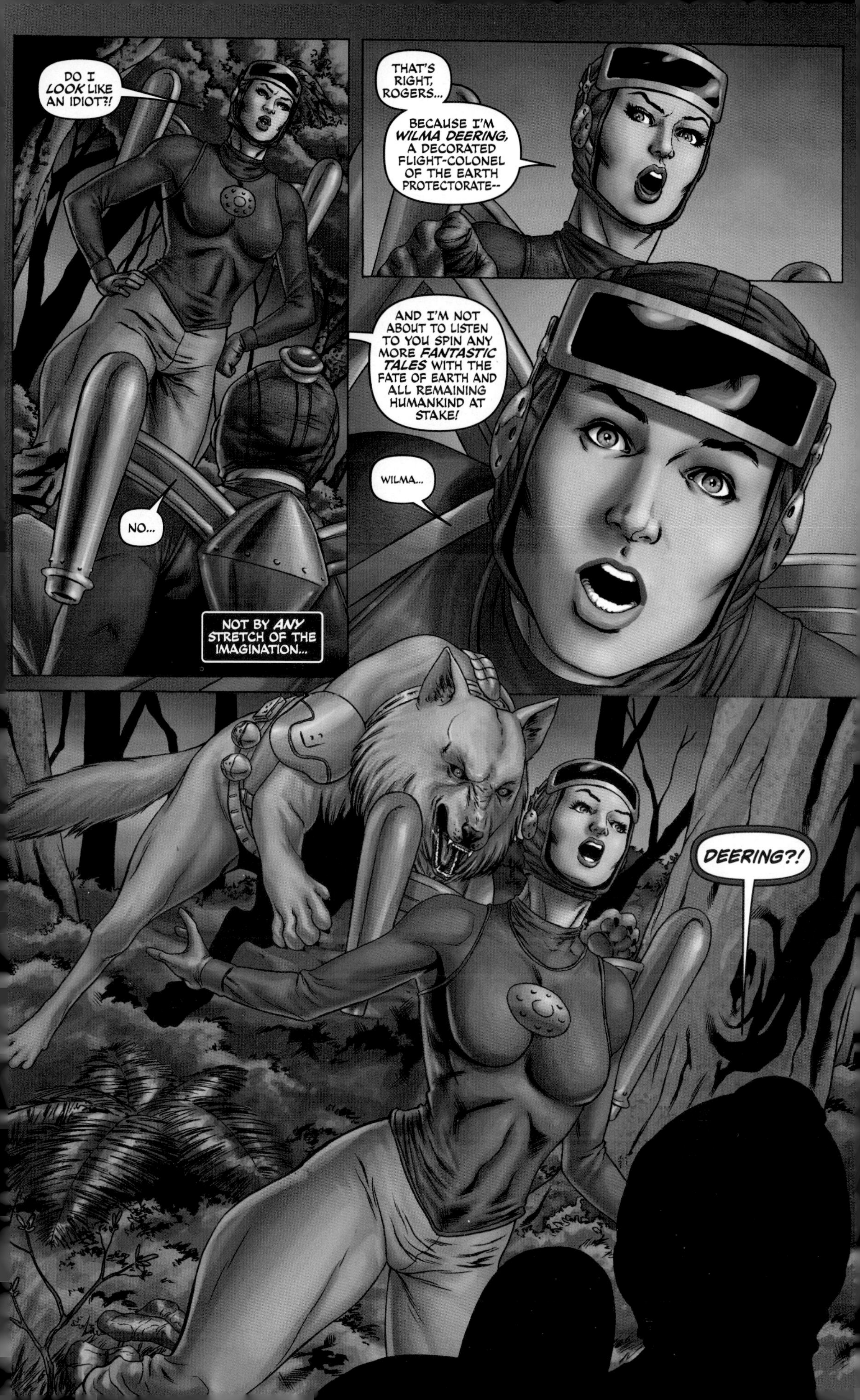
DO I *LOOK* LIKE AN IDIOT?!
NO...
NOT BY *ANY* STRETCH OF THE IMAGINATION...
THAT'S RIGHT, ROGERS...
BECAUSE I'M *WILMA DEERING,* A DECORATED FLIGHT-COLONEL OF THE EARTH PROTECTORATE--
AND I'M NOT ABOUT TO LISTEN TO YOU SPIN ANY MORE *FANTASTIC TALES* WITH THE FATE OF EARTH AND ALL REMAINING HUMANKIND AT STAKE!
WILMA...
DEERING?!

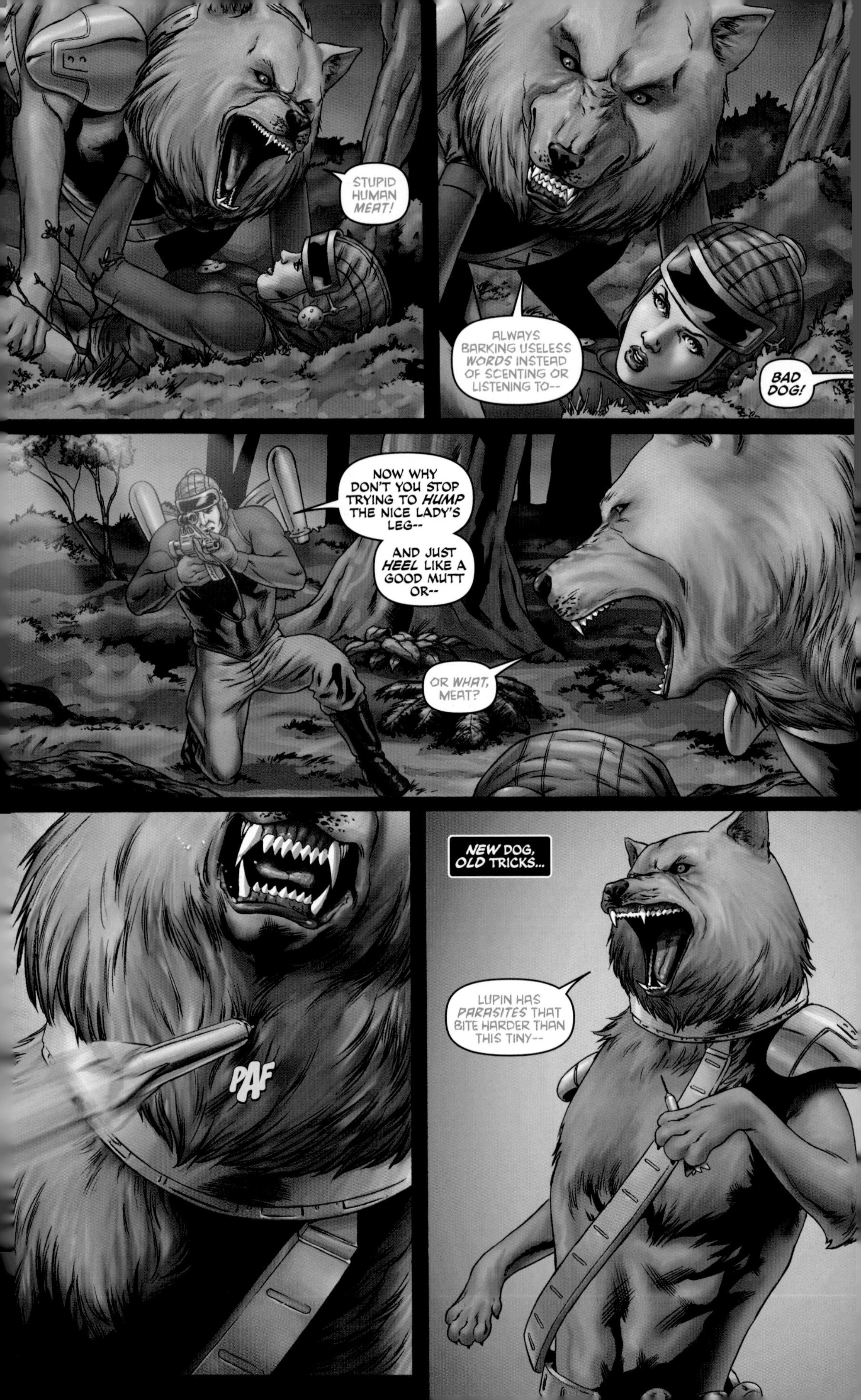
STUPID HUMAN MEAT!
ALWAYS BARKING USELESS WORDS INSTEAD OF SCENTING OR LISTENING TO--
BAD DOG!
NOW WHY DON'T YOU STOP TRYING TO HUMP THE NICE LADY'S LEG--
AND JUST HEEL LIKE A GOOD MUTT OR--
OR WHAT, MEAT?
PAF
NEW DOG, OLD TRICKS...
LUPIN HAS PARASITES THAT BITE HARDER THAN THIS TINY--

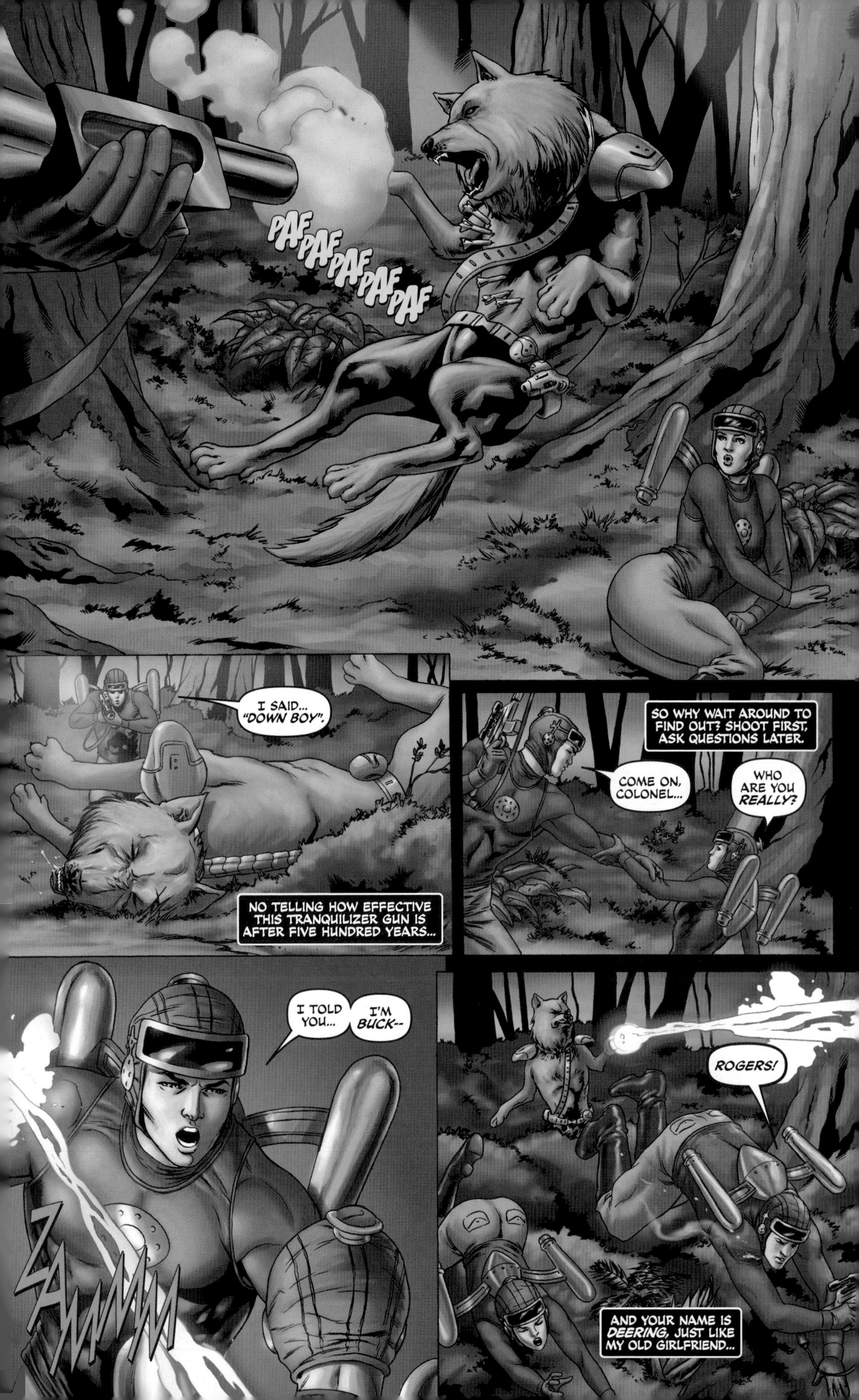
PAF PAF PAF PAF PAF PAF
I SAID... "DOWN BOY".
NO TELLING HOW EFFECTIVE THIS TRANQUILIZER GUN IS AFTER FIVE HUNDRED YEARS...
SO WHY WAIT AROUND TO FIND OUT? SHOOT FIRST, ASK QUESTIONS LATER.
COME ON, COLONEL...
WHO ARE YOU REALLY?
I TOLD YOU...
I'M BUCK--
ZAMMM
ROGERS!
AND YOUR NAME IS DEERING, JUST LIKE MY OLD GIRLFRIEND...

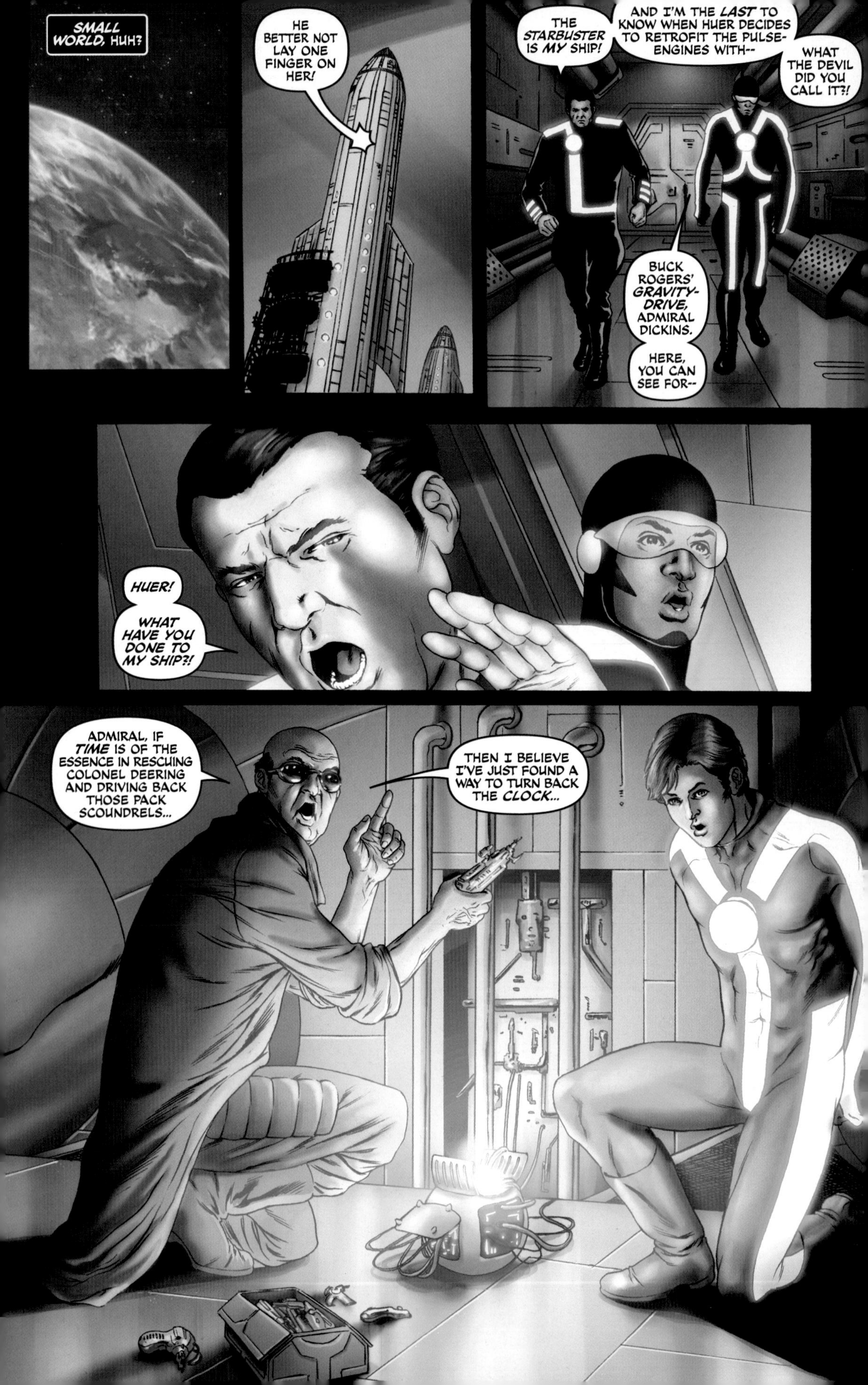
SMALL WORLD, HUH?
HE BETTER NOT LAY ONE FINGER ON HER!
THE STARBUSTER IS MY SHIP!
AND I'M THE LAST TO KNOW WHEN HUER DECIDES TO RETROFIT THE PULSE-ENGINES WITH--
WHAT THE DEVIL DID YOU CALL IT?!
BUCK ROGERS' GRAVITY-DRIVE, ADMIRAL DICKINS.
HERE, YOU CAN SEE FOR--
HUER!
WHAT HAVE YOU DONE TO MY SHIP?!
ADMIRAL, IF TIME IS OF THE ESSENCE IN RESCUING COLONEL DEERING AND DRIVING BACK THOSE PACK SCOUNDRELS...
THEN I BELIEVE I'VE JUST FOUND A WAY TO TURN BACK THE CLOCK...

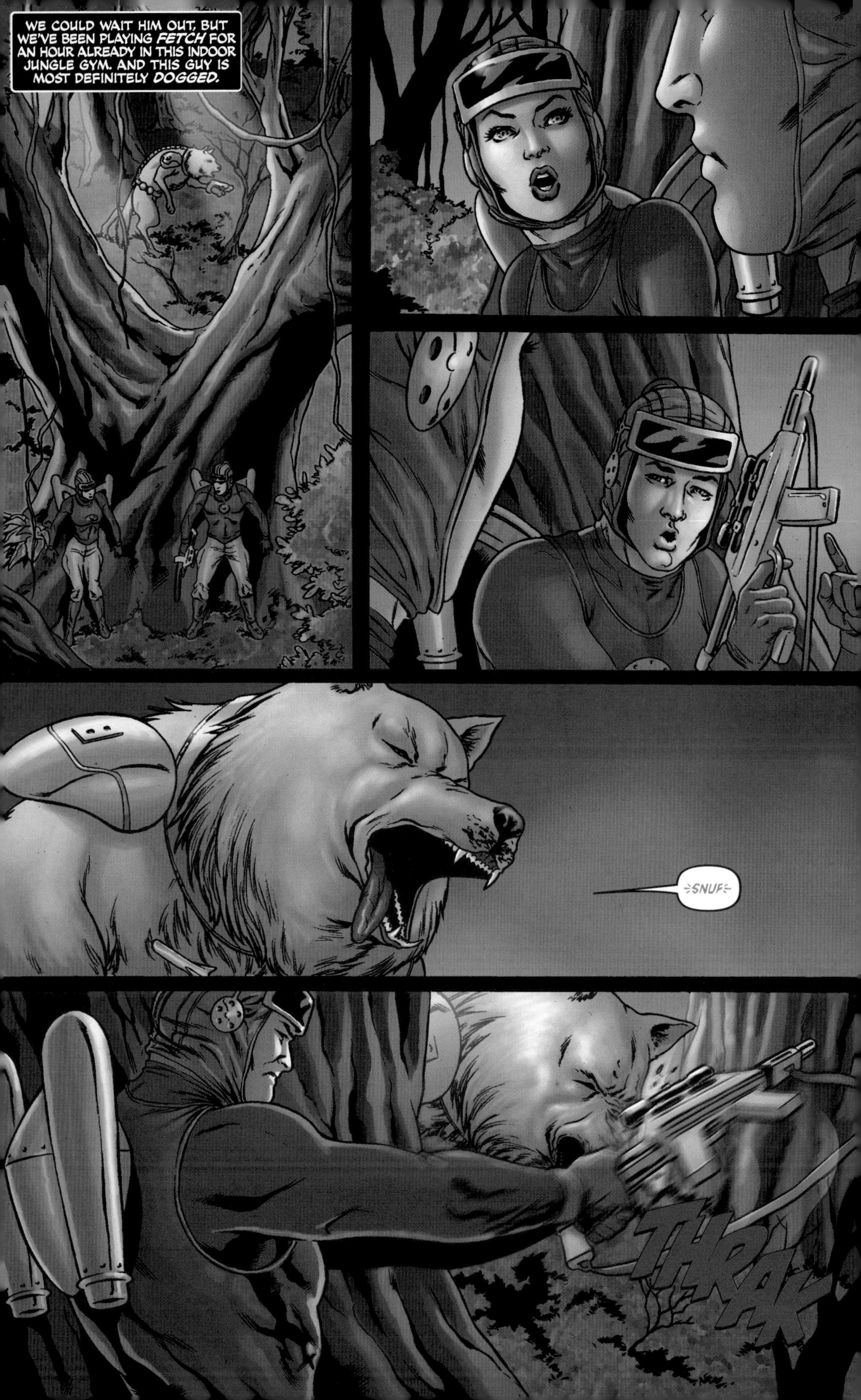
WE COULD WAIT HIM OUT, BUT WE'VE BEEN PLAYING *FETCH* FOR AN HOUR ALREADY IN THIS INDOOR JUNGLE GYM. AND THIS GUY IS MOST DEFINITELY *DOGGED.*
SNUF
THRAK

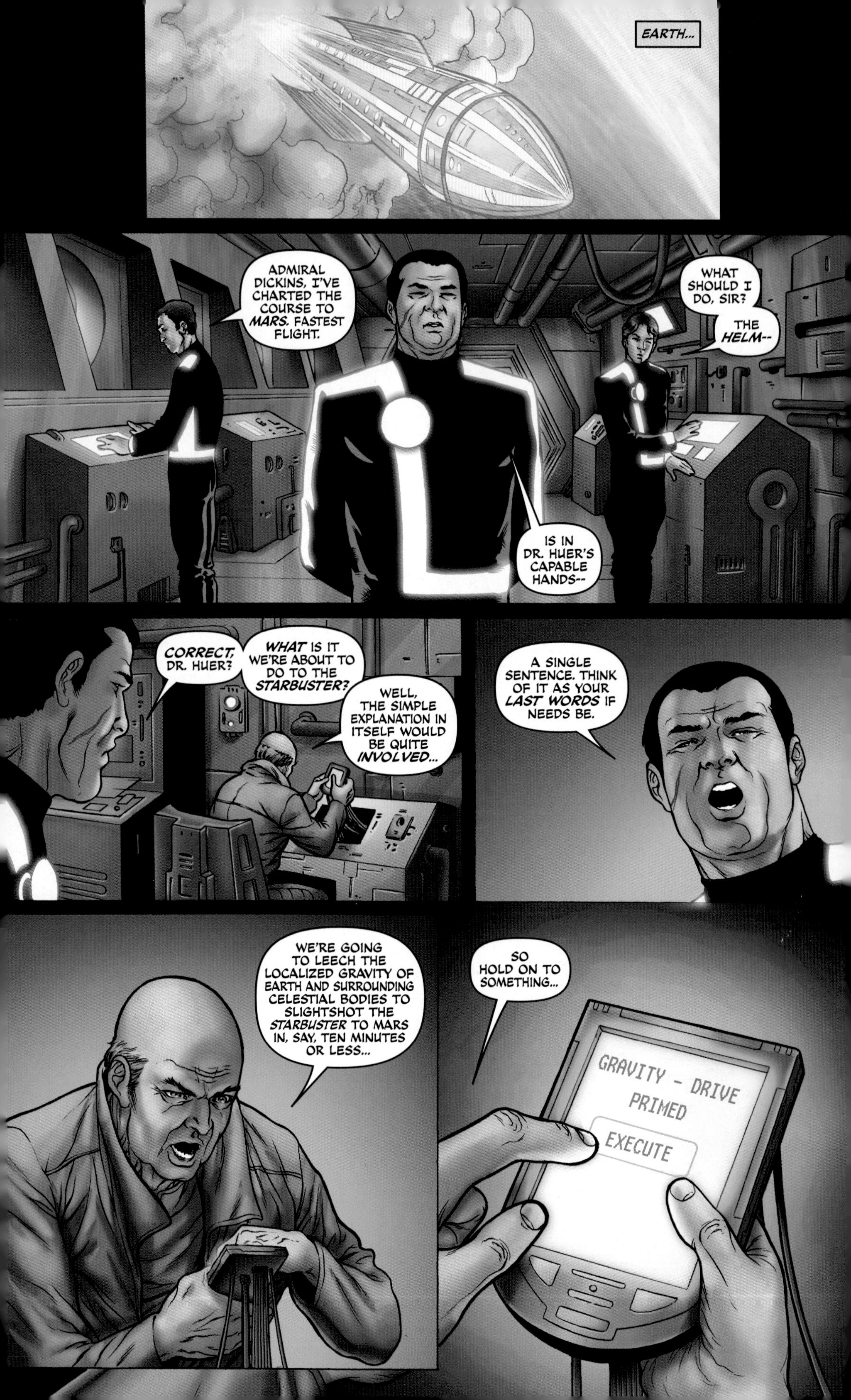
EARTH...
ADMIRAL DICKINS, I'VE CHARTED THE COURSE TO MARS. FASTEST FLIGHT.
WHAT SHOULD I DO, SIR?
THE HELM--
IS IN DR. HUER'S CAPABLE HANDS--
CORRECT, DR. HUER?
WHAT IS IT WE'RE ABOUT TO DO TO THE STARBUSTER?
WELL, THE SIMPLE EXPLANATION IN ITSELF WOULD BE QUITE INVOLVED...
A SINGLE SENTENCE. THINK OF IT AS YOUR LAST WORDS IF NEEDS BE.
WE'RE GOING TO LEECH THE LOCALIZED GRAVITY OF EARTH AND SURROUNDING CELESTIAL BODIES TO SLIGHTSHOT THE STARBUSTER TO MARS IN, SAY, TEN MINUTES OR LESS...
SO HOLD ON TO SOMETHING...
GRAVITY - DRIVE
PRIMED
EXECUTE

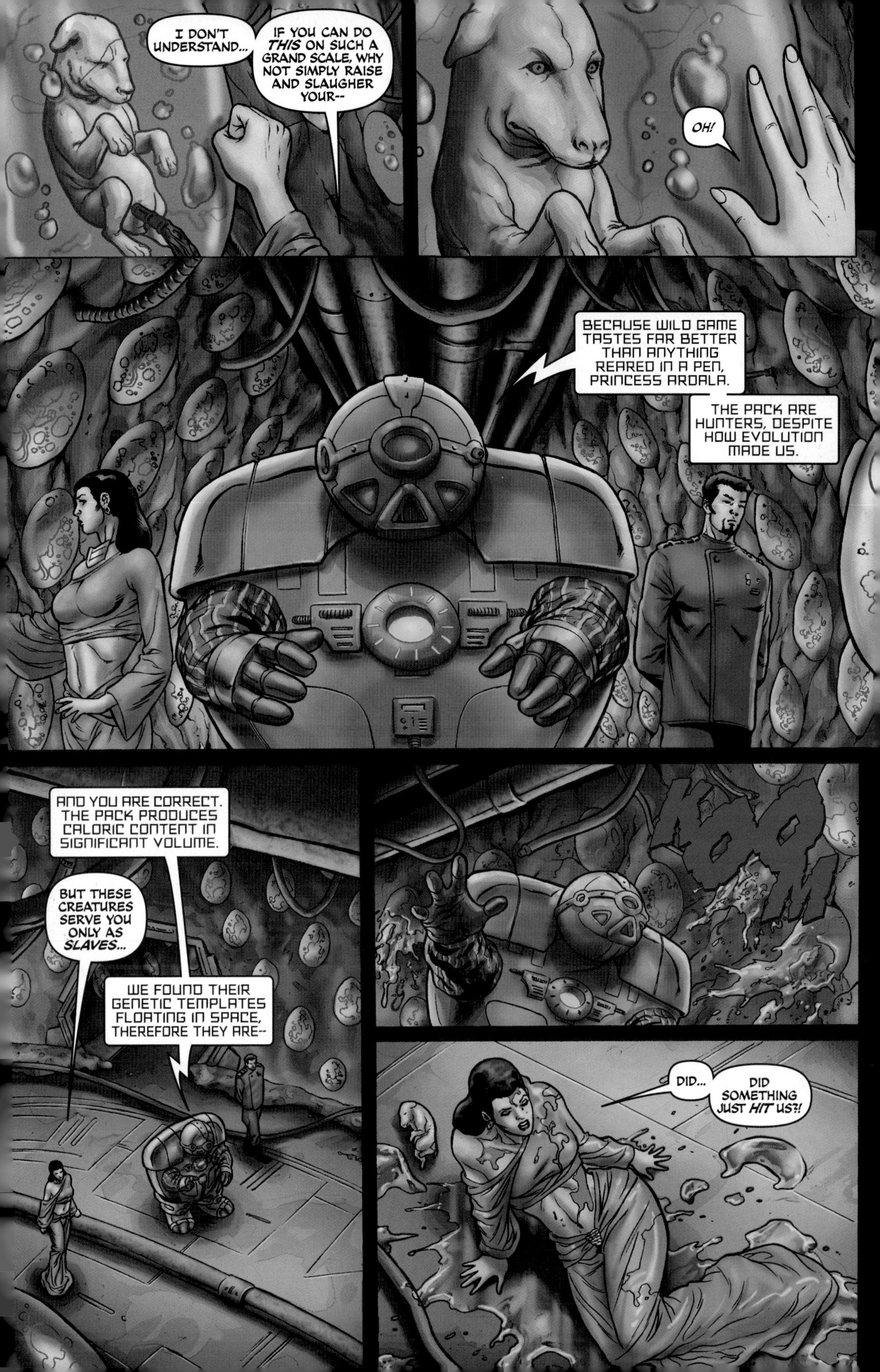
I DON'T UNDERSTAND...
IF YOU CAN DO THIS ON SUCH A GRAND SCALE, WHY NOT SIMPLY RAISE AND SLAUGHER YOUR--
OH!
BECAUSE WILD GAME TASTES FAR BETTER THAN ANYTHING REARED IN A PEN, PRINCESS ARDALA.
THE PACK ARE HUNTERS, DESPITE HOW EVOLUTION MADE US.
AND YOU ARE CORRECT. THE PACK PRODUCES CALORIC CONTENT IN SIGNIFICANT VOLUME.
BUT THESE CREATURES SERVE YOU ONLY AS SLAVES...
WE FOUND THEIR GENETIC TEMPLATES FLOATING IN SPACE, THEREFORE THEY ARE--
DID...
DID SOMETHING JUST HIT US?!

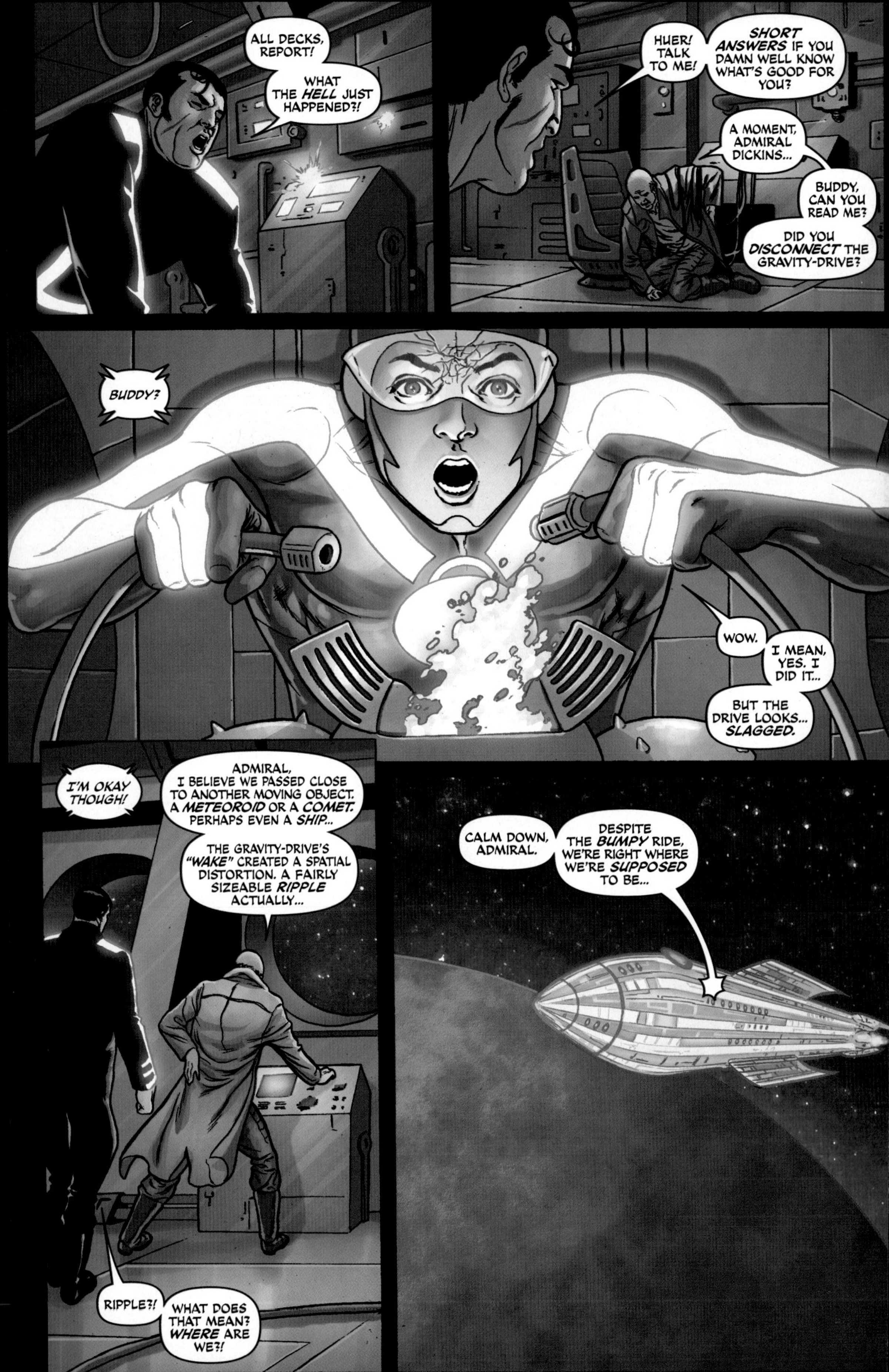
ALL DECKS, REPORT!
WHAT THE *HELL* JUST HAPPENED?!
HUER! TALK TO ME!
SHORT ANSWERS IF YOU DAMN WELL KNOW WHAT'S GOOD FOR YOU?
A MOMENT, ADMIRAL DICKINS...
BUDDY, CAN YOU READ ME?
DID YOU *DISCONNECT* THE GRAVITY-DRIVE?
BUDDY?
WOW.
I MEAN, YES. I DID IT...
BUT THE DRIVE LOOKS... *SLAGGED.*
I'M OKAY THOUGH!
ADMIRAL, I BELIEVE WE PASSED CLOSE TO ANOTHER MOVING OBJECT. A *METEOROID* OR A *COMET.* PERHAPS EVEN A *SHIP*...
THE GRAVITY-DRIVE'S *"WAKE"* CREATED A SPATIAL DISTORTION. A FAIRLY SIZEABLE *RIPPLE* ACTUALLY...
RIPPLE?!
WHAT DOES THAT MEAN? *WHERE* ARE WE?!
CALM DOWN, ADMIRAL.
DESPITE THE *BUMPY* RIDE, WE'RE RIGHT WHERE WE'RE *SUPPOSED* TO BE...

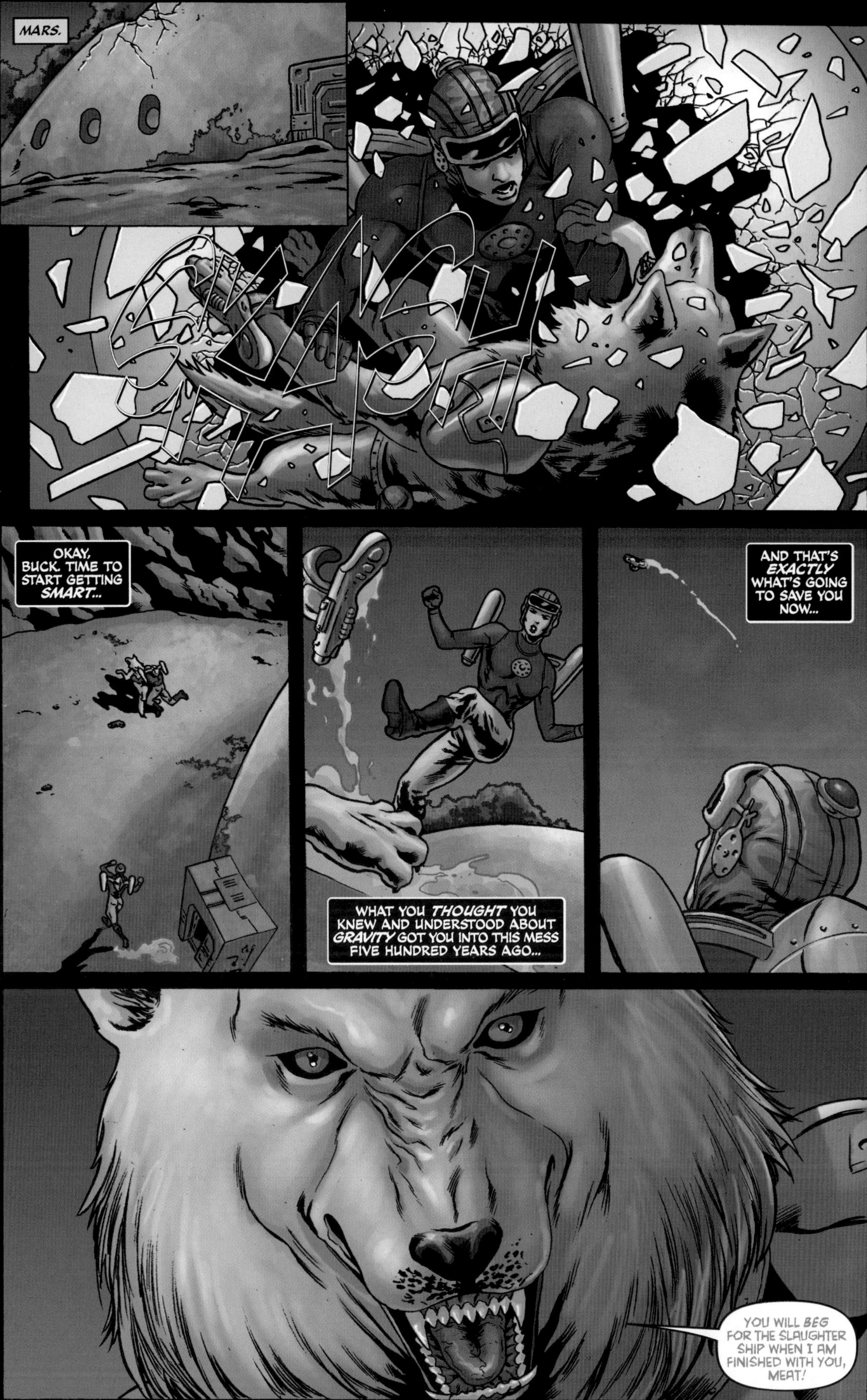
MARS.
SMASH
SMASH
OKAY, BUCK. TIME TO START GETTING SMART...
WHAT YOU THOUGHT YOU KNEW AND UNDERSTOOD ABOUT GRAVITY GOT YOU INTO THIS MESS FIVE HUNDRED YEARS AGO...
AND THAT'S EXACTLY WHAT'S GOING TO SAVE YOU NOW...
YOU WILL BEG FOR THE SLAUGHTER SHIP WHEN I AM FINISHED WITH YOU, MEAT!

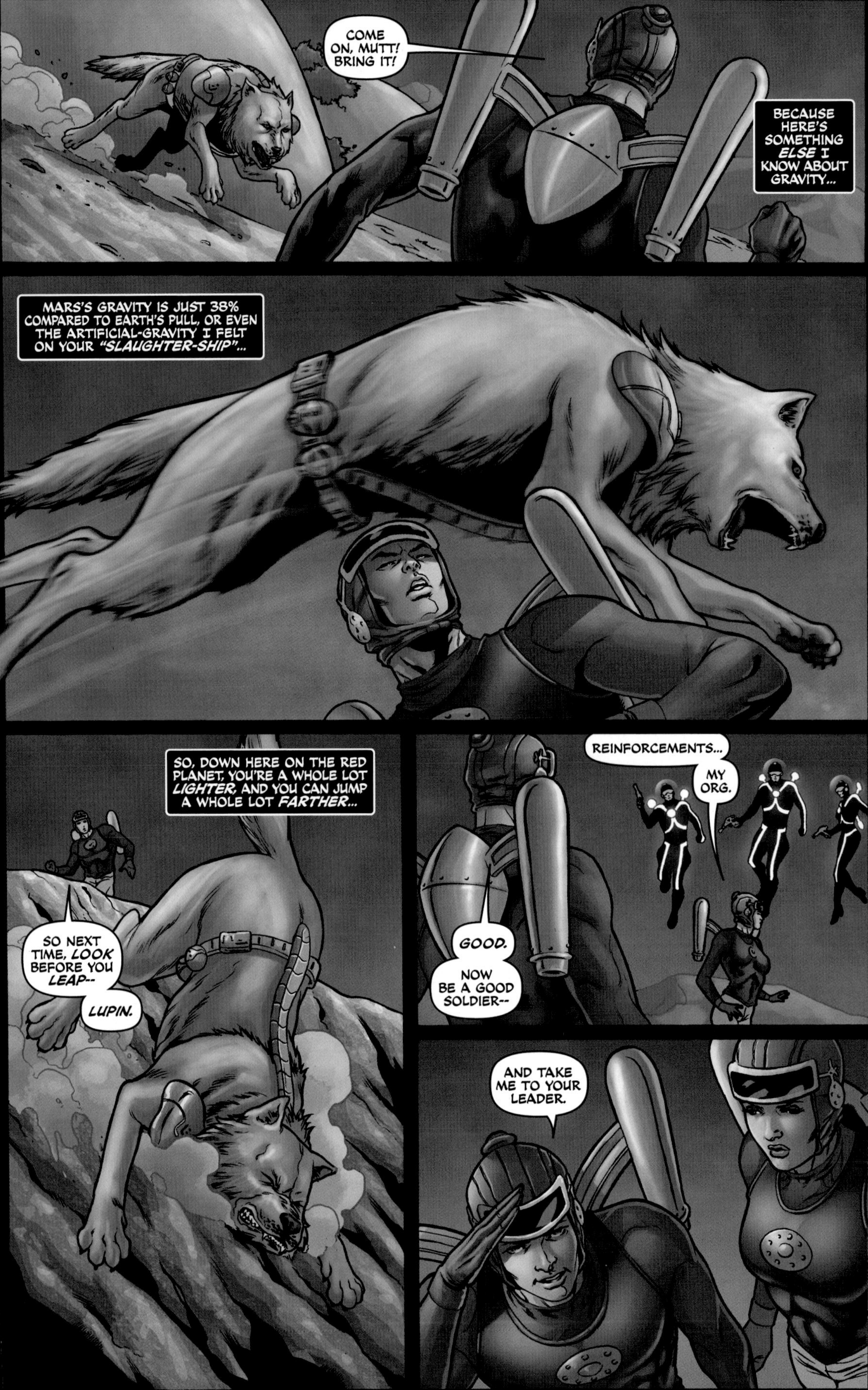
COME ON, MUTT! BRING IT!
BECAUSE HERE'S SOMETHING *ELSE* I KNOW ABOUT GRAVITY...
MARS'S GRAVITY IS JUST 38% COMPARED TO EARTH'S PULL, OR EVEN THE ARTIFICIAL-GRAVITY I FELT ON YOUR *"SLAUGHTER-SHIP"*...
SO, DOWN HERE ON THE RED PLANET, YOU'RE A WHOLE LOT *LIGHTER,* AND YOU CAN JUMP A WHOLE LOT *FARTHER*...
SO NEXT TIME, *LOOK* BEFORE YOU *LEAP*--
LUPIN.
REINFORCEMENTS...
MY ORG.
GOOD.
NOW BE A GOOD SOLDIER--
AND TAKE ME TO YOUR LEADER.

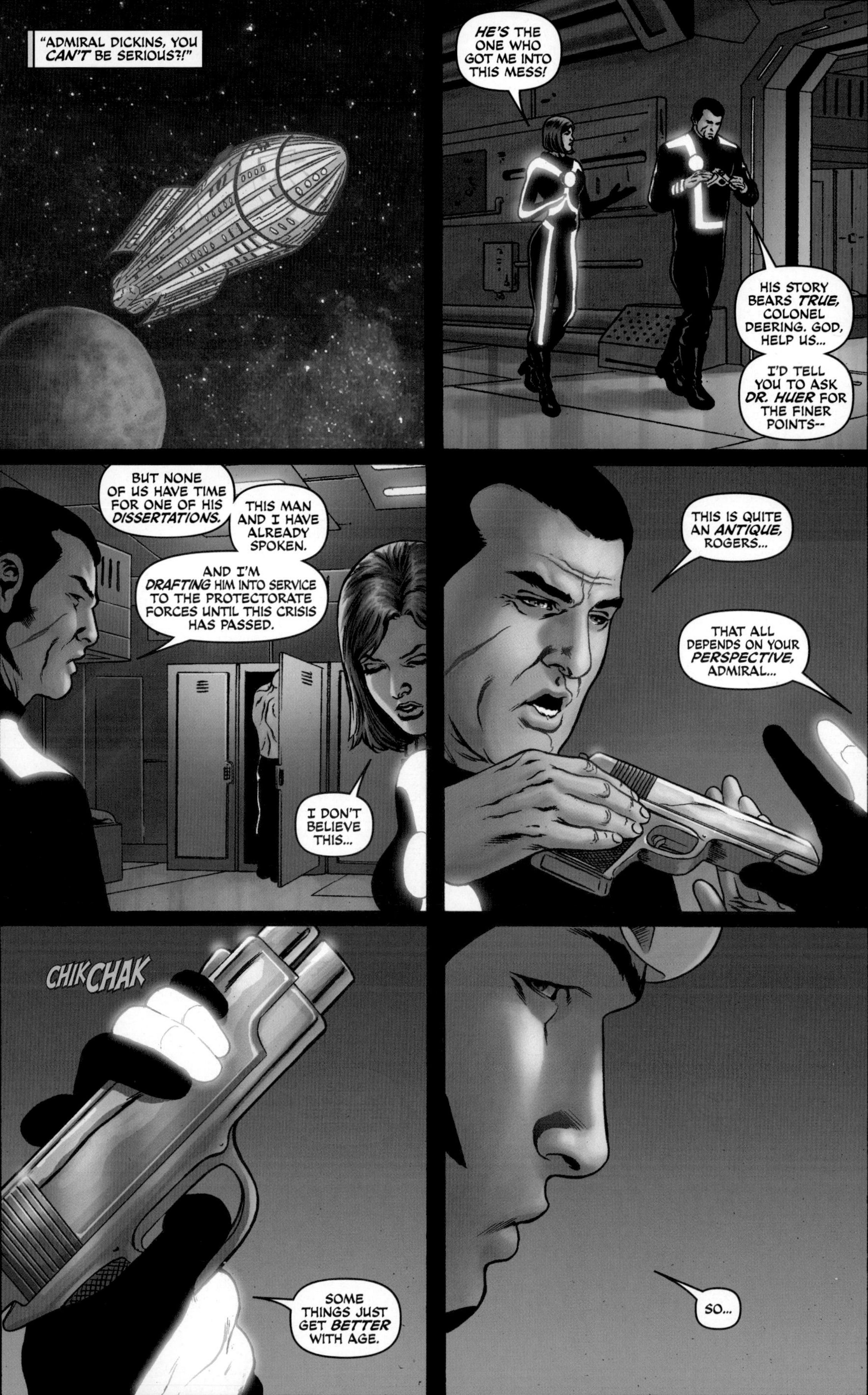
"ADMIRAL DICKINS, YOU CAN'T BE SERIOUS?!"
HE'S THE ONE WHO GOT ME INTO THIS MESS!
HIS STORY BEARS TRUE, COLONEL DEERING. GOD, HELP US...
I'D TELL YOU TO ASK DR. HUER FOR THE FINER POINTS--
BUT NONE OF US HAVE TIME FOR ONE OF HIS DISSERTATIONS.
THIS MAN AND I HAVE ALREADY SPOKEN.
AND I'M DRAFTING HIM INTO SERVICE TO THE PROTECTORATE FORCES UNTIL THIS CRISIS HAS PASSED.
I DON'T BELIEVE THIS...
THIS IS QUITE AN ANTIQUE, ROGERS...
THAT ALL DEPENDS ON YOUR PERSPECTIVE, ADMIRAL...
CHIK CHAK
SOME THINGS JUST GET BETTER WITH AGE.
SO...

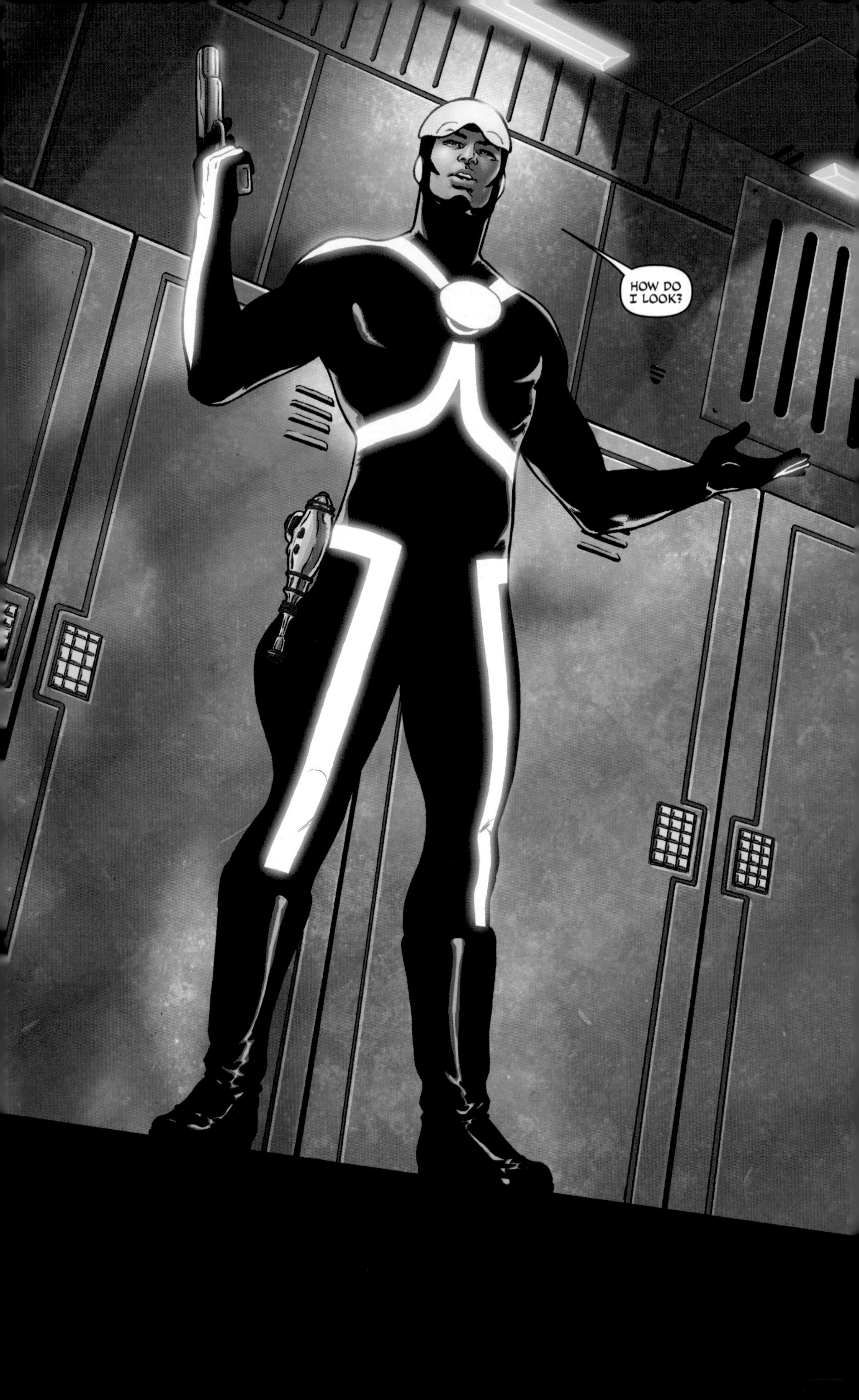
HOW DO I LOOK?

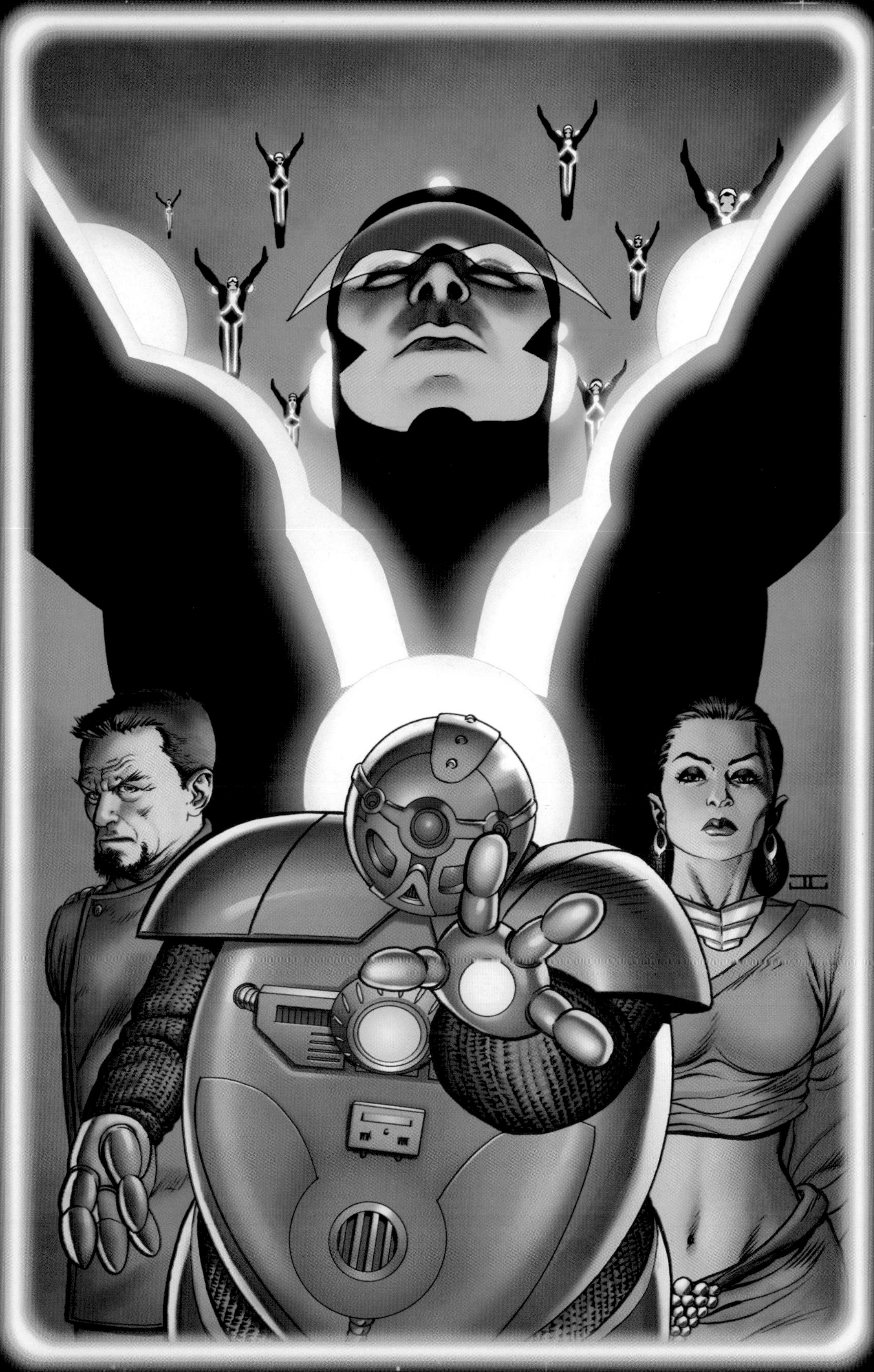

ISSUE FIVE: The Caloric Standard

COVER BY JOHN CASSADAY

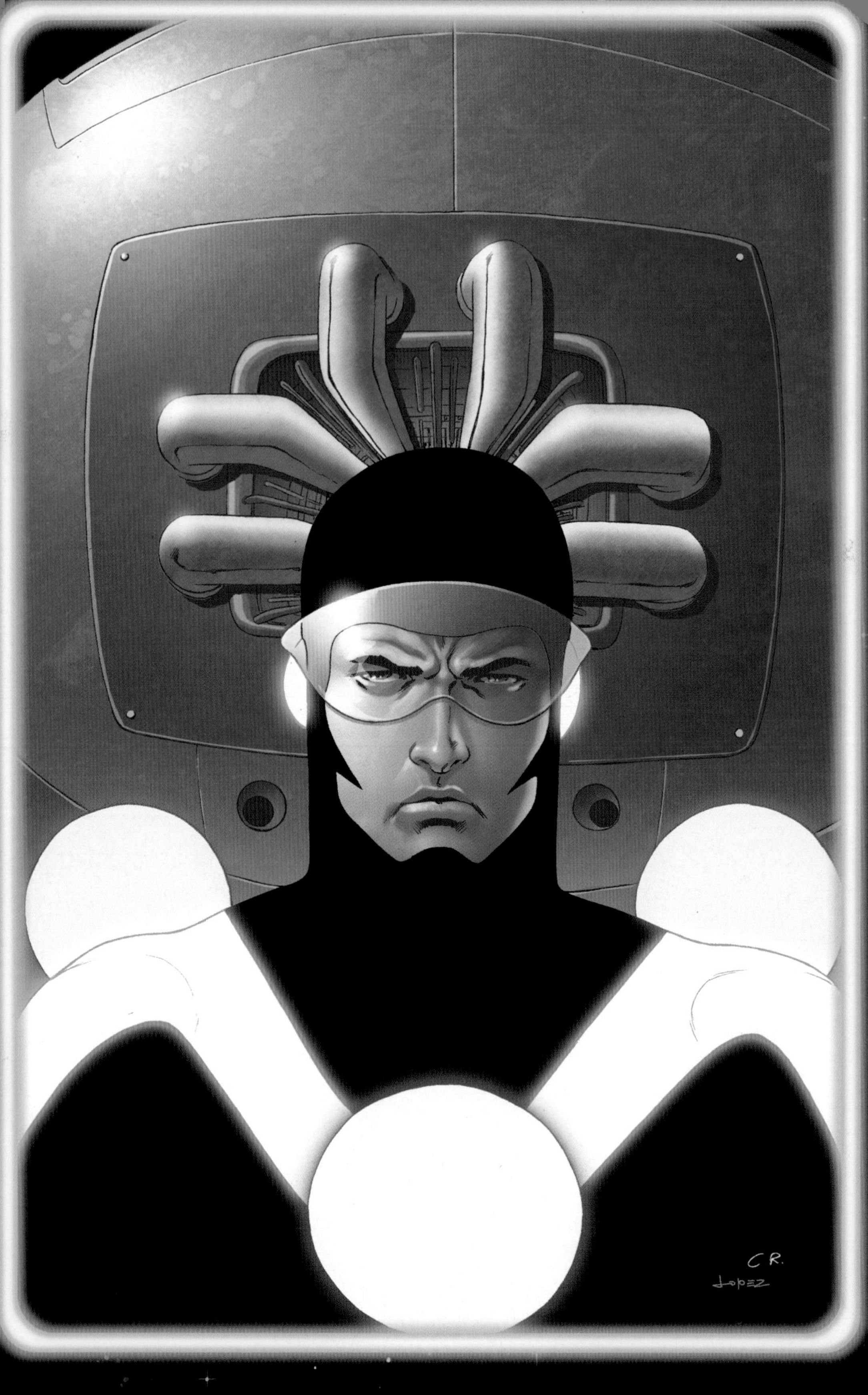
CR.
Lopez

ALTERNATE COVER BY CARLOS RAFAEL

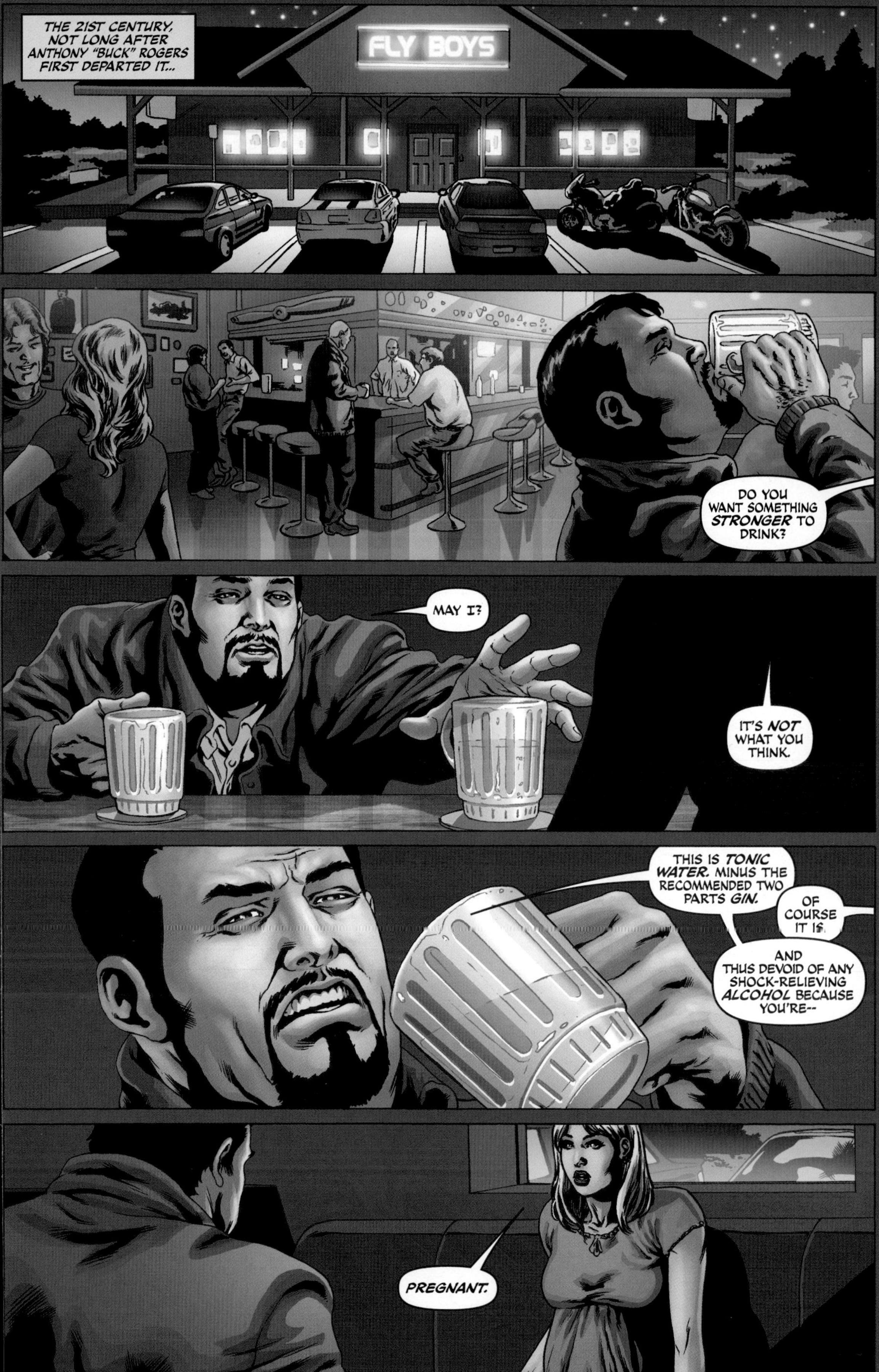
THE 21ST CENTURY, NOT LONG AFTER ANTHONY "BUCK" ROGERS FIRST DEPARTED IT...
FLY BOYS
DO YOU WANT SOMETHING STRONGER TO DRINK?
MAY I?
IT'S NOT WHAT YOU THINK.
THIS IS TONIC WATER. MINUS THE RECOMMENDED TWO PARTS GIN.
OF COURSE IT IS.
AND THUS DEVOID OF ANY SHOCK-RELIEVING ALCOHOL BECAUSE YOU'RE--
PREGNANT.

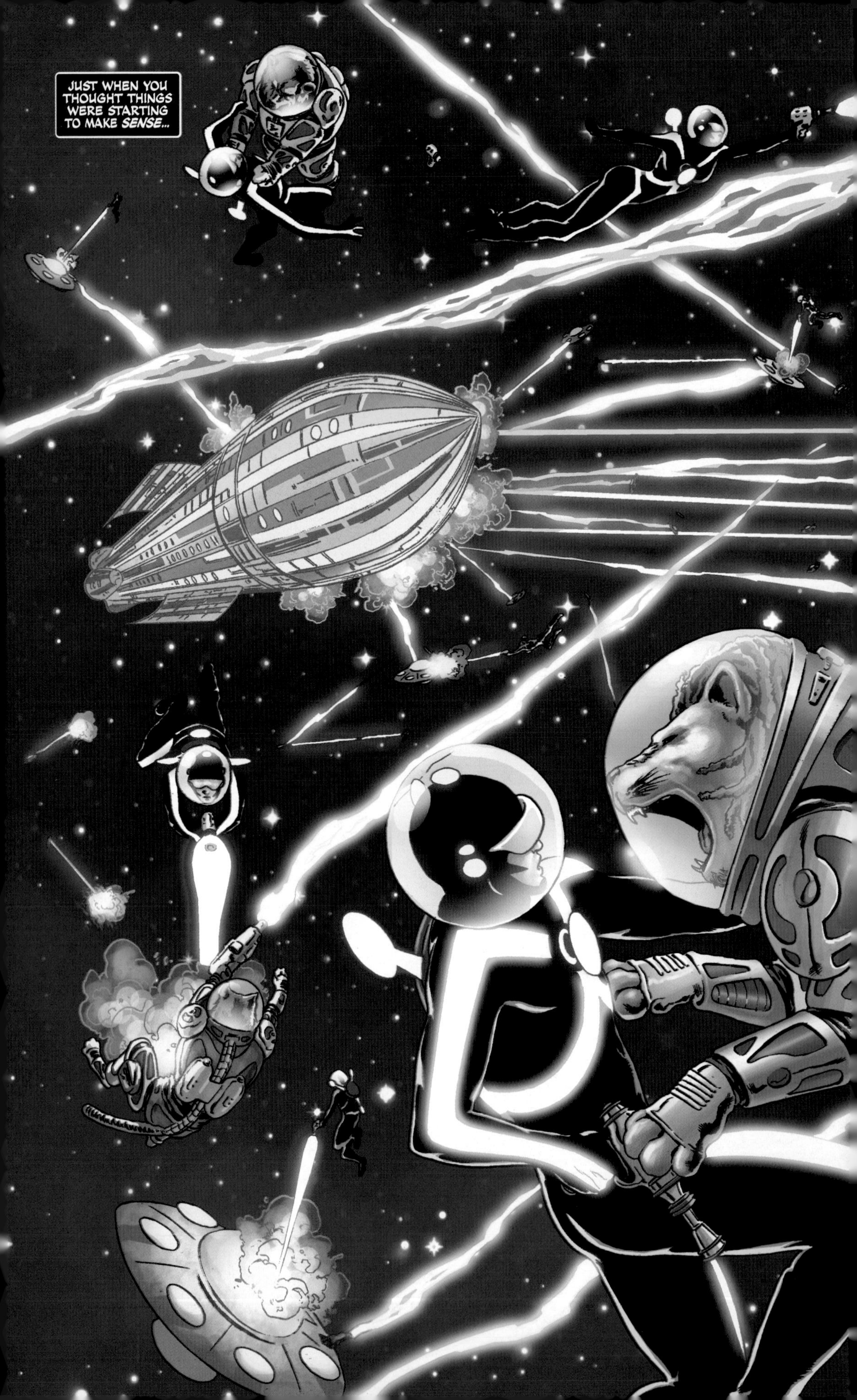
JUST WHEN YOU THOUGHT THINGS WERE STARTING TO MAKE *SENSE*...

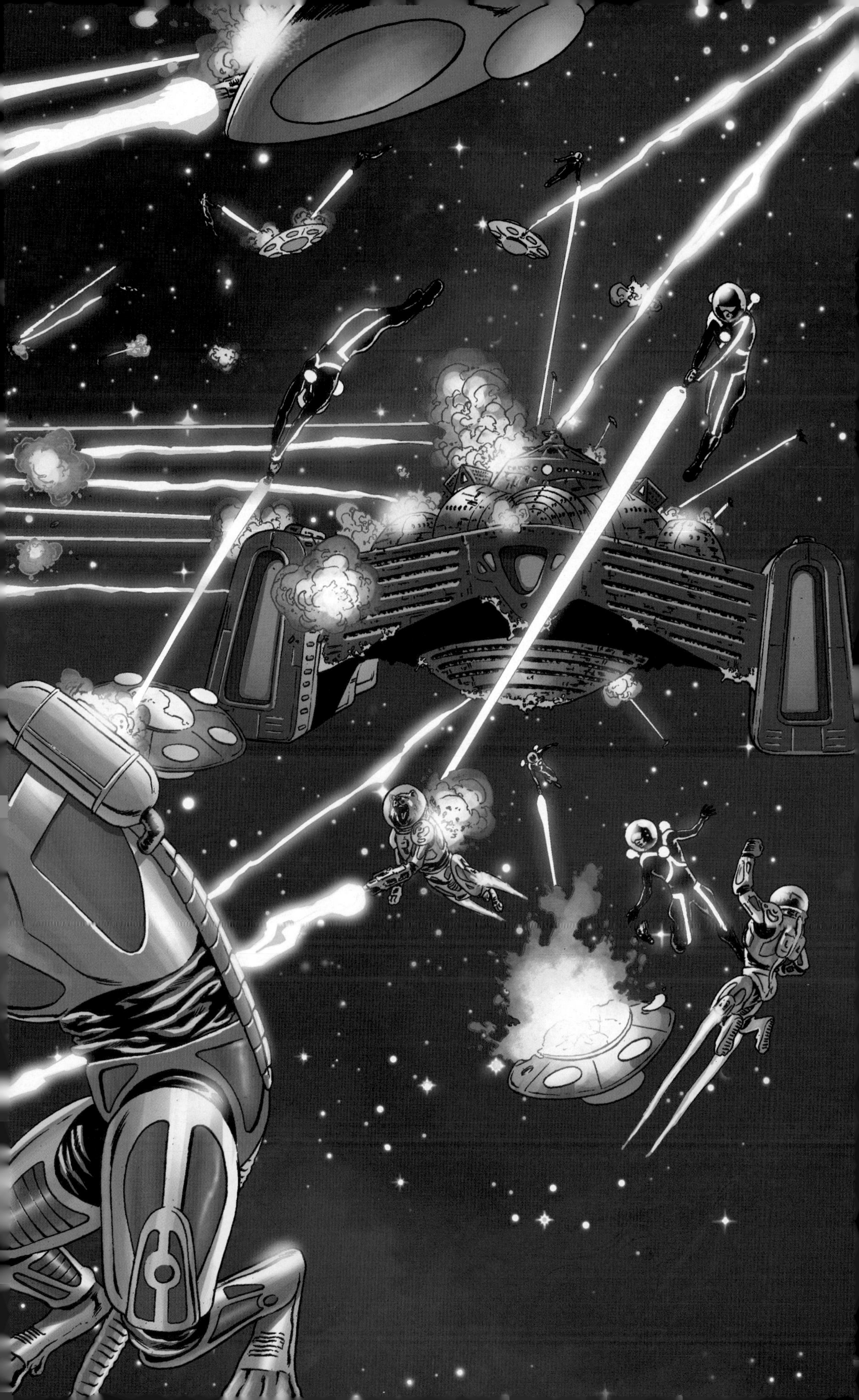

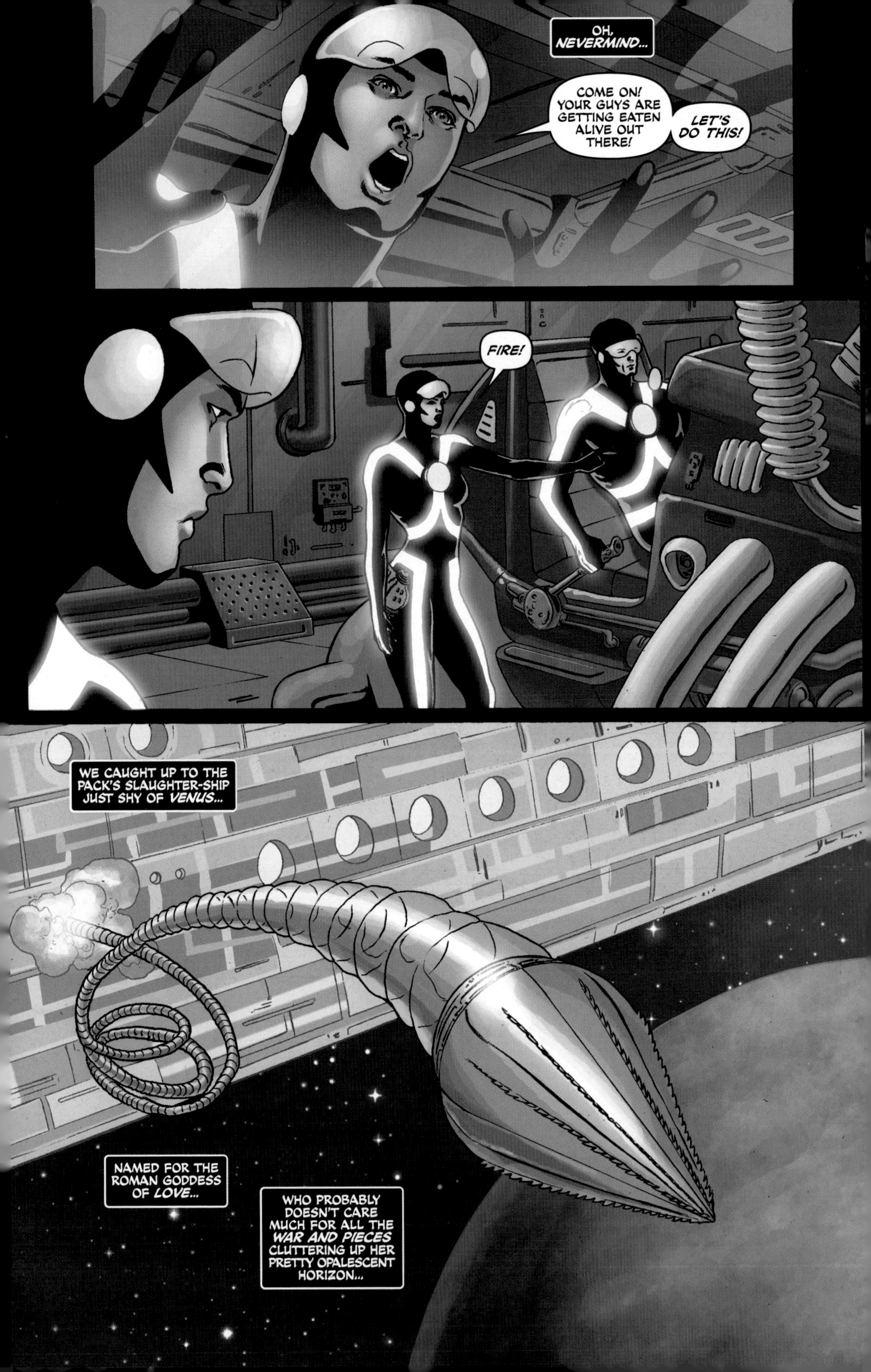
OH, NEVERMIND...
COME ON! YOUR GUYS ARE GETTING EATEN ALIVE OUT THERE!
LET'S DO THIS!
FIRE!
WE CAUGHT UP TO THE PACK'S SLAUGHTER-SHIP JUST SHY OF VENUS...
NAMED FOR THE ROMAN GODDESS OF LOVE...
WHO PROBABLY DOESN'T CARE MUCH FOR ALL THE WAR AND PIECES CLUTTERING UP HER PRETTY OPALESCENT HORIZON...

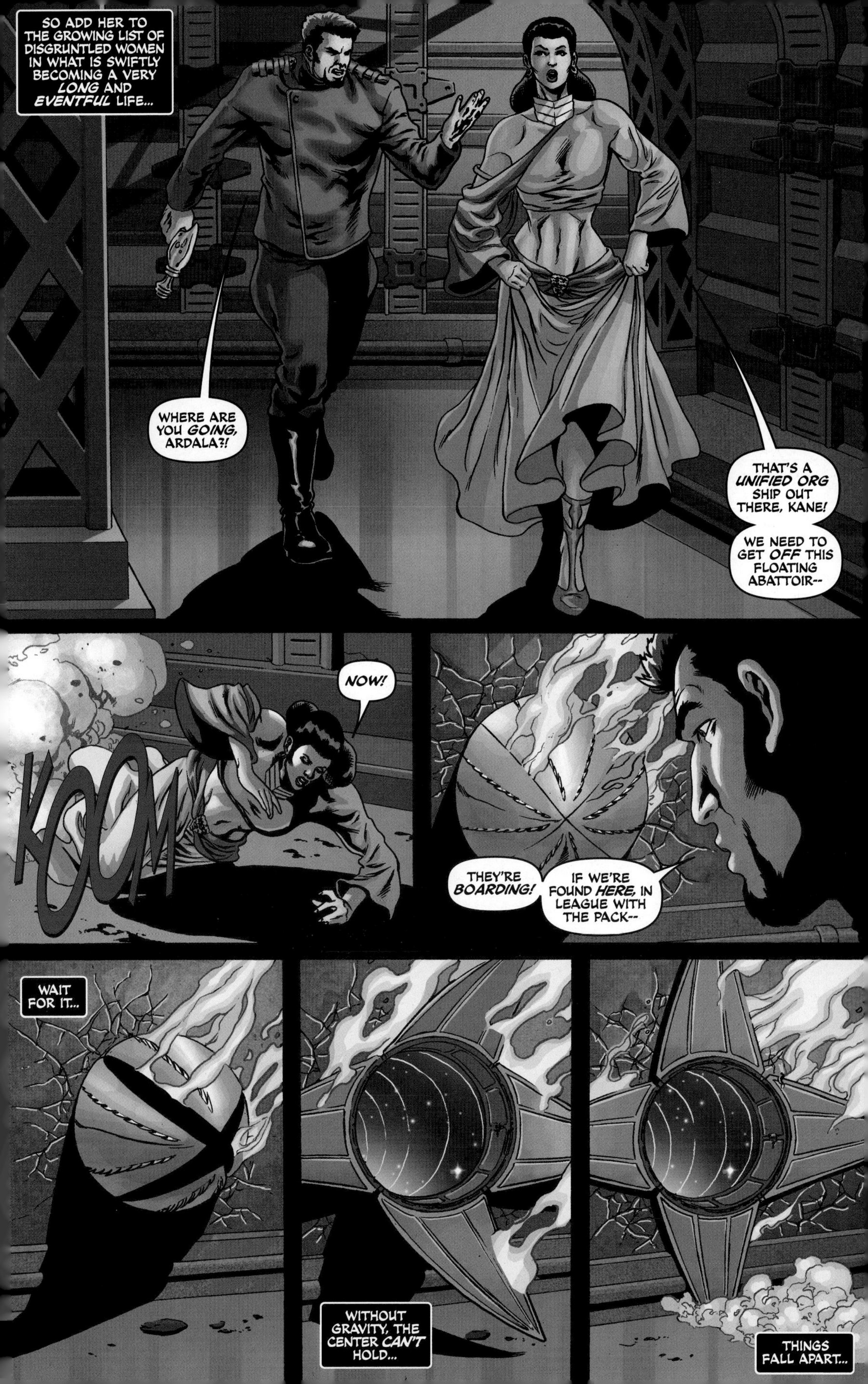
SO ADD HER TO THE GROWING LIST OF DISGRUNTLED WOMEN IN WHAT IS SWIFTLY BECOMING A VERY LONG AND EVENTFUL LIFE...
WHERE ARE YOU GOING, ARDALA?!
THAT'S A UNIFIED ORG SHIP OUT THERE, KANE!
WE NEED TO GET OFF THIS FLOATING ABATTOIR--
NOW!
KOOM
THEY'RE BOARDING!
IF WE'RE FOUND HERE, IN LEAGUE WITH THE PACK--
WAIT FOR IT...
WITHOUT GRAVITY, THE CENTER CAN'T HOLD...
THINGS FALL APART...

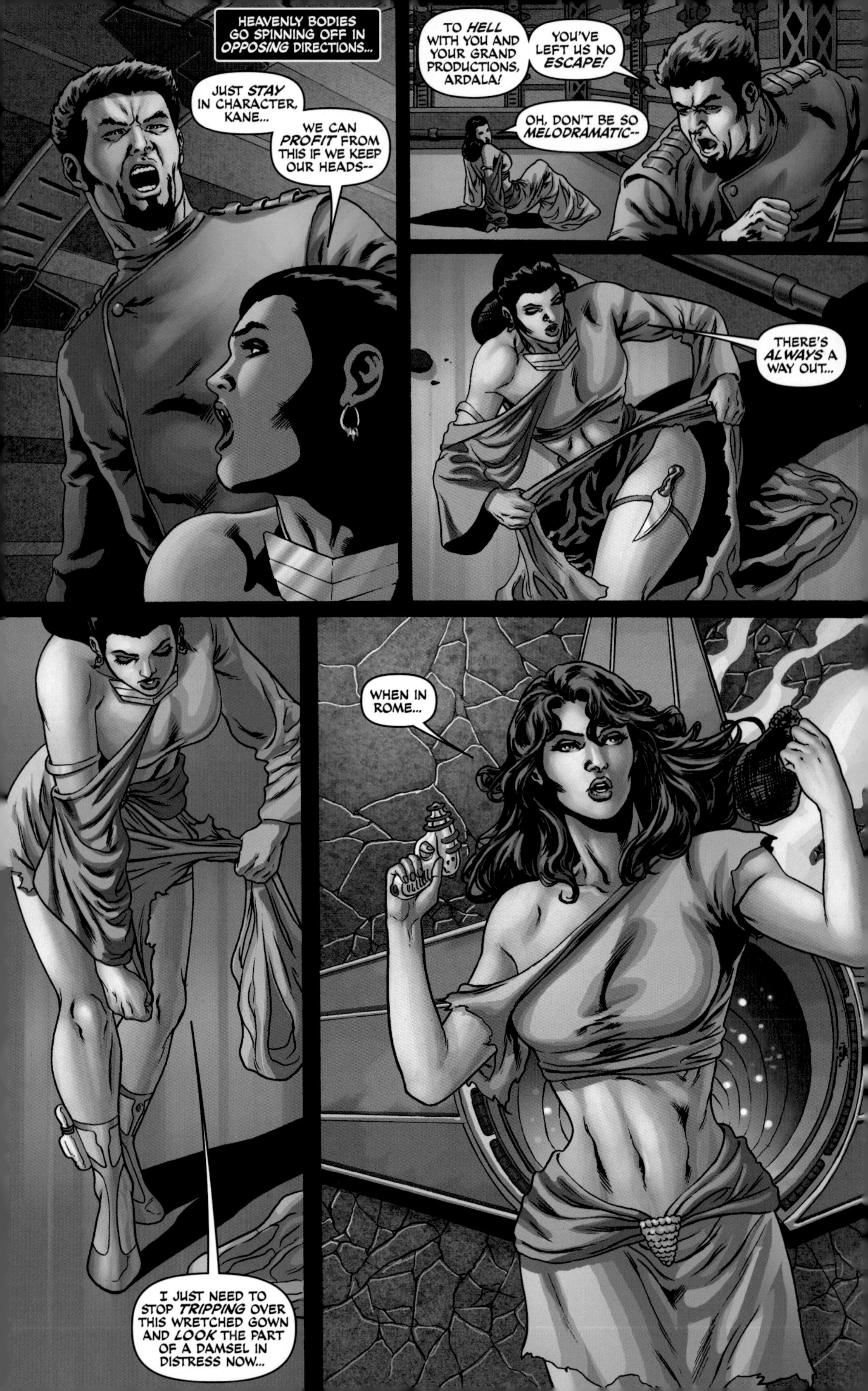
HEAVENLY BODIES GO SPINNING OFF IN OPPOSING DIRECTIONS...
JUST STAY IN CHARACTER, KANE...
WE CAN PROFIT FROM THIS IF WE KEEP OUR HEADS--
TO HELL WITH YOU AND YOUR GRAND PRODUCTIONS, ARDALA!
YOU'VE LEFT US NO ESCAPE!
OH, DON'T BE SO MELODRAMATIC--
THERE'S ALWAYS A WAY OUT...
I JUST NEED TO STOP TRIPPING OVER THIS WRETCHED GOWN AND LOOK THE PART OF A DAMSEL IN DISTRESS NOW...
WHEN IN ROME...

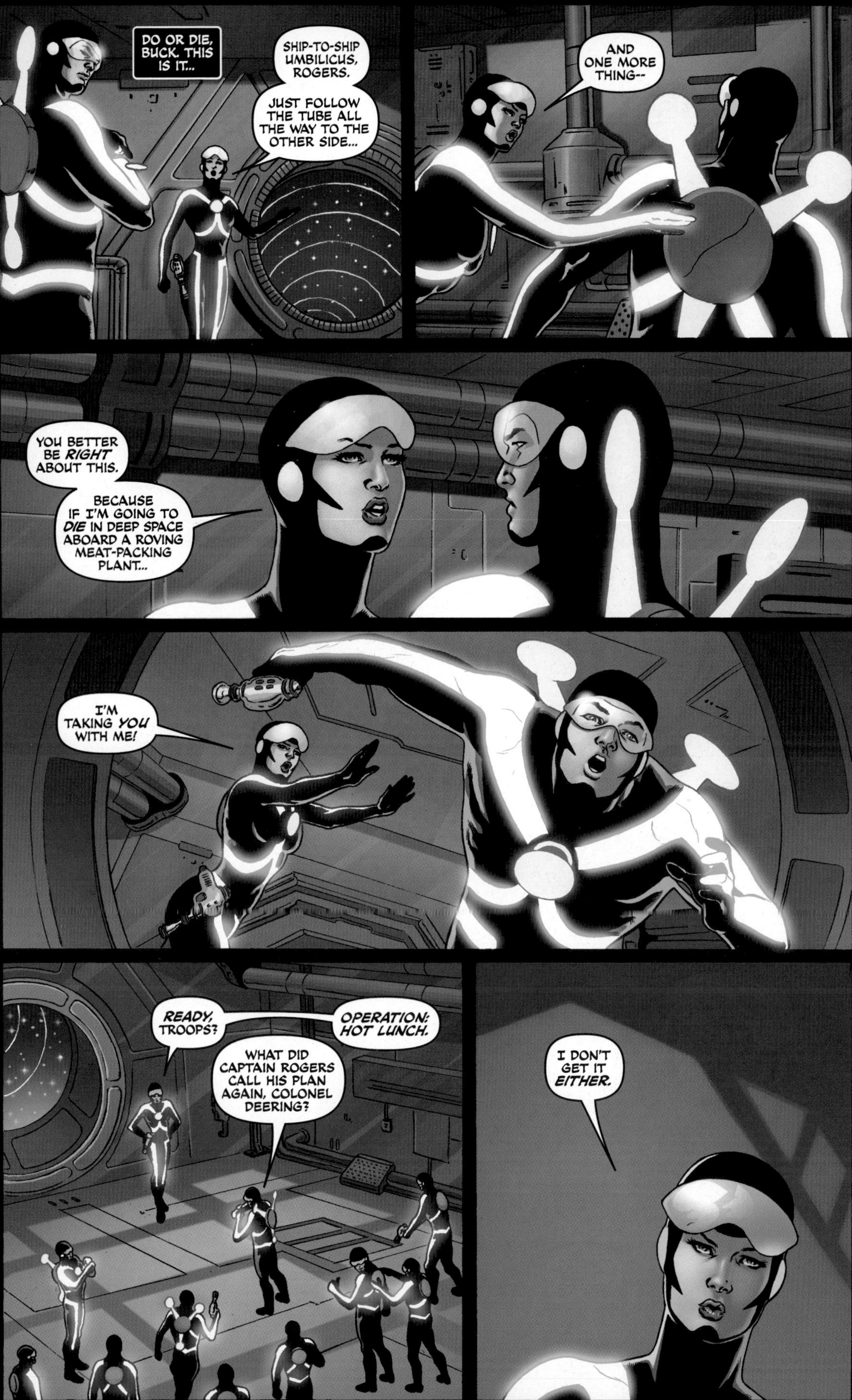
DO OR DIE, BUCK. THIS IS IT...
SHIP-TO-SHIP UMBILICUS, ROGERS.
JUST FOLLOW THE TUBE ALL THE WAY TO THE OTHER SIDE...
AND ONE MORE THING--
YOU BETTER BE *RIGHT* ABOUT THIS.
BECAUSE IF I'M GOING TO *DIE* IN DEEP SPACE ABOARD A ROVING MEAT-PACKING PLANT...
I'M TAKING *YOU* WITH ME!
READY, TROOPS?
OPERATION: HOT LUNCH.
WHAT DID CAPTAIN ROGERS CALL HIS PLAN AGAIN, COLONEL DEERING?
I DON'T GET IT *EITHER.*

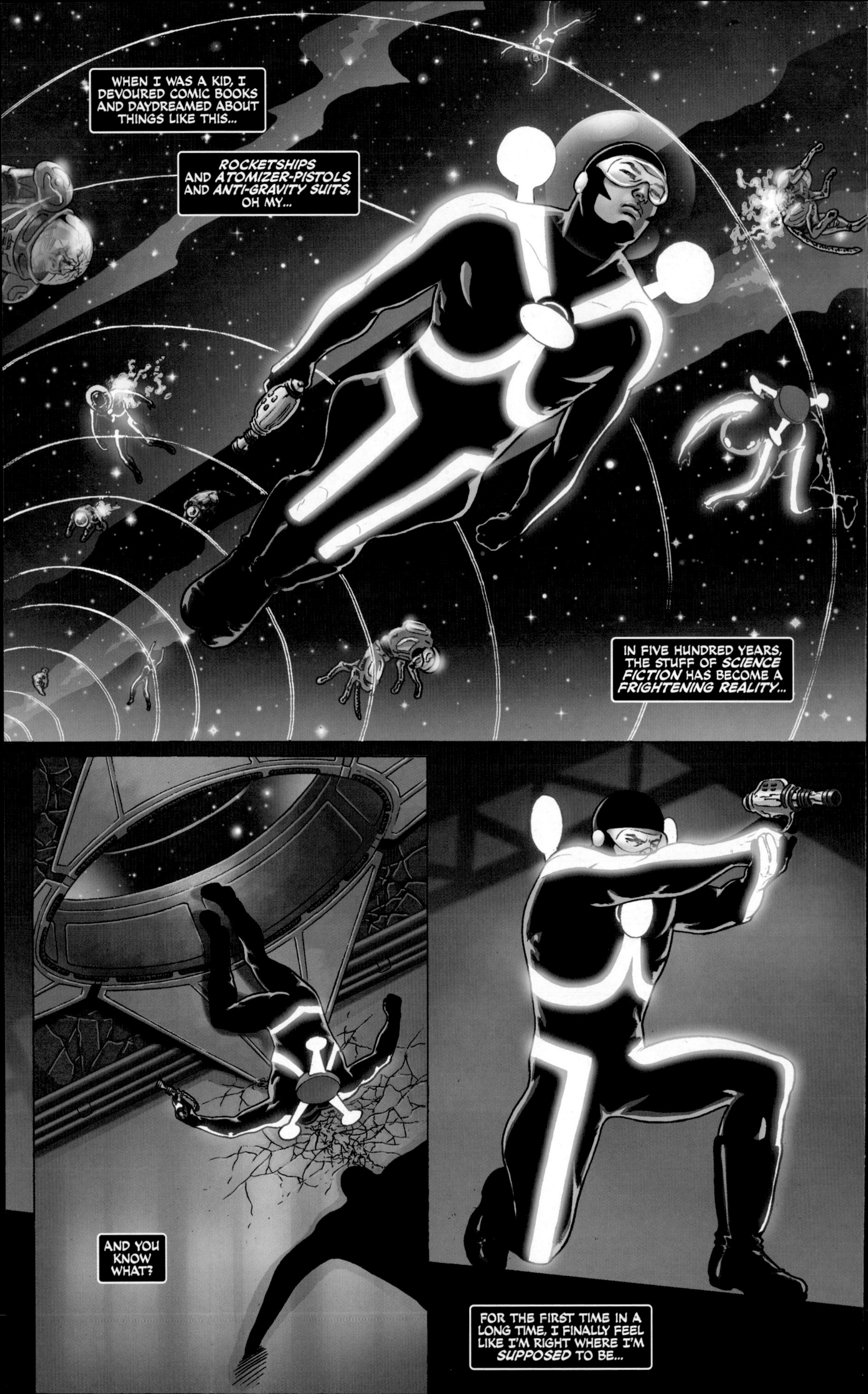
WHEN I WAS A KID, I DEVOURED COMIC BOOKS AND DAYDREAMED ABOUT THINGS LIKE THIS...
ROCKETSHIPS AND ATOMIZER-PISTOLS AND ANTI-GRAVITY SUITS, OH MY...
IN FIVE HUNDRED YEARS, THE STUFF OF SCIENCE FICTION HAS BECOME A FRIGHTENING REALITY...
AND YOU KNOW WHAT?
FOR THE FIRST TIME IN A LONG TIME, I FINALLY FEEL LIKE I'M RIGHT WHERE I'M SUPPOSED TO BE...

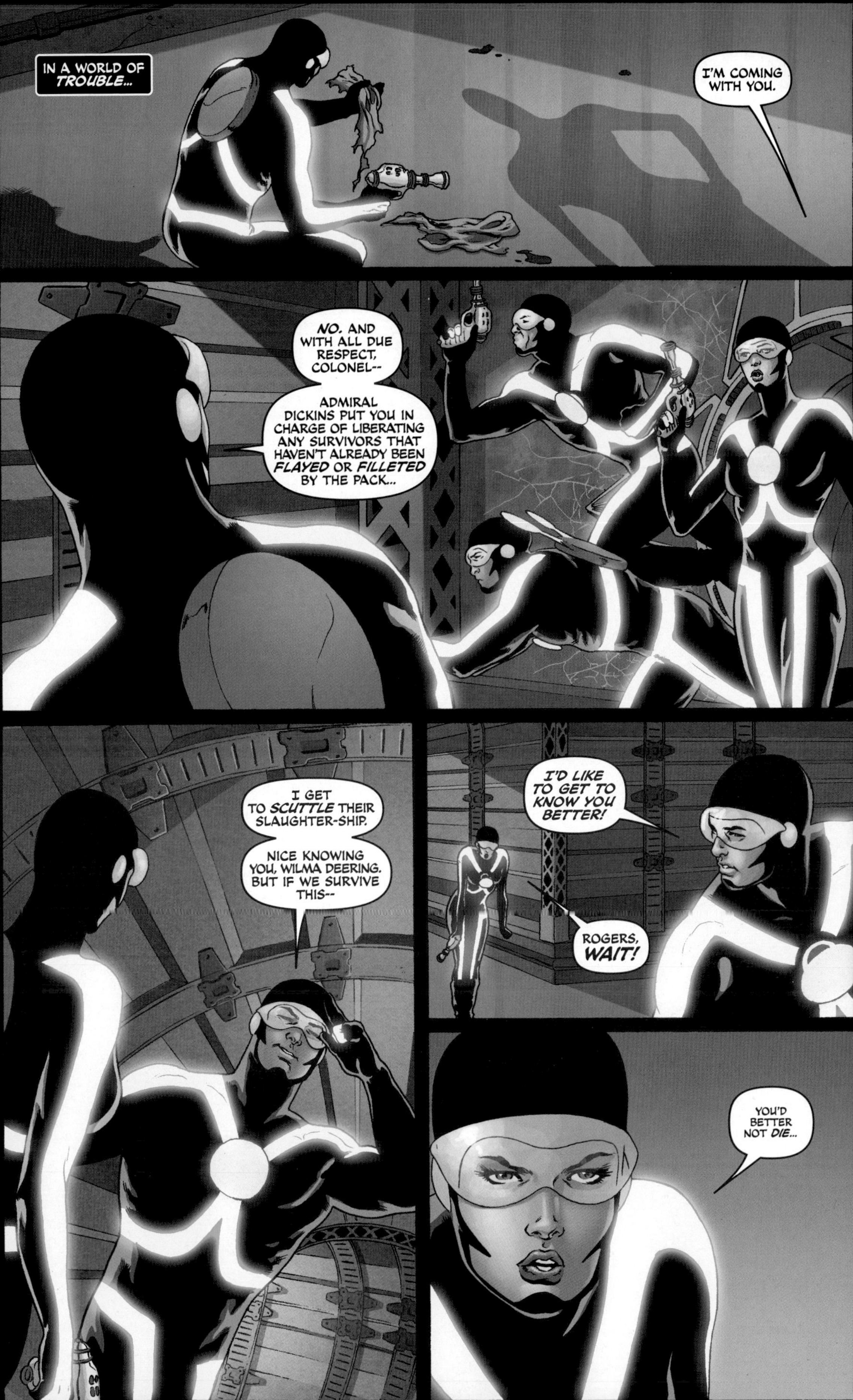
IN A WORLD OF TROUBLE...
I'M COMING WITH YOU.
NO. AND WITH ALL DUE RESPECT, COLONEL--
ADMIRAL DICKINS PUT YOU IN CHARGE OF LIBERATING ANY SURVIVORS THAT HAVEN'T ALREADY BEEN FLAYED OR FILLETED BY THE PACK...
I GET TO SCUTTLE THEIR SLAUGHTER-SHIP.
NICE KNOWING YOU, WILMA DEERING. BUT IF WE SURVIVE THIS--
I'D LIKE TO GET TO KNOW YOU BETTER!
ROGERS, WAIT!
YOU'D BETTER NOT DIE...

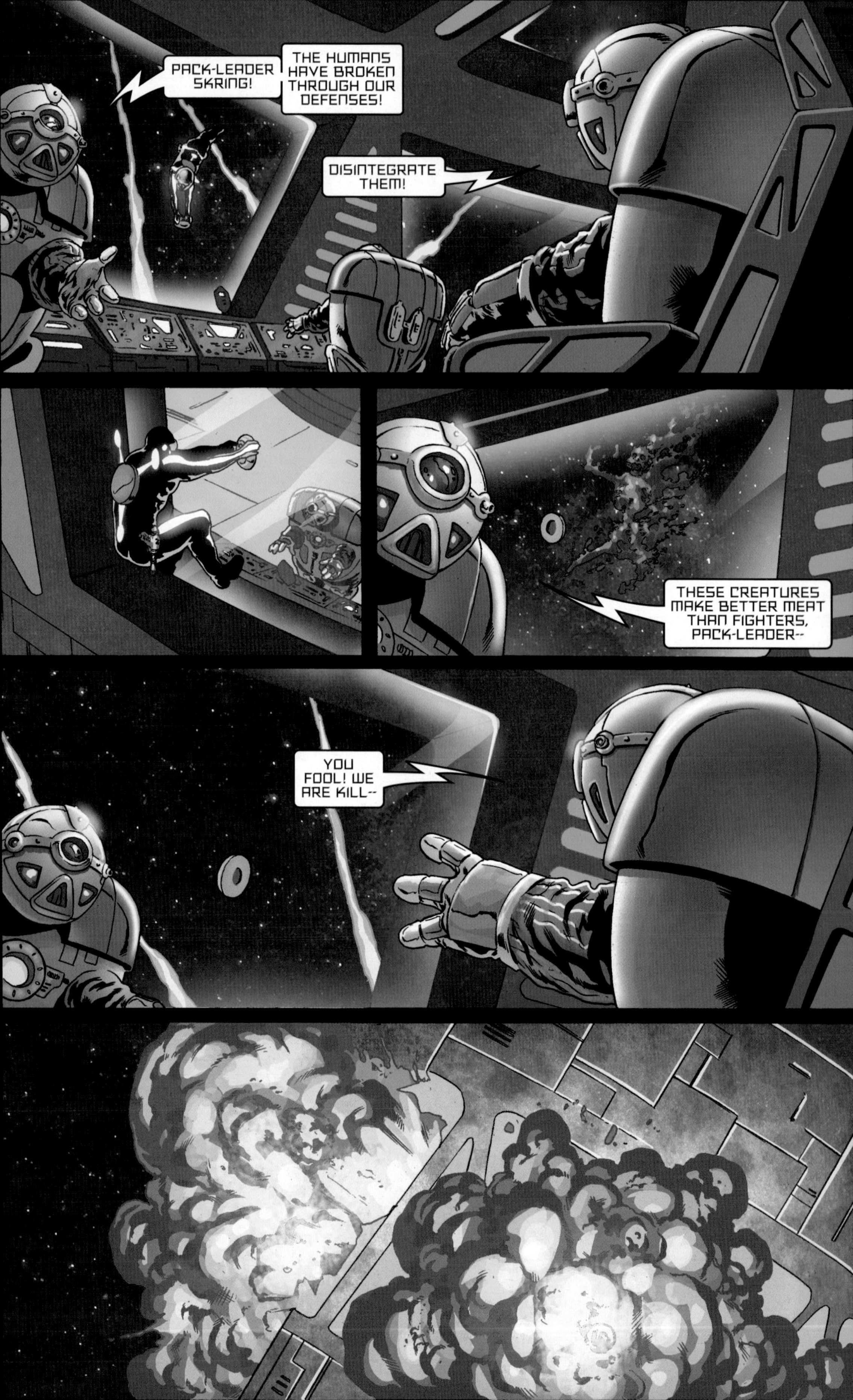
PACK-LEADER SKRING!
THE HUMANS HAVE BROKEN THROUGH OUR DEFENSES!
DISINTEGRATE THEM!
THESE CREATURES MAKE BETTER MEAT THAN FIGHTERS, PACK-LEADER--
YOU FOOL! WE ARE KILL--

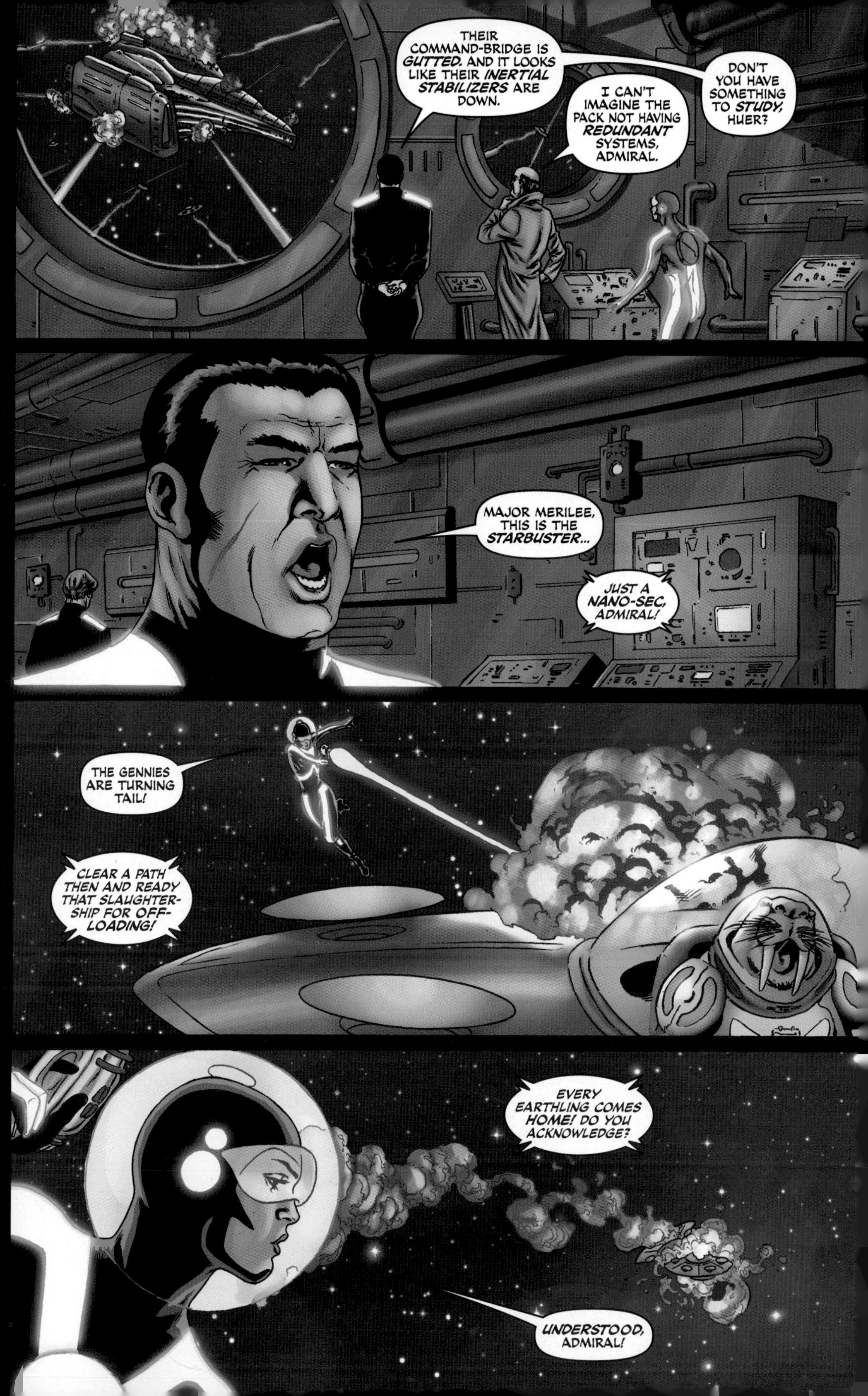
THEIR COMMAND-BRIDGE IS *GUTTED.* AND IT LOOKS LIKE THEIR *INERTIAL STABILIZERS* ARE DOWN.
I CAN'T IMAGINE THE PACK NOT HAVING *REDUNDANT* SYSTEMS, ADMIRAL.
DON'T YOU HAVE SOMETHING TO *STUDY,* HUER?
MAJOR MERILEE, THIS IS THE *STARBUSTER*...
JUST A *NANO-SEC,* ADMIRAL!
THE GENNIES ARE TURNING TAIL!
CLEAR A PATH THEN AND READY THAT SLAUGHTER-SHIP FOR OFF-LOADING!
EVERY EARTHLING COMES *HOME!* DO YOU ACKNOWLEDGE?
UNDERSTOOD, ADMIRAL!

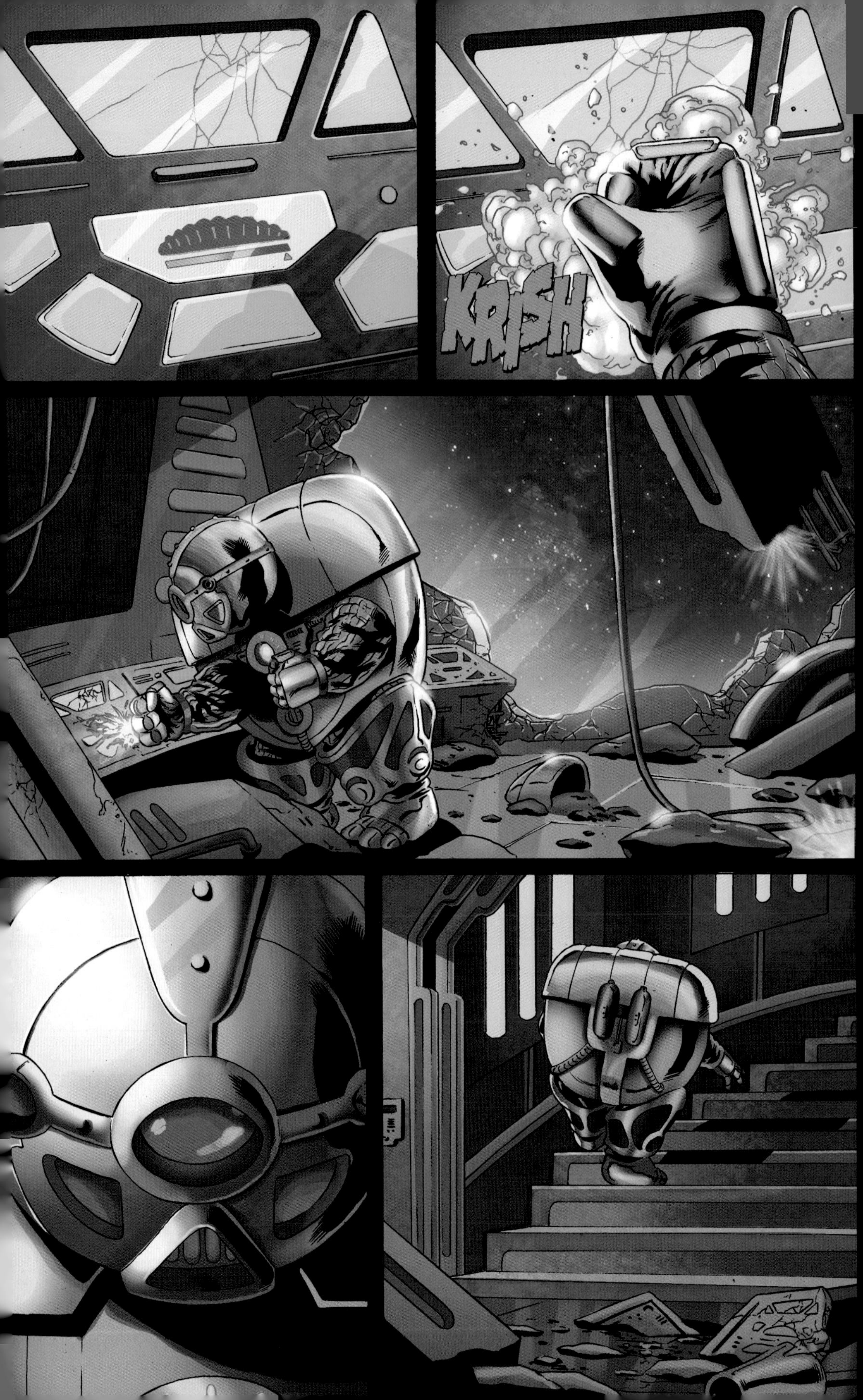
KRISH

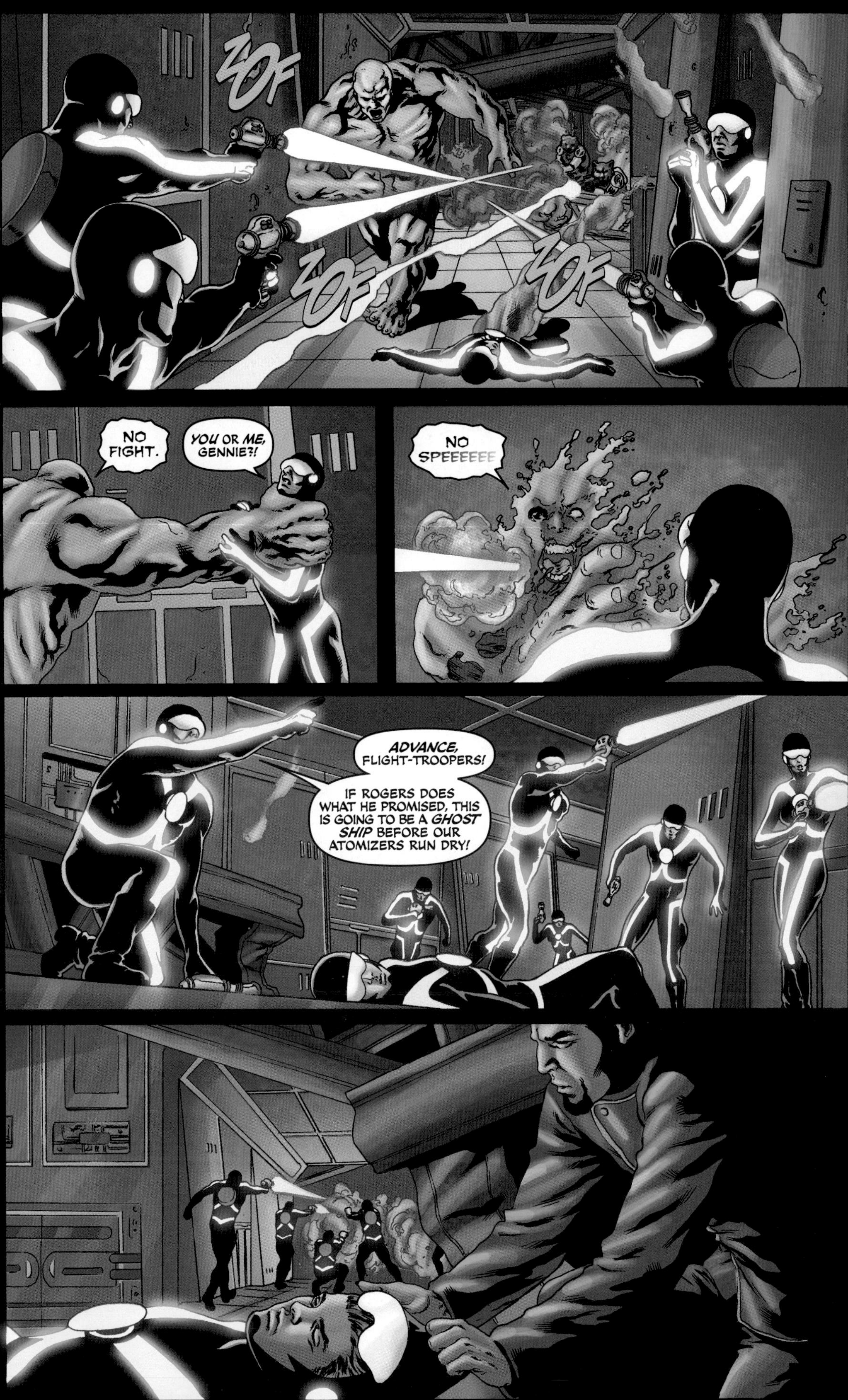
ZOF
ZOF
ZOF
NO FIGHT.
YOU OR ME, GENNIE?!
NO SPEEEEEE
ADVANCE, FLIGHT-TROOPERS!
IF ROGERS DOES WHAT HE PROMISED, THIS IS GOING TO BE A GHOST SHIP BEFORE OUR ATOMIZERS RUN DRY!

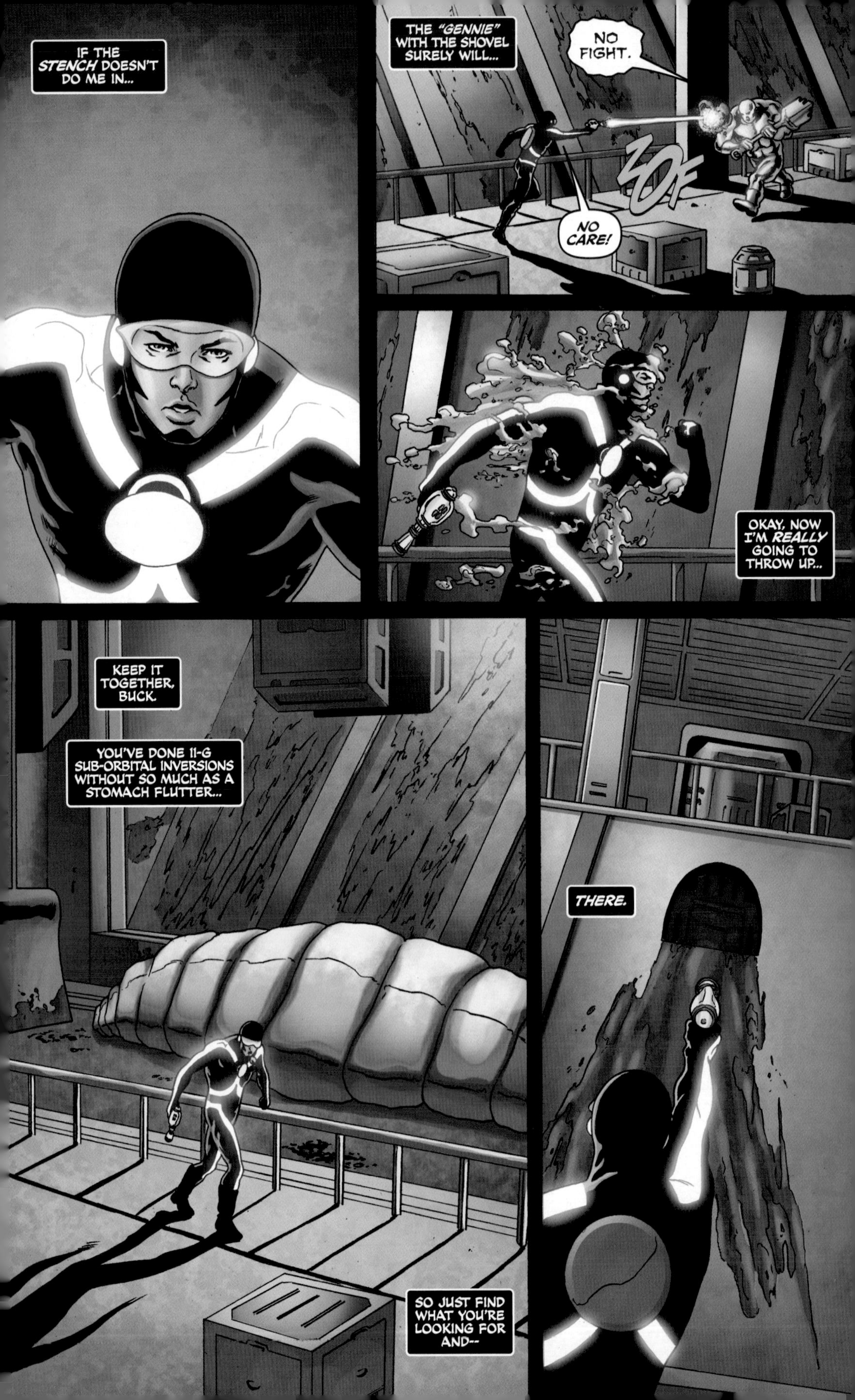
IF THE STENCH DOESN'T DO ME IN...
THE "GENNIE" WITH THE SHOVEL SURELY WILL...
NO FIGHT.
ZOOF
NO CARE!
OKAY, NOW I'M REALLY GOING TO THROW UP...
KEEP IT TOGETHER, BUCK.
YOU'VE DONE 11-G SUB-ORBITAL INVERSIONS WITHOUT SO MUCH AS A STOMACH FLUTTER...
SO JUST FIND WHAT YOU'RE LOOKING FOR AND--
THERE.

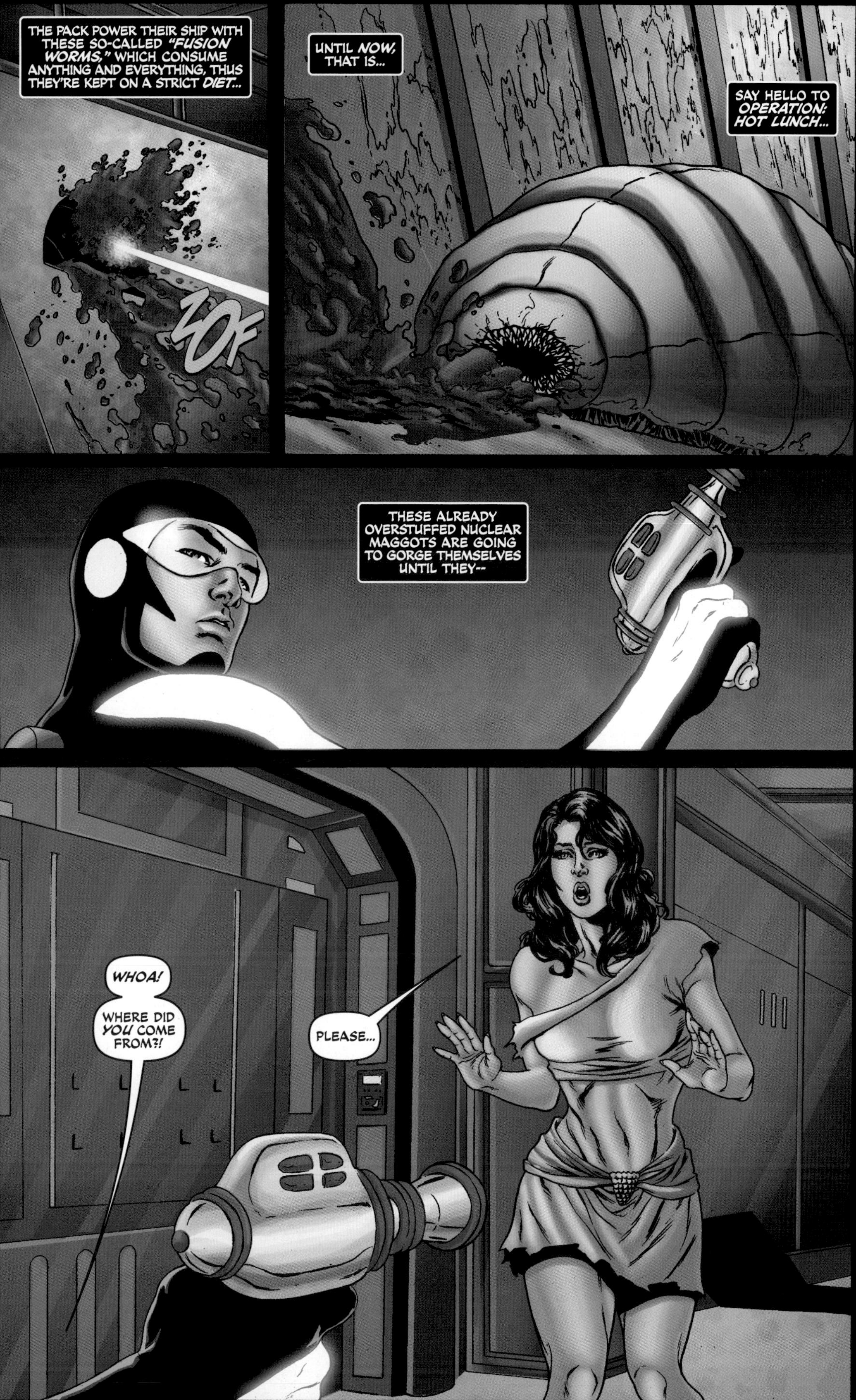
THE PACK POWER THEIR SHIP WITH THESE SO-CALLED *"FUSION WORMS,"* WHICH CONSUME ANYTHING AND EVERYTHING, THUS THEY'RE KEPT ON A STRICT *DIET*...
ZOF
UNTIL *NOW*, THAT IS...
SAY HELLO TO *OPERATION: HOT LUNCH*...
THESE ALREADY OVERSTUFFED NUCLEAR MAGGOTS ARE GOING TO GORGE THEMSELVES UNTIL THEY--
WHOA!
WHERE DID *YOU* COME FROM?!
PLEASE...

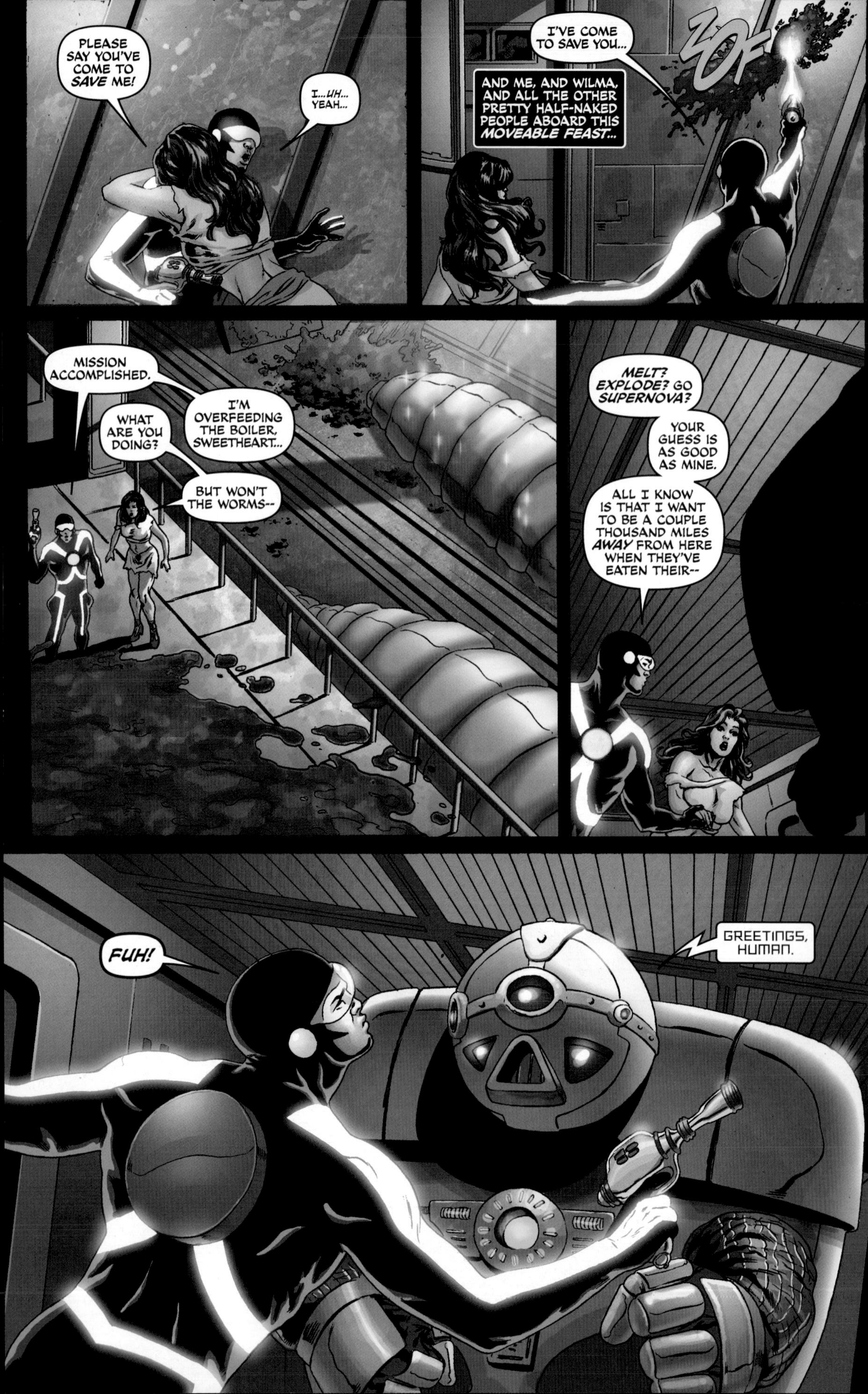
PLEASE SAY YOU'VE COME TO SAVE ME!
I...UH... YEAH...
I'VE COME TO SAVE YOU...
AND ME, AND WILMA, AND ALL THE OTHER PRETTY HALF-NAKED PEOPLE ABOARD THIS MOVEABLE FEAST...
ZOOF
MISSION ACCOMPLISHED.
WHAT ARE YOU DOING?
I'M OVERFEEDING THE BOILER, SWEETHEART...
BUT WON'T THE WORMS--
MELT? EXPLODE? GO SUPERNOVA?
YOUR GUESS IS AS GOOD AS MINE.
ALL I KNOW IS THAT I WANT TO BE A COUPLE THOUSAND MILES AWAY FROM HERE WHEN THEY'VE EATEN THEIR--
FUH!
GREETINGS, HUMAN.

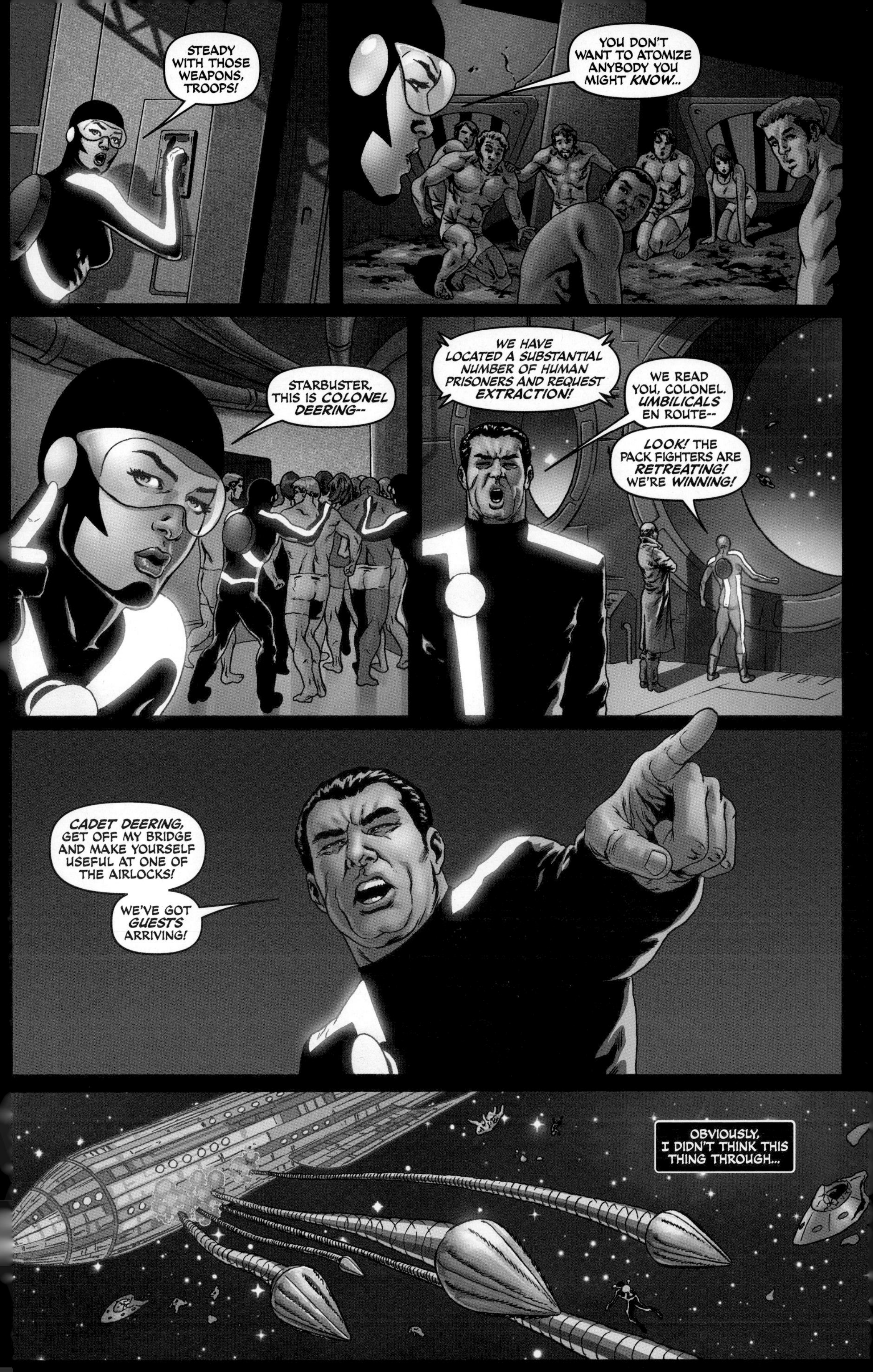
STEADY WITH THOSE WEAPONS, TROOPS!
YOU DON'T WANT TO ATOMIZE ANYBODY YOU MIGHT KNOW...
STARBUSTER, THIS IS COLONEL DEERING--
WE HAVE LOCATED A SUBSTANTIAL NUMBER OF HUMAN PRISONERS AND REQUEST EXTRACTION!
WE READ YOU, COLONEL. UMBILICALS EN ROUTE--
LOOK! THE PACK FIGHTERS ARE RETREATING! WE'RE WINNING!
CADET DEERING, GET OFF MY BRIDGE AND MAKE YOURSELF USEFUL AT ONE OF THE AIRLOCKS!
WE'VE GOT GUESTS ARRIVING!
OBVIOUSLY, I DIDN'T THINK THIS THING THROUGH...

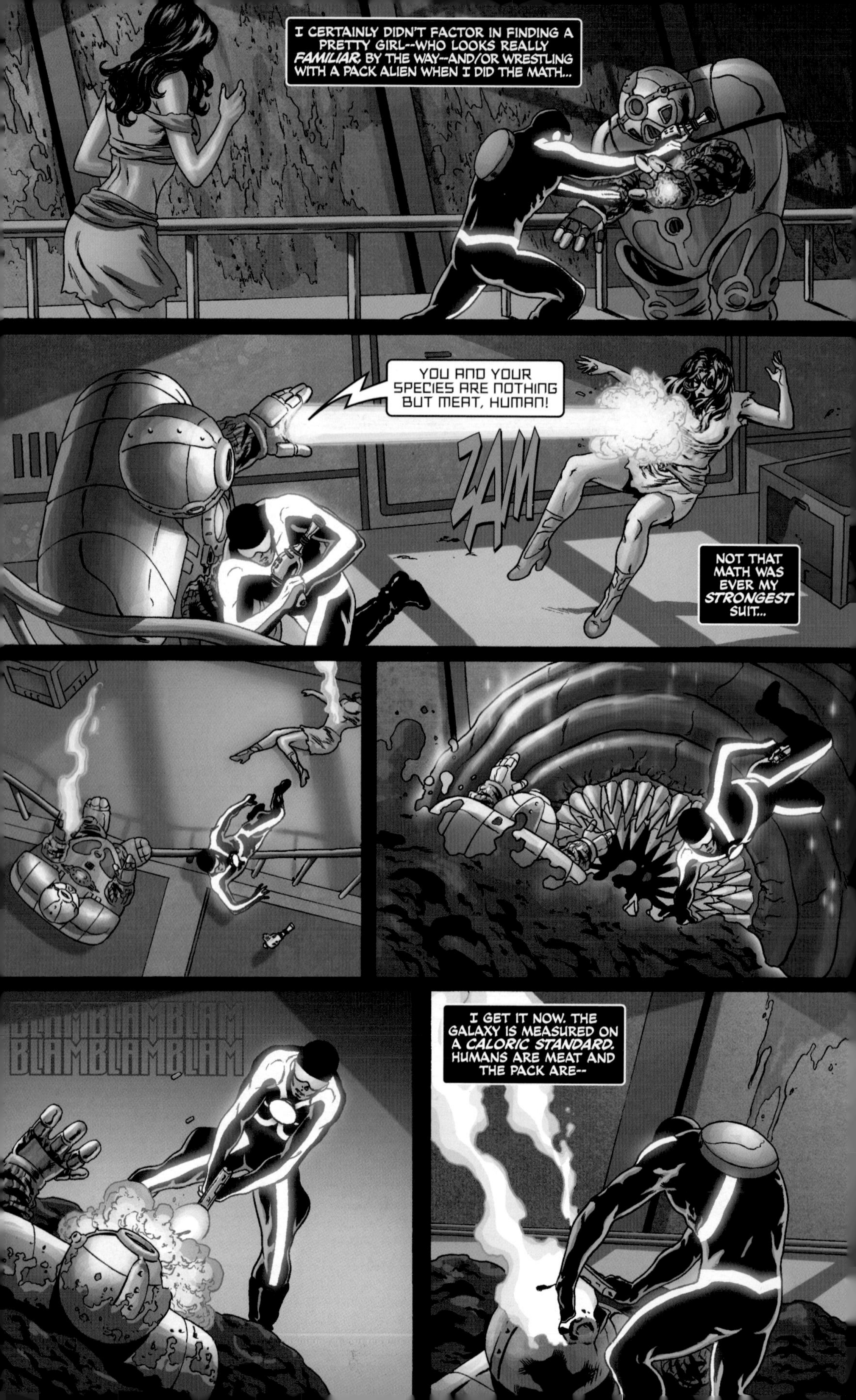

I CERTAINLY DIDN'T FACTOR IN FINDING A PRETTY GIRL--WHO LOOKS REALLY *FAMILIAR,* BY THE WAY--AND/OR WRESTLING WITH A PACK ALIEN WHEN I DID THE MATH...
YOU AND YOUR SPECIES ARE NOTHING BUT MEAT, HUMAN!
ZAM
NOT THAT MATH WAS EVER MY *STRONGEST* SUIT...
BLAMBLAMBLAM BLAMBLAMBLAM
I GET IT NOW. THE GALAXY IS MEASURED ON A *CALORIC STANDARD.* HUMANS ARE MEAT AND THE PACK ARE--

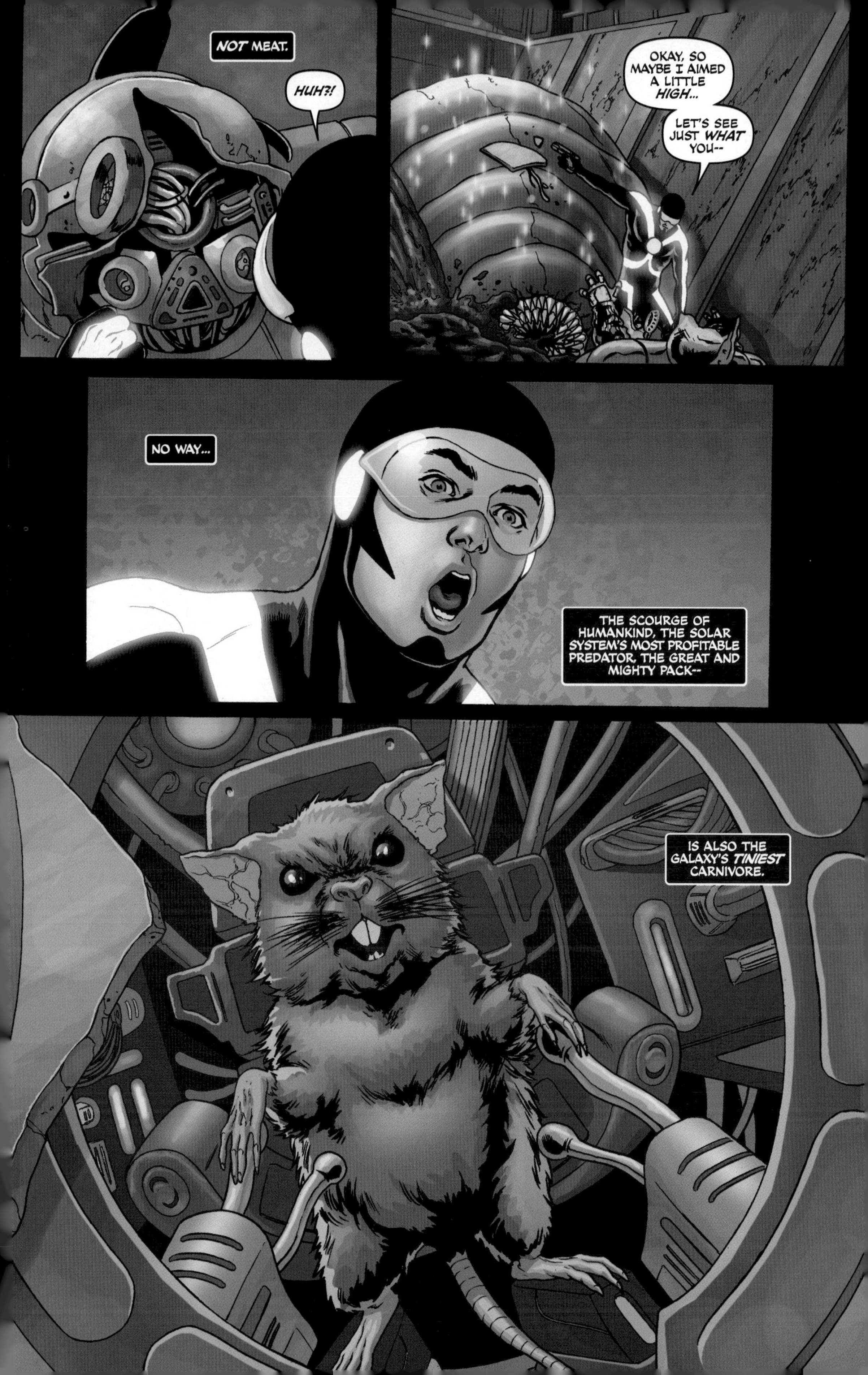

NOT MEAT.
HUH?!
OKAY, SO MAYBE I AIMED A LITTLE HIGH...
LET'S SEE JUST WHAT YOU--
NO WAY...
THE SCOURGE OF HUMANKIND, THE SOLAR SYSTEM'S MOST PROFITABLE PREDATOR, THE GREAT AND MIGHTY PACK--
IS ALSO THE GALAXY'S TINIEST CARNIVORE.

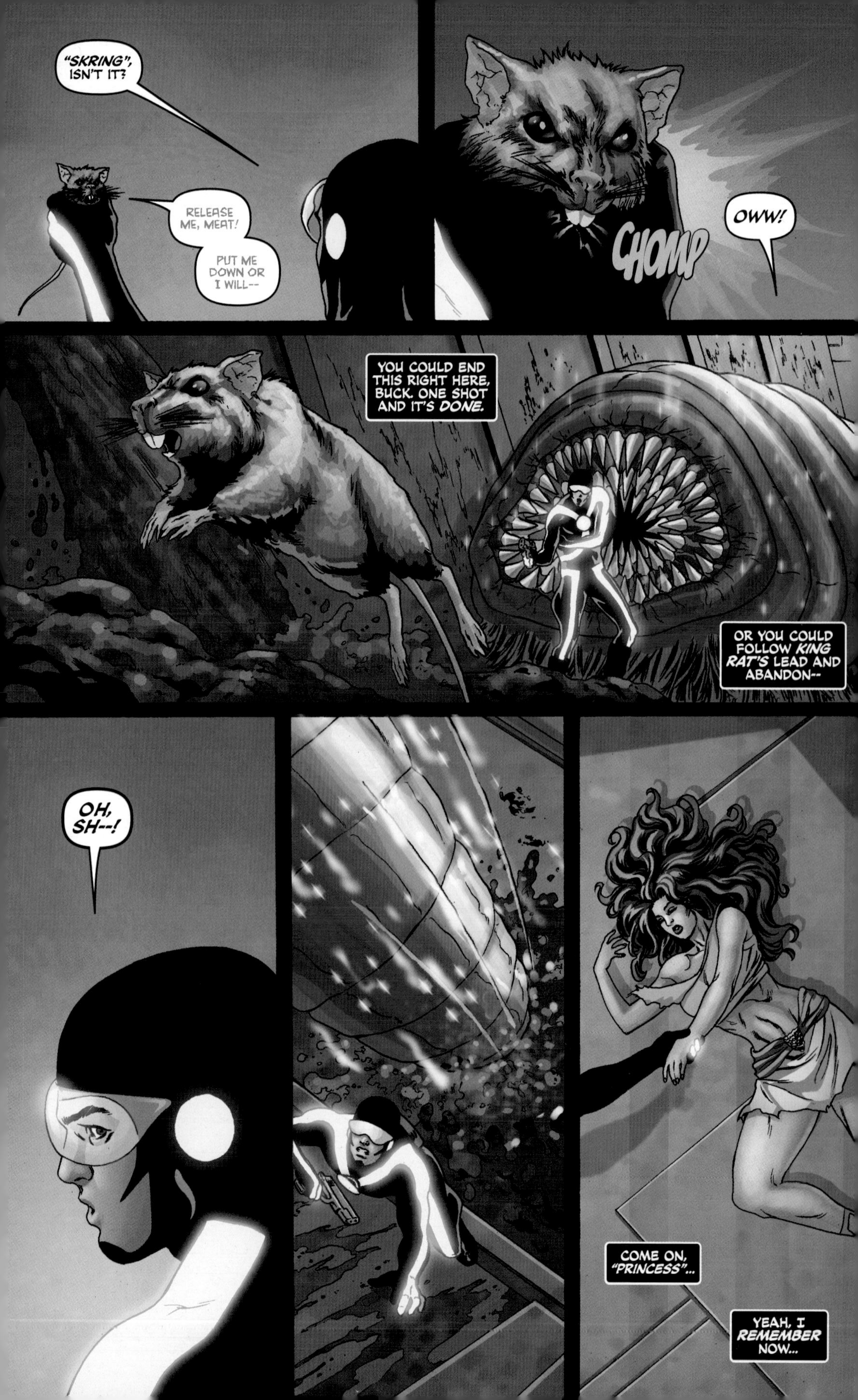
"SKRING", ISN'T IT?
RELEASE ME, MEAT!
PUT ME DOWN OR I WILL--
CHOMP
OWW!
YOU COULD END THIS RIGHT HERE, BUCK. ONE SHOT AND IT'S DONE.
OR YOU COULD FOLLOW KING RAT'S LEAD AND ABANDON--
OH, SH--!
COME ON, "PRINCESS"...
YEAH, I REMEMBER NOW...

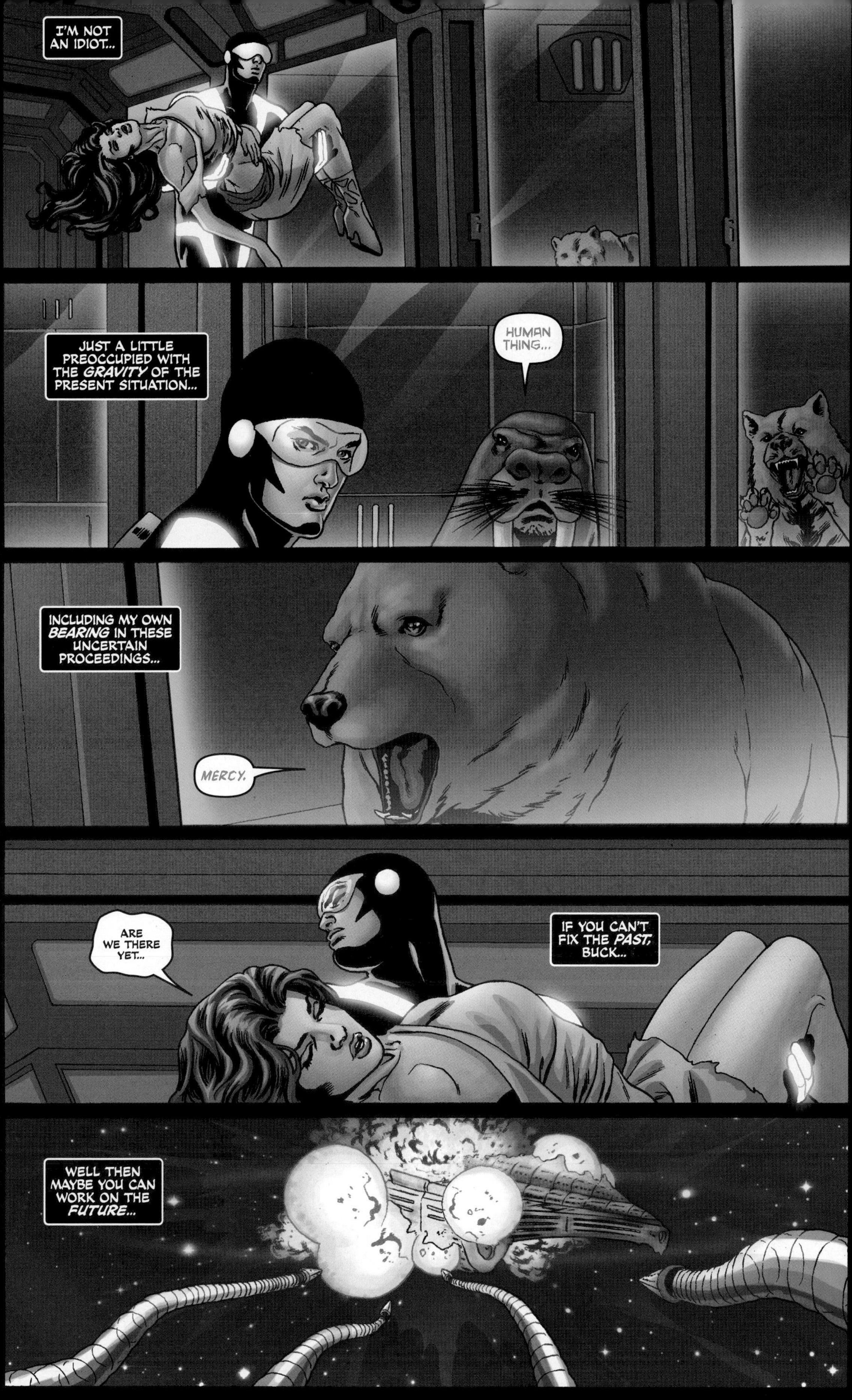
I'M NOT AN IDIOT...
JUST A LITTLE PREOCCUPIED WITH THE *GRAVITY* OF THE PRESENT SITUATION...
HUMAN THING...
INCLUDING MY OWN *BEARING* IN THESE UNCERTAIN PROCEEDINGS...
MERCY.
ARE WE THERE YET...
IF YOU CAN'T FIX THE *PAST,* BUCK...
WELL THEN MAYBE YOU CAN WORK ON THE *FUTURE*...

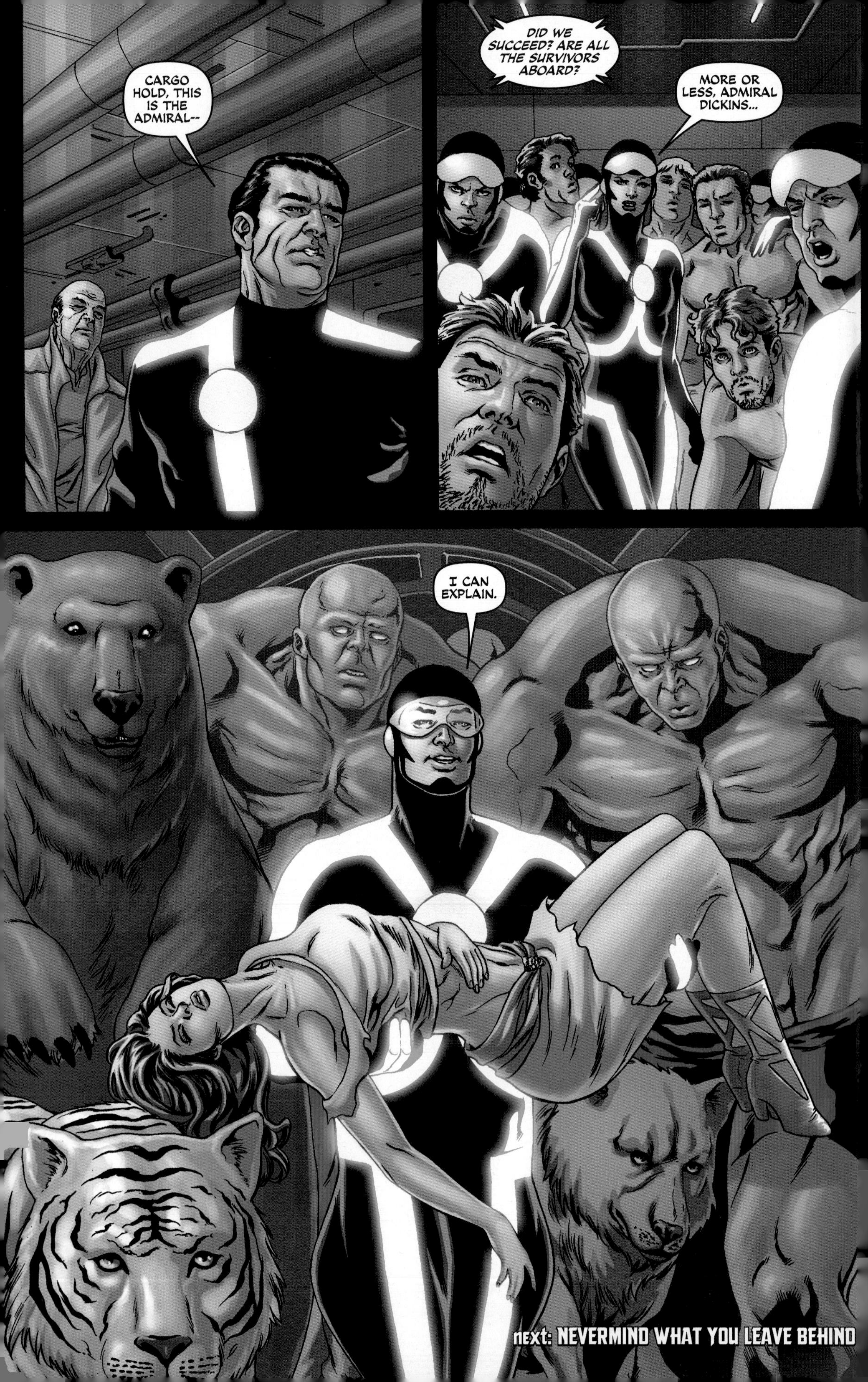
CARGO HOLD, THIS IS THE ADMIRAL--
DID WE SUCCEED? ARE ALL THE SURVIVORS ABOARD?
MORE OR LESS, ADMIRAL DICKINS...
I CAN EXPLAIN.
next: NEVERMIND WHAT YOU LEAVE BEHIND

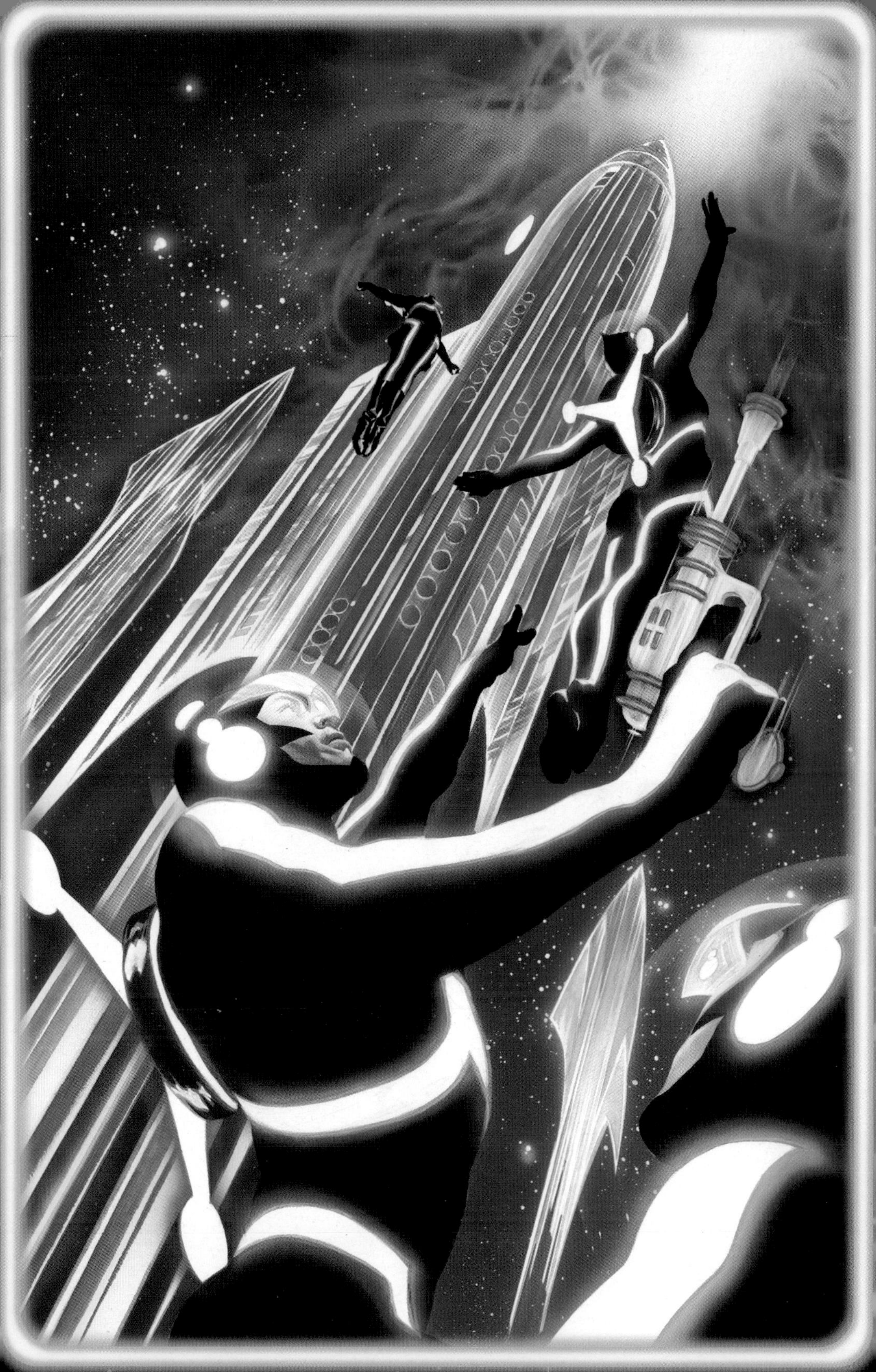

ALTERNATE #1 COVER BY ALEX ROSS

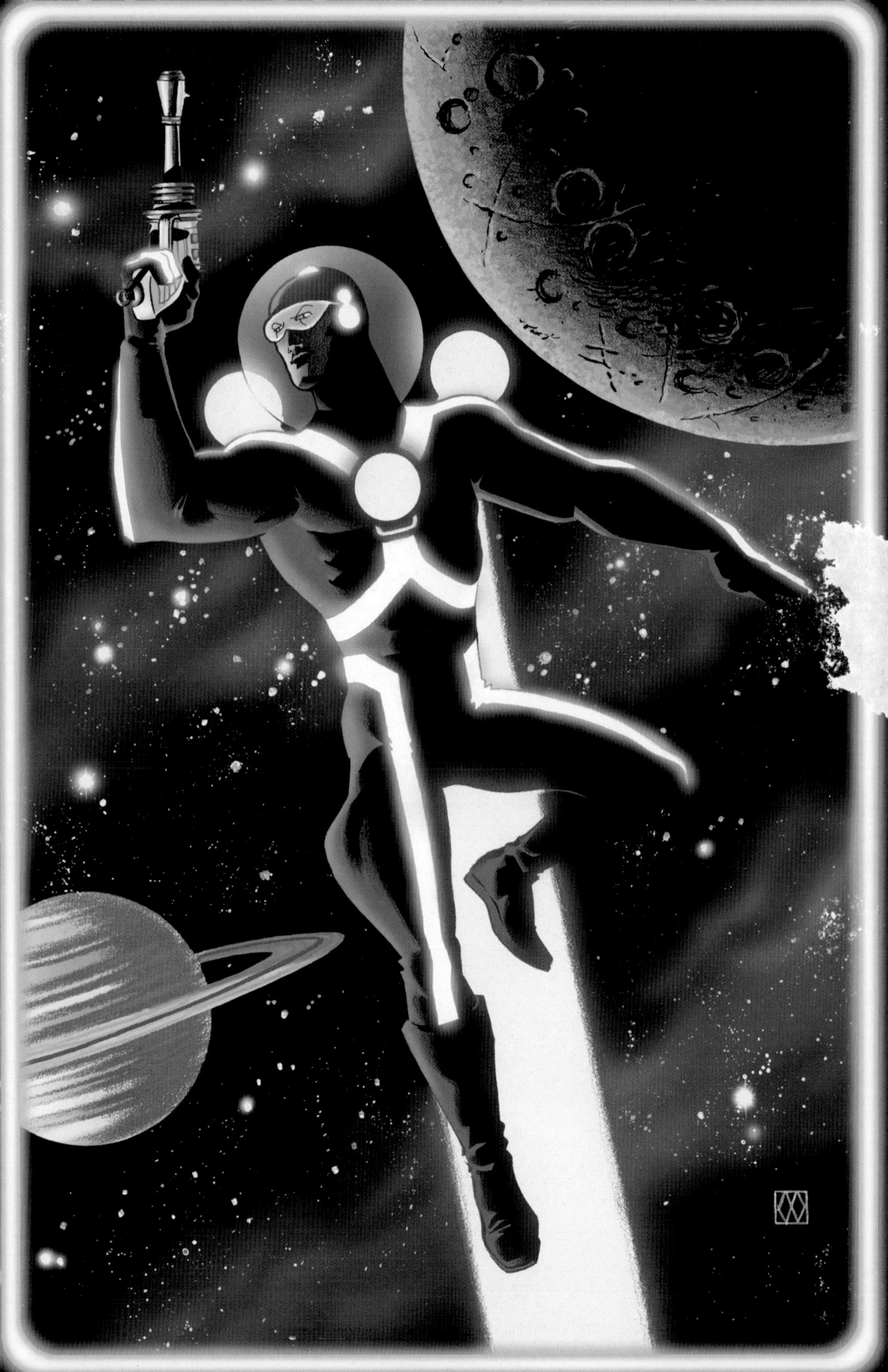

ALTERNATE #1 COVER BY MATT WAGNER

SKETCHES AND DESIGNS

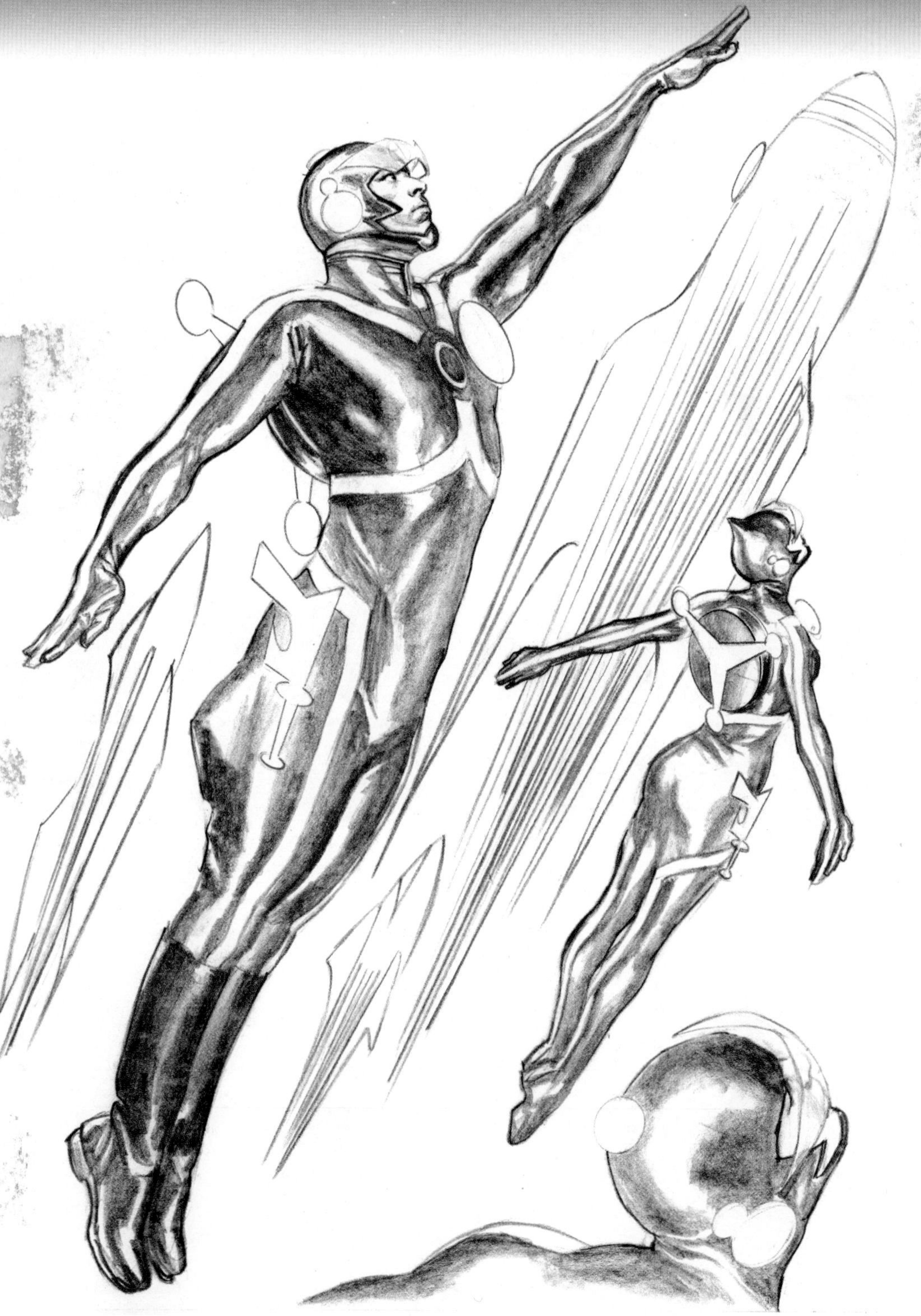

ORIGINAL DESIGNS BY ALEX ROSS

SKETCHES AND DESIGNS

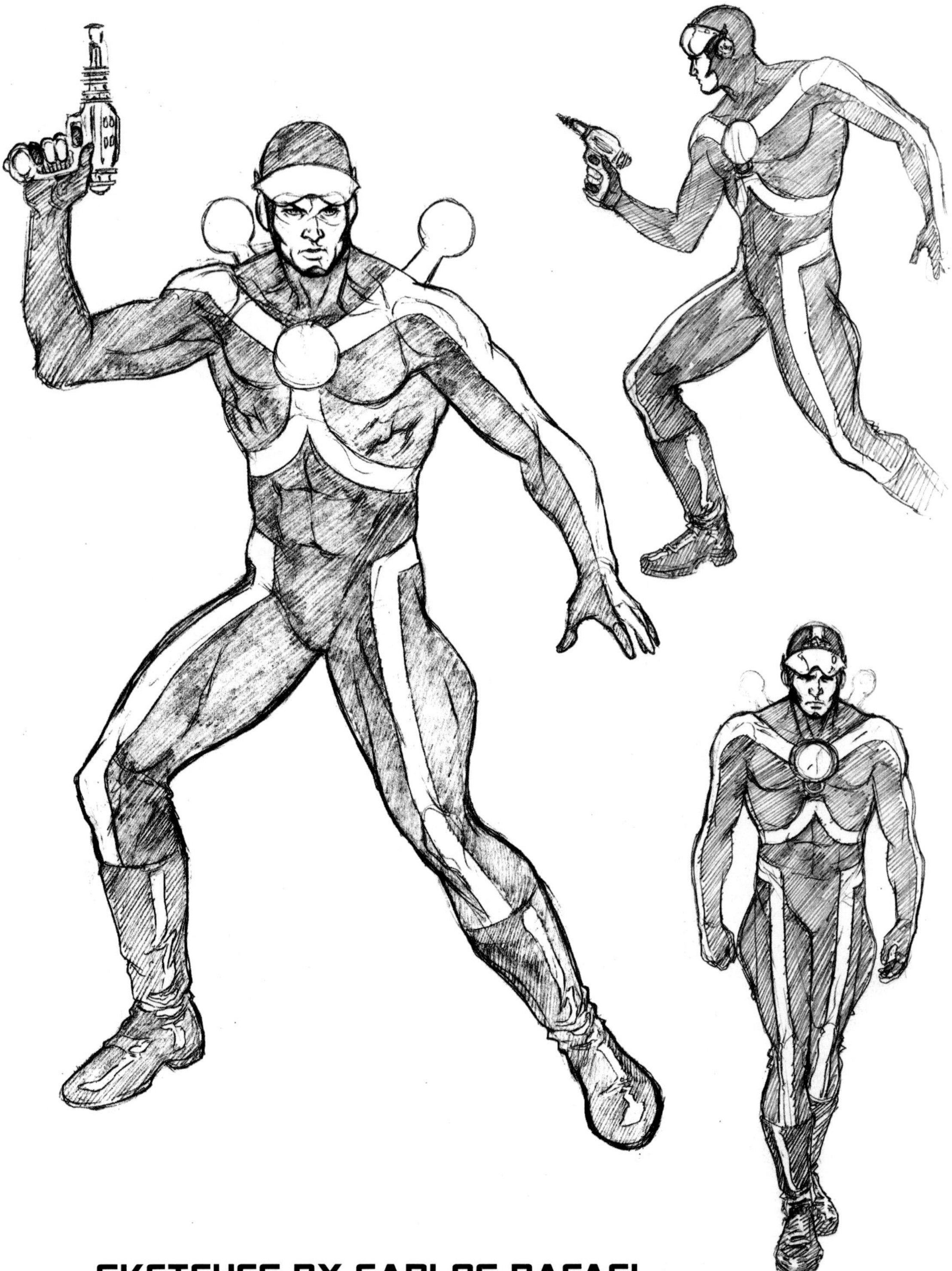

SKETCHES BY CARLOS RAFAEL

SKETCHES AND DESIGNS

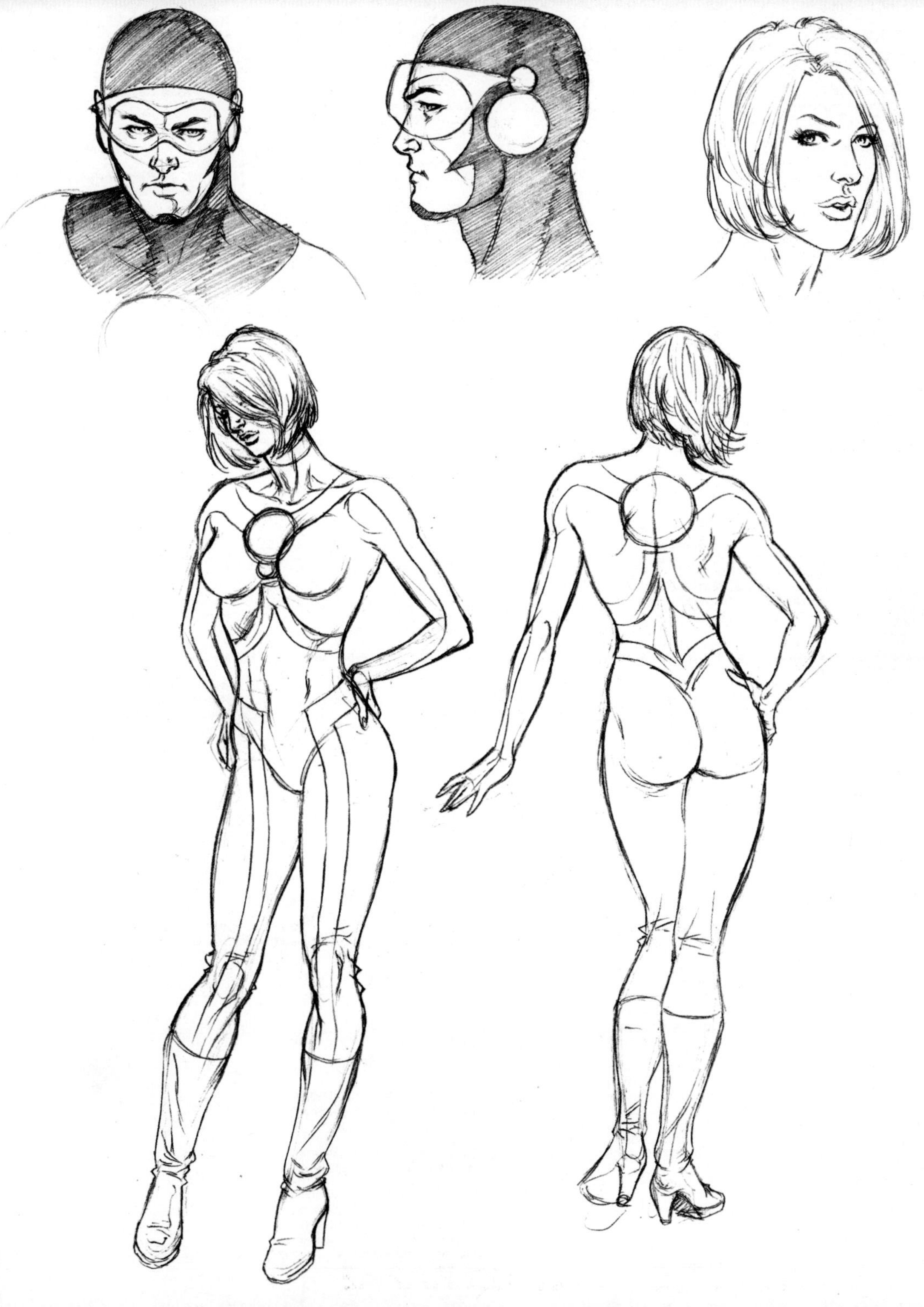

CURRENTLY AVAILABLE AND UPCOMING COLLECTIONS FROM DYNAMITE ENTERTAINMENT

Adventures of Red Sonja Vol. 1
Thomas, Thorne, More

Adventures of Red Sonja Vol. 2
Thomas, Thorne, More

Adventures of Red Sonja Vol. 3
Thomas, Thorne, More

American Flagg! Definitive Collection Vol. 1
Chaykin

Army of Darkness: Movie Adaptation
Raimi, Raimi, Bolton

Army of Darkness: Ashes to Ashes
Hartnell, Bradshaw

Army of Darkness: Shop 'Till You Drop Dead
Kuhoric, Bradshaw, Greene

Army of Darkness vs. Re-Animator
Kuhoric, Bradshaw, Greene

Army of Darkness: Old School & More
Kuhoric, Sharpe

Army of Darkness: Ash vs. The Classic Monsters
Kuhoric, Sharpe, Blanco

Army of Darkness: From The Ashes
Kuhoric, Blanco

Army of Darkness: The Long Road Home
Kuhoric, Raicht, Blanco

Army of Darkness: Home Sweet Hell
Kuhoric, Raicht, Perez

Army of Darkness: Hellbillies & Deadnecks
Kuhoric, Raicht, Cohn

Army of Darkness Omnibus Vol. 1
Hartnell, Kuhoric, Kirkman, more

Army of Darkness vs. Xena Vol. 1: Why Not?
Layman, Jerwa, Montenegro

Xena vs. Army of Darkness Vol. 2: What...Again?!
Jerwa, Serrano, Montenegro

Bad Boy 10th Anniv. Edition
Miller, Bisley

Borderline Vol. 1
Risso, Trillo

Borderline Vol. 2
Risso, Trillo1

Borderline Vol. 3
Risso, Trillo

The Boys Vol. 1: The Name of the Game
Ennis, Robertson

The Boys Vol. 2: Get Some
Ennis, Robertson, Snejbjerg

The Boys Vol. 3: Good For The Soul
Ennis, Robertson

The Boys Vol. 4: We Gotta Go Now
Ennis, Robertson

The Boys Vol. 5: Herogasm
Ennis, McCrea

The Boys Definitive Edition Vol. 1
Ennis, Robertson

The Boys Definitive Edition Vol. 2
Ennis, Robertson

Buck Rogers Vol. 1: Future Shock
Beatty, Rafael

Classic Battlestar Galactica Vol. 1
Remender, Rafael

Classic Battlestar Galactica Vol. 2: Cylon Apocalypse
Grillo-Marxuach, Rafael

The Complete Dracula
Stoker, Moore, Reppion, Worley

Dan Dare Omnibus
Ennis, Erskine

Darkman vs. Army of Darkness
Busiek, Stern, Fry

Darkness vs. Eva Vol. 1
Moore, Reppion, Salazar

Dead Irons
Kuhoric, Alexander, Lee

Dreadstar The Definitive Collection
Starlin

Dreadstar: The Beginning
Starlin

Eduardo Risso's Tales of Terror
Risso, Trillo

Garth Ennis' Battlefields Vol. 1: The Night Witches
Ennis, Braun

Garth Ennis' Battlefields Vol. 2: Dear Billy
Ennis, Snejbjerg

Garth Ennis' Battlefields Vol. 3: The Tankies
Ennis, Ezquerra

Garth Ennis' The Complete Battlefields Vol. 1
Ennis, Braun, Snejbjerg, Ezquerra

Hellshock
Lee, Chung

Highlander Vol. 1: The Coldest War
Oeming, Jerwa, Moder, Sharpe

Highlander Vol. 2: Dark Quickening
Jerwa, Laguna

Highlander Vol. 3: Armageddon
Jerwa, Rafael

Highlander Way Of The Sword
Krul, Rafael

Jungle Girl Vol. 1
Cho, Murray, Batista

Jungle Girl Season 2
Cho, Murray, Batista

Just A Pilgrim
Ennis, Ezquerra

Kid Kosmos: Cosmic Guard
Starlin

Kid Kosmos: Kidnapped
Starlin

The Lone Ranger Vol. 1: Now & Forever
Matthews, Cariello, Cassaday

The Lone Ranger Vol. 2: Lines Not Crossed
Matthews, Cariello, Cassaday, Pope

The Lone Ranger Vol. 3: Scorched Earth
Matthews, Cariello, Cassaday

The Lone Ranger Definitive Edition Vol. 1
Matthews, Cariello, Cassaday

The Man With No Name Vol. 1: Saints and Sinners
Gage, Dias

The Man With No Name Vol. 2: Holliday in the Sun
Lieberman, Wolpert, Bernard

Masquerade Vol. 1
Ross, Hester, Paul

Mercenaries Vol. 1
Reed, Salazar

Monster War
Golden, Chin, more

New Battlestar Galactica Vol. 1
Pak, Raynor

New Battlestar Galactica Vol. 2
Pak, Raynor

New Battlestar Galactica Vol. 3
Pak, Raynor, Lau

New Battlestar Galactica Complete Omnibus V1
Pak, Raynor, Jerwa, Lau

New Battlestar Galactica: Zarek
Jerwa, Batista

New Battlestar Galactica: Season Zero Vol. 1
Jerwa, Herbert

New Battlestar Galactica: Season Zero Vol. 2
Jerwa, Herbert

New Battlestar Galactica Origins: Baltar
Fahey, Lau

New Battlestar Galactica Origins: Adama
Napton, Lau

New Battlestar Galactica Origins: Starbuck & Helo
Fahey, Lau

New Battlestar Galactica: Ghosts
Jerwa, Lau

New Battlestar Galactica: Cylon War
Ortega, Nylund, Raynor

New Battlestar Galactica: The Final Five
Fahey, Reed, Raynor

Essential Painkiller Jane Vol. 1
Quesada, Palmiotti, Leonardi, more

Painkiller Jane Vol. 1: The Return
Quesada, Palmiotti, Moder

Painkiller Jane Vol. 2: Everything Explodes
Quesada, Palmiotti, Moder

Painkiller Jane vs. Terminator
Palmiotti, Raynor

Power & Glory
Chaykin

Project Superpowers Chapter 1
Ross, Krueger, Paul, Sadowski

Project Superpowers Chapter 2 Vol. 1
Ross, Krueger, Salazar

Raise The Dead
Moore, Reppion, Petrus

Red Sonja She-Devil With a Sword Vol. 1
Oeming, Carey, Rubi

Red Sonja She-Devil With a Sword Vol. 2: Arrowsmiths
Oeming, Rubi, more6

Red Sonja She-Devil With a Sword Vol. 3: The Rise of Kulan Gath
Oeming, Rubi, more

Red Sonja She-Devil With a Sword Vol. 4: Animals & More
Oeming, Homs, more

Red Sonja She-Devil With a Sword Vol. 5: World On Fire
Oeming, Reed, Homs

Red Sonja She-Devil With a Sword Vol. 6: Death
Marz, Ortega, Reed, more

Red Sonja She-Devil With a Sword Vol. 7: Born Again
Reed, Geovani

Red Sonja She-Devil With a Sword Omnibus Vol. 1
Oeming, Carey, Rubi, more

Red Sonja vs. Thulsa Doom Vol. 1
David, Lieberman, Conrad

Savage Red Sonja: Queen of the Frozen Wastes
Cho, Murray, Homs

Red Sonja: Travels
Marz, Ortega, Thomas, more

Sword of Red Sonja: Doom of the Gods (Red Sonja vs. Thulsa Doom 2)
Lieberman, Antonio

Savage Tales of Red Sonja
Marz, Gage, Ortega, more

Scout Vol. 1
Truman

Scout Vol. 2
Truman

Sherlock Holmes Vol. 1: The Trial of Sherlock Holmes
Moore, Reppion, Campbell

Six From Sirius
Moench, Gulacy

Street Magik
Lieberman, McCarthy, Buchemi

Super Zombies
Guggenheim, Gonzales, Rubi

Terminator: Infinity
Furman, Raynor

Terminator: Revolution
Furman, Antonio

Witchblade: Shades of Gray
Moore, Reppion, Segovia, Geovani

Xena Vol. 1: Contest of Pantheons
Layman, Neves

Xena Vol. 2: Dark Xena
Layman, Champagne, Salonga

Zorro Vol. 1: Year One Trail of the Fox
Wagner, Francavilla

Zorro Vol. 2: Clashing Blades
Wagner, Razek